THE Mythic Journey

THE Mythic Journey

THE MEANING OF MYTH
AS A GUIDE FOR LIFE

Liz Greene and Juliet Sharman-Burke

A Fireside Book
Published by Simon & Schuster

To my Father and Mother, who first told me myths and fairy tales, with love. JULIET SHARMAN-BURKE

To Charles and Suzi, with love, for their friendship. LIZ GREENE

FIRESIDE
Rockefeller Center
1230 Avenue of the Americas
New York, NY 10020

1 3 5 7 9 10 8 6 4 2

Library of Congress Cataloging-in-Publication Data is available.

ISBN 0-684-86947-0

AN EDDISON·SADD EDITION
Edited, designed and produced by
Eddison Sadd Editions Limited
St Chad's House, 148 King's Cross Road
London WC1X 9DH

Phototypeset in Quadraat using QuarkXPress on Apple Macintosh.
Origination by Bright Arts, Singapore
Printed by Craft Print, Singapore

FRONTISPIECE *The figures of myth embody every dimension of human experience and, like mirrors, reflect back to us, gently but profoundly, the secret patterns of our own souls.*
Narcissus, Giovanni Antonio Boltraffio (1467–1516)

PAGE 7 *The gods were imaged in the ancient world as a huge, loving, quarrelling, rumbustious family, revealing themselves in human form yet larger, brighter and more radiant than any mortal being.*
The Feast of the Gods, Hendrik van Balen the Elder (1575–1632)

CONTENTS

INTRODUCTION

Myth is the original self-help psychology. For centuries, human beings have used myths, fairy tales and folklore to explain life's mysteries and make them bearable – from why the seasons change, through complex relationship issues, to the enigma of death. Jesus explained his teachings through parables, giving his followers difficult problems in an easy-to-understand form. Plato communicated abstruse philosophical concepts through simple myths and allegories. In ancient Hindu medicine, when someone with mental or emotional difficulties consulted a doctor, the physician prescribed a story on which to meditate, thus helping the patient to find his or her own solution to the problem. It is often our linear, causally bound, rational thinking that obscures the deeper meaning and resolution of life's dilemmas. Myths have the mysterious capacity to contain and communicate paradoxes, allowing us to see through, around and over the dilemma to the real heart of the matter.

Over the following pages, we will explore significant myths, some well-known and others less familiar, from Greco-Roman, Hebrew, Egyptian, Hindu, Native American, Maori, Celtic and Norse, as well as other sources, which relate to the various stages of life and the important challenges all human beings encounter. Rather than following the familiar format of a 'mythological dictionary' which gives snippets of

interpretation for each of a long list of ancient deities and heroes, we will follow, instead, the format of a human life, weaving the ancient tales around fundamental human experiences, beginning with family relationships and ending with death as the final mythic journey. Each part of the book can be read and reread independently of the others; but as a whole, the book takes the reader on a journey through the major rites of passage of a human life.

Each part focuses on a particular area of life and the characteristic conflicts and joys we all encounter. Specific myths are, in turn, used to illustrate particular issues, both positive and negative, relevant to that sphere of life. The story is told first, and then a psychological overview is given which helps us to understand the deeper meaning and application of the myth to our own lives.

The purpose of this book is to show you how mythic stories and imagery can bring relief from internal conflicts and help you to discover greater depth, richness and meaning in life. One of the great healing functions of myth is to show us that we are not alone with our feelings, fears, conflicts and aspirations. We learn from myth that sibling rivalry is as old as time; that Oedipus is alive and well and is not limited to the psychoanalytic couch; that the eternal triangle is indeed eternal and has been written about since human beings first learned to write; that beauty, talent, power and wealth bring their own forms of suffering; and that in the darkness of loneliness, failure and loss we have always discovered light and new hope.

PART I

IN THE BEGINNING

Family life is the most fundamental of life's experiences. Regardless of the nature of our background, we have all had parents – present, absent, loving or unloving – and Mother Earth and Father Sky are the great mythic symbols of the origin of the world as well as our own beginnings. We have all come from somewhere and, whatever we make of ourselves later in life, we cannot undo the past. We inherit not only genetic patterns from our family backgrounds, but also psychological patterns, and the individuals we become are partly our own creation and partly the legacy of the past. Myths do not give us easy solutions to family difficulties. They portray family dynamics just as they are, with all their joys, sorrows and complexities. Yet there is a mysterious, transformative power which lies embedded in these stories. Although the archetypal dynamics of family life are eternal, change and healing are always possible – within ourselves if not in our external circumstances.

Birth is a universal human experience. The Madonna, pregnant with the unborn Christ, reflects an archetypal image of serene expectancy.

DETAIL *Madonna del Parto, Piero della Francesca (c.1410/20–92)*

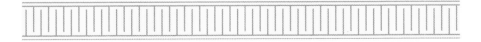

Chapter One

PARENTS AND CHILDREN

Myth offers us a vast array of stories about parent–child relationships. From the hilarious squabblings of the Olympian gods to the tragic destinies of kingly dynasties, the human imagination has always found both solace and enlightenment in creating tales about mothers, fathers, sons, daughters, and the mystery of what binds us together through unbreakable emotional cords. There is no parent–child dilemma that does not have a mythic counterpart, and no resolution of conflict that is not reflected in mythic tales.

THETIS AND ACHILLES

Great expectations

THE FIRST OF OUR FAMILY MYTHS TELLS US ABOUT HOW PARENTS EXPECT NOTHING LESS THAN EVERYTHING FROM THEIR CHILDREN. PERHAPS THE MOST IMPORTANT THEME IN THIS GREEK STORY IS THE AMBITION THETIS HAS FOR HER CHILD – SHE WANTS HIM TO BE A GOD. THIS STORY HAS A SAD ENDING, BUT IT CONVEYS PROFOUND INSIGHT INTO THE SECRET HOPES, DREAMS AND LONGINGS WE MAY UNKNOWINGLY ASK OUR CHILDREN TO CARRY – SOMETIMES TO THEIR COST.

T hetis was the great goddess of the sea and ruled over all that moved in its depths. But it was time she married, and Zeus, king of the gods, had received a prophecy that, if Thetis married a god, she would bear a son who would be greater than Zeus himself. Worried about losing his position, Zeus espoused the sea-goddess to a mortal man called Peleus. This mixed marriage was not unsuccessful,

and the two settled down relatively comfortably – although Peleus sometimes resented his wife's supernatural powers, and Thetis sometimes felt she had married beneath her station.

In time, Thetis bore a son, whom she called Achilles. Because he was fathered by a mortal, he was a mortal child, allotted his time on earth by the Fates, as are all mortal beings. But Thetis was not content with this prospect. Being immortal herself, she did not wish to remain eternally young while watching her son grow old and die. So she secretly carried the newborn child to the River Styx, in whose waters lay the gift of immortality. She held the child by one heel and dipped him in the waters, believing thereby that she had made him immortal. But the heel by which she held him remained untouched by the waters of Styx, and therefore Achilles was vulnerable through this one place.

When he reached adulthood and fought in the Trojan War, Achilles received his death wound through an arrow in the heel. Although Achilles achieved great glory and was remembered forever, Thetis could not cheat the Fates, nor turn that which was human into the stuff of the gods.

COMMENTARY: *Many parents unconsciously wish their children to be divine, although usually not as literally as Thetis. We do not hope that our children will live forever, but we may want them to be better than other children, more beautiful, more gifted, more brilliant, unique and special, and exempt from the ordinary limitations of life. No child can live up to such unconscious expectations, and any child may suffer because his or her ordinary humanity is overlooked in the parents' strenuous efforts to produce something superhuman. We may also hope that our children will somehow redeem us – make good what we ourselves have spoiled, or live out what we have been denied in life. We may make sacrifices in the hope that our children will provide meaning for our own lives, rather than allowing them to live theirs. And when they stumble and fall, as all humans do, or show insufficient gratitude for our efforts, we may feel outraged and disappointed. All this can be read into the story of Thetis and Achilles.*

Thetis, the goddess mother who wants her child to be divine like her rather than mortal like his father, is also an image of a certain attitude towards

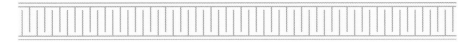

mothering. If a mother wishes to wholly possess her child, and is unwilling or unable to share the child's love, then many problems may ensue. The marriage of Thetis and Peleus, with Achilles as its progeny, portrays a marriage in which there is an imbalance between the parents. Thetis feels superior to Peleus and hopes that her child will take after her. This is a common enough dilemma; we may secretly fantasize a child's identity, rather than recognizing that two parents have contributed to the child's existence. This can happen when a marriage is unhappy or unfulfilled. Fathers may also idealize their daughters as Thetis does her son, and may unconsciously strive to separate mother and daughter so that no outsider can mar the unity of the father–daughter bond. (See Orion and Oenopion, pages 19–22.)

All these are dilemmas of parenting which, rather than being pathological, are merely human. But myths are about human beings, even when their main characters are gods. How do we deal with these issues of over-expectation and possessiveness? If we bring children into the world, we owe them fairness and justice in our emotional dealings with them. First and foremost, we need to be conscious of our hidden feelings. If we know we are expecting too much from our children, we can show them love even when they are not achieving what we hope, and we can also encourage them to follow the path of their own hearts and souls rather than the one we ourselves wish we could have followed. Feelings which are conscious and contained do not destroy. Unconscious feelings, which result in unconscious behavior, can cause great injury to a child. No parent's life is perfect and we all harbor unrealistic hopes for our children. This is human and natural. But our children are not divine, nor are they on this earth for our greater glory or the redemption of our own lives. In the marriage of Thetis and Peleus, created through the wisdom of Zeus, lies a profound image of the mixture of human and divine which stands behind every human being's origin. Every child partakes of both. If we can remember this and allow our offspring to be the humans that they are, then this ancient myth can help us to be wiser and more generous parents.

Unable to countenance the possibility of a mortal child, Thetis dipped her son Achilles in the waters of the Styx to give him eternal life.

Thetis Immerses the Infant Achilles into the Water of the Styx, Antonio Balestra (1666–1740)

HERA AND HEPHAISTOS

The ugly duckling

THE STORY OF HERA AND HEPHAISTOS IS ANOTHER TALE ABOUT PARENTAL
EXPECTATIONS. HERE IT IS NOT IMMORTALITY THAT IS EXPECTED OF THE CHILD,
BUT RATHER PHYSICAL BEAUTY BEFITTING AN OLYMPIAN. UNLIKE MANY STORIES
OF THE GODS, THIS ONE HAS A HAPPY ENDING – HEPHAISTOS IS ULTIMATELY
RECOGNIZED FOR HIS GREAT TALENT AND IS GIVEN AN HONORED PLACE IN THE
FAMILY. BUT HE MUST SUFFER TO EARN THIS PLACE, AND HIS SUFFERING IS UNJUST.

Zeus and Hera, king and queen of the gods, conceived their son
Hephaistos in an excess of passion before they were married.
Sadly, this child was born ill-made. His feet were twisted, and his
stumbling gait and dislocated hips aroused the unquenchable laughter of
all the immortals when he walked among them. Hera, ashamed that with
all her beauty and grandeur she should produce such an imperfect
progeny, tried to rid herself of him. She threw him from the heights of
Olympus into the sea, where he was taken in by Thetis, ruler of the sea.

For nine years, the boy remained hidden away beneath the waters. But
Hephaistos was as gifted as he was ugly, and he spent the time forging a
thousand ingenious objects for his friends the sea-nymphs. He was also,
understandably, furious at the treatment he had received and, as he grew
stronger in body and mind, he planned a cunning revenge. One day Hera
received a gift from her absent son – an exquisite golden throne, beautifully wrought and decorated. She sat on it with delight, but, when she
tried to rise again, she was suddenly gripped by invisible bands. In vain
the other gods tried to extricate her from the throne. Only Hephaistos was
capable of releasing her, but he refused to leave the depths of the ocean.
The war-god Ares, his irascible brother, tried to drag him up by force, but
Hephaistos threw burning brands at him. Dionysus, Hephaistos' half-
brother and god of wine, was more successful: he made Hephaistos
drunk, slung him across the back of a mule, and brought him to Olympus.

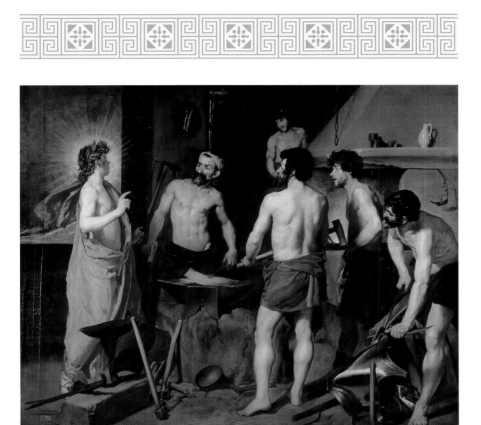

Hephaistos was as gifted as he was ugly, and he worked hard to create many beautiful and useful objects for the other gods.

DETAIL The Forge of Vulcan, Diego Velazquez (1599–1660)

But Hephaistos still refused to cooperate unless his demands were met. He asked for the loveliest of the goddesses, Aphrodite, for a bride. From then on, there was peace between Hera and her son. Forgetting his former rancor, Hephaistos, at peril of his life, attempted to defend his mother when she was being beaten by Zeus. Irritated, Zeus seized his son by one foot and flung him from the courts of heaven. But Hephaistos was taken up to Olympus again and made peace with his father, and forever afterwards Hephaistos played the role of peacemaker among the immortals.

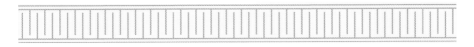

COMMENTARY: This tale speaks of how we may want our children to be a reflection of ourselves, not what they actually are. How many parents, themselves physically attractive, want a son or daughter who is beautiful and will reflect their greater glory? Or perhaps we hope our children will carry on an undeveloped talent of our own, or take over the family business. Whatever we are or would like to be, we hope that our children will be extensions of ourselves, and we may hurt them before we discover their true worth.

This tale is complex and has many subtle motifs. Hephaistos, unloved and unwelcome, finds friendship and support with the sea-gods, who accept him in their underwater domain. Often a child who is not appreciated within the immediate family will be fortunate enough to find an understanding grandparent, uncle or teacher who can recognize and encourage his or her abilities. And we should not be surprised if we discover that the child upon whom we place unfair expectations bears resentment and anger towards us. Hephaistos' revenge is ingenious. He does not wish to destroy his mother; he wishes to be welcomed by her. To accomplish this, he tricks her into bondage.

What is this bondage from which no god can release her? Hera, although she has been harsh and rejecting, is nevertheless not immune to feelings of obligation to her offspring. She is not evil; she is simply vain and self-centered, as human beings so often are. Hephaistos reminds her of the indestructible debt of parenting, which, in human terms, is experienced as what we call guilt. When we experience guilt towards our children, we may know deep down that we have been culpable of failing to recognize the real identity and value of the child. We can only be released when we become conscious of how we have treated those we profess to love, and can offer acceptance rather than imposing expectations.

Hephaistos' forgiving nature also tells us something about the power of love to surmount family conflicts and hurts. Children can forgive their parents a great many acts of omission as well as commission, if they know these acts were committed unwittingly, and if there is some remorse and understanding shown. A genuine apology goes a long way towards healing wounds. This story teaches us that hurts in childhood are not irrevocable. And it encourages us to seek the real value of those we love, even if they do not fulfill the image of what we wish and hope they will be.

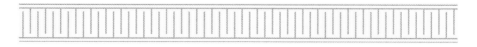

ORION AND OENOPION

A father's possession of his daughter

THIS UNHAPPY GREEK MYTH CONCERNS A FATHER'S ATTEMPT TO POSSESS HIS
DAUGHTER, AND THE DESTRUCTION HE UNLEASHES WHEN A SUITOR APPEARS TO
TAKE HIS BELOVED CHILD AWAY. IT REVEALS THE DARKER UNDERCURRENTS THAT
CAN EXIST IN THE PARENT–CHILD BOND. BUT, ALTHOUGH THE TALE PORTRAYS
SAVAGE EMOTIONS AND EXTREME CIRCUMSTANCES NOT LIKELY TO BE MET IN
EVERYDAY LIFE, NEVERTHELESS, IT OFFERS INSIGHT INTO THE EMOTIONAL
CONFUSION AND BLINDNESS WHICH AFFLICT US WHEN WE SEEK, CONSCIOUSLY OR
UNCONSCIOUSLY, TO POSSESS OUR CHILDREN.

Orion the hunter was reputed to be the most handsome man alive. One day he fell in love with Merope, the daughter of Oenopion. But Oenopion was no mere mortal; he was of immortal descent, being a son of Dionysus, god of wine and ecstasy; and the intense passions of his father were at work deep within him.

Oenopion promised Orion that the hunter could have Merope's hand in marriage, but only if he were able to rid the countryside of the fearsome wild beasts which threatened the lives of the inhabitants. This was no problem for an experienced hunter, and Orion gladly accepted the challenge. Having completed his task, he reported back to Oenopion, eager to receive his prize. But Oenopion found reasons to delay the marriage – there were still more bears, wolves and lions which lurked in the hills. Oenopion really had no intention of giving his daughter away in marriage, because secretly he was in love with her himself.

Orion became increasingly frustrated with the situation. Once more he scoured the hills for wild beasts, and once more Oenopion found reasons to delay the marriage. One night, Orion got very drunk on Oenopion's finest wine (and the wine of a son of Dionysus was fine indeed, and stronger than most) and, in a thoroughly intoxicated state, he burst into Merope's room and raped her. As a result of this violent act, Oenopion felt

Oenopion demanded that, in order to win his daughter's hand, Orion the hunter must scour the land of the fearsome wild beasts which threatened the people.

Wild Boar and Wolf, Friedrich Gauermann (1807–62)

himself justified in revenging himself on Orion. He forced more wine into Orion until the hunter fell into a drunken stupor. Then Oenopion gouged out Orion's eyes and flung him blind and unconscious upon the seashore. Eventually, through the aid of the gods, Orion got his sight back and lived to pursue many more adventures. What happened to poor Merope we do not know – raped, abandoned and imprisoned by a father who never had any intention of letting her become a woman in her own right.

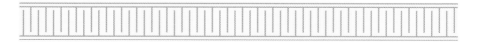

COMMENTARY: The story of Orion is relevant not only to pathological emotional patterns within the family. A healthy bond of love and affection between a father and his daughter may, if exacerbated by unconsciousness, lead to trouble. The father is usually his daughter's first love, and in his little girl many a father sees a magical image of beauty and youth which encapsulates all his most cherished romantic dreams. This is natural and joyful, and does not in any way imply abuse or sickness. But if the father's marriage is unhappy or he cannot accept the rewards of an ordinary human marriage and persists in wanting a magical 'soul bond', he may seek this fantasy of perfect love in his daughter. Then he may find it hard to allow her an independent existence. It takes a generous heart to let a beloved daughter go, especially to a young man as handsome as Orion. Orion's good looks and youthful virility serve as a painful reminder that Oenopion is no longer as young as he used to be, and that his beloved little girl is now a woman who wants a potent young man of her own. There is no mention of Merope's mother in the myth. This father and daughter live in a world of their own, which is the psychological reality of many fathers who relate better to their daughters than to their wives.

The father who tries to turn his daughter into a soulmate may inadvertently inflict lasting damage on her. This may be revealed through the time-honored tactic of insisting that the daughter's chosen partner 'isn't good enough'. If a father sets impossible ideals for his daughter, how can she ever leave him and live happily with a partner of her own? The greater the love, the greater the potential damage arising from unconsciousness; for a daughter who loves and admires her father will listen to his apparent 'wisdom' and will then see every prospective suitor as impossibly flawed.

Oenopion apparently wishes Merope to have a husband. This husband must meet certain standards. And how can any father be blamed for wanting the best for his child? In this way, the father's unconscious possessiveness is concealed by a mask of good intentions. And he may ensure that no one will ever be good enough for his daughter. He then justifies destroying all potential relationships she might make — subtly or obviously — because he believes that he has her best interests at heart. Orion becomes infuriated because Oenopion keeps moving the goal posts, and ultimately he rapes Merope. This gives Oenopion the perfect excuse for ridding

himself of the criminal. But, all along, Oenopion has no intention of letting his precious daughter go, because he wants her for himself.

The great poet Kahlil Gibran (1883–1931) once wrote that our children are born through us but are not of us. Yet a lonely father may feel justified in treating his daughter as a precious object to be possessed by him alone. The young can only move forward in life if their elders permit them free passage. If a daughter is driven by a father's jealousy to choose between father and lover, then her happiness is ruined and the rewards of her love are soured. Children should not be forced to make such a choice; everyone's heart is torn by the coercions of jealousy. Every father holds in his hand the key to his daughter's fulfillment by allowing her to enjoy the love of both father and husband. It is a hard challenge for any father, yet the rewards are great. But we may need to recognize and contain our secret envy and jealousy. As the myth tells us, such feelings are ancient, universal and quintessentially human. But possession is really all about power; and love and power cannot coexist.

THESEUS AND HIPPOLYTUS

Father–son rivalry

THIS GREEK MYTH DESCRIBES THE CORROSIVE JEALOUSY A FATHER FEELS TOWARDS THE SON HE FEARS WILL SUPPLANT HIM IN BEAUTY, STRENGTH AND SEXUAL PROWESS. THE ARCHETYPAL THEME OF THE OLDER MAN WHO FEARS HIS NEW YOUNG WIFE'S SUSCEPTIBILITY TO THE ATTRACTIONS OF A SON BY A FORMER MARRIAGE MAY BE FOUND IN MANY TALES. BUT WHAT IS UNIQUE TO THIS GRIM DEMISE OF A GREAT MYTHIC HERO IS THE WAY IN WHICH JEALOUSY BLINDS THESEUS TO THE TRUTH. WITHOUT THIS BLINDNESS, A NEW MARRIAGE WOULD HAVE NO POWER TO DESTROY THE FATHER–SON BOND.

he great hero Theseus, son of the god Poseidon, became king of Attica after conquering the terrible Minotaur. He ruled his country justly and wisely. But he was unlucky in love, and, in the

end, jealousy of his own offspring proved to be his undoing. His tempestuous affair with the Cretan princess Ariadne, who helped him destroy the Minotaur, ended in tears, and he abandoned her. His passionate liaison with Hippolyta, queen of the Amazons, ended tragically with her death, although she bore him a son, Hippolytus. Finally, he married Phaedra, Ariadne's sister. By this time, Theseus' son Hippolytus was a strong and beautiful youth, fair-haired and grey-eyed, taller and more kingly than his father. This noble young man was devoted to horsemanship and to the chaste cult of the goddess Artemis.

Soon Phaedra, Theseus' new wife, was seized with a consuming passion for her stepson and enlisted her old nurse to plead her cause with the handsome young prince. Upon his shocked refusal she hanged herself, leaving a letter accusing him of her rape. Theseus, convinced by the fact of her death and blinded by a deep, albeit secret, jealousy of the son who now threatened to outshine him in beauty and prowess, drove his son out of the kingdom and invoked the death-curse entrusted to him by his father Poseidon. As Hippolytus drove his chariot along the rocky coastal road from Athens, the god sent a huge wave, bearing on its crest a gigantic sea-bull, which stampeded the horses. The young man's battered corpse was brought back to Theseus, who had learned the truth too late.

After this, Theseus' luck forsook him. Bereft of the beloved son who would have inherited his kingdom, he took to piracy and, while attempting to abduct the queen of the underworld, was confined in torment in the realm of the dead for four years. On his return, he found Athens sunk in lawlessness and sedition. Turning his back on his kingdom, he travelled to the island of Skyros where, through his host's treachery, he fell from a high rock into the sea.

COMMENTARY: *This tale may be enacted on a psychological level in everyday family life. Many a man, accustomed to power and recognition in the world, identifies his masculinity with external achievement. He may experience ageing as a kind of humiliation and fear that lack of potency – worldly, sexual or both – will diminish his value in his own and others' eyes. A son who is just beginning*

Theseus invoked the death-curse against his son, and the god Poseidon sent a huge wave bearing a giant sea-bull which stampeded Hippolytus' horses and destroyed him.

The Death of Hippolytus, Peter Paul Rubens (1577–1640)

to set out on his life's journey – virile, full of promise and with the potential to achieve more than his father – may invoke the corrosive acid of jealousy, even in the midst of great love. If this happens without the father's awareness, then the father may, without meaning to, invoke a 'curse' on his son. He may become withdrawn or overly critical, resenting the bond between his wife and his son. He may crush the child's dreams and aspirations, and seek, unconsciously but with destructive intent, to undermine the young man's confidence so that the older man can retain his feeling of power and control.

The effects of such unconscious jealousy on a child can be catastrophic for him. A young man struggling against secret enmity from his father may persistently find himself failing – at school, at work, in his personal life – because somewhere

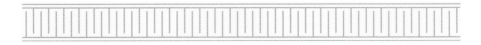

inside he feels that he must do as his father wishes and does not dare to unseat his father from the throne of authority. He may be impelled to become the failure his father unconsciously wishes him to be, even if, on the conscious level, the father expects and encourages success in his son. Such a son may also find himself consistently embroiled in quarrels with authority and may end up acting out all the weakness and confusion which his father projects onto him – be it unconsciously – as a means of avoiding the inevitable weakness and confusion of his own ageing process.

Such a pattern is by no means uncommon; and it is not evil, but merely human. It is a great challenge to any father to find the generosity of heart to allow his son to surpass him – and to accept gracefully the passage of time and the manner in which the world, however unfairly, favors the young. It is also a great challenge to accept the bond between one's wife and one's son as legitimate and worthy of support, rather than as a threat to one's own emotional security. This requires a profound letting go and a trust in life which, if it can be achieved, can provide the support and encouragement which every son needs from his father. It can also generate a deep serenity and inner strength in the father who, recognizing that he has fulfilled his own youthful potentials to the best of his ability, can make peace with what has not been achieved, and move creatively and hopefully into the next phase of life.

OSIRIS, ISIS AND HORUS

The divine child brings eternal hope

THIS TALE FROM ANCIENT EGYPT TEACHES US ABOUT THE CHILD AS AN IMAGE OF HOPE AND RENEWAL, GIVING US THE COURAGE TO SURMOUNT OBSTACLES AND WIN THROUGH TO PEACE AND CONTENTMENT. OSIRIS, ISIS AND HORUS HAVE BEEN LIKENED BY SOME SCHOLARS TO THE CHRISTIAN TRINITY, BECAUSE OF THE DIVINE CHILD WHO REDEEMS SUFFERING AND VANQUISHES EVIL. PSYCHOLOGICALLY, THIS DIVINE FAMILY CAN TELL US MUCH ABOUT THE SENSE OF HOPE AND MEANING WHICH WE EXPERIENCE THROUGH OUR CHILDREN.

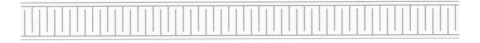

O siris was the first child of Father Earth and Mother Sky. The young god was handsome of countenance and vastly taller than human beings. He took Isis – his sister, the goddess of the Moon – as his wife. Together they taught the people of Egypt how to fashion agricultural implements and produce bread, wine and beer. Isis taught women to grind corn, spin flax and weave cloth. Osiris built the first temples and sculptured the first divine images, thus teaching human beings about the gods. He was called 'The Good One' because he was the enemy of violence, and it was by gentleness alone that he made his will known. But it was not long before Osiris became the victim of a plot by his evil younger brother Set, who was jealous of his power. Set was rough and wild; he had torn himself prematurely from his mother's womb and was determined to rule the world in Osiris' place. He invited Osiris to a banquet and then murdered him, locking the corpse in a coffer which he flung into the Nile.

When Isis heard the news that Osiris had been murdered, she was overwhelmed with grief. She cut off her hair, tore her robes and, at once, set forth in search of the coffer. It had been carried out to sea and borne across the waves to Byblos, where it came to rest at the base of a tamarisk tree. The tree grew with such astonishing speed that the chest was entirely enclosed within its trunk. Meanwhile, the king of Byblos had ordered that the tree be cut down to serve as a prop for the roof of his palace. When this was done, the marvellous tree gave off so exquisite a scent that its reputation reached the ears of Isis, who immediately understood its significance. Without delay, she set off for Byblos, drew the coffer from the trunk of the tree and bore it back to Egypt. But Set, knowing what was afoot, found the coffer where Isis had hidden it in a swamp, opened it and hacked the body of his brother into fourteen pieces which he scattered far and wide.

Isis could not be discouraged. She searched for the precious fragments of her husband and found them all – except for the phallus, which had been swallowed by a Nile crab. A potent sorceress, the goddess then reconstituted the body of Osiris, joining all the fragments together and

26

making a new phallus out of clay. She then performed the rites of embalmment which would restore the murdered god to eternal life. While he slept awaiting his rebirth, Isis lay with him and conceived the divine child Horus, who at birth was likened to a falcon whose eyes shone with the light of the Sun and the Moon.

Resurrected and thenceforward secure from the threat of death, Osiris could have regained his rulership of the world. But he was saddened by the power of evil which he had experienced on earth and he retired to the underworld, where he warmly welcomed the souls of the just and reigned over the dead.

It was left to Osiris' son Horus to avenge the savage act which had resulted in his father's death and dismemberment. Horus was brought up in seclusion, for his mother feared the machinations of Set. He was extremely weak at birth and escaped the dangers which threatened him only with the help of his mother's magic powers. He was bitten by savage beasts, stung by scorpions, burnt, and attacked by pains in the entrails, all through the agency of Set. Yet, despite these sufferings, he grew strong, and Osiris appeared to him frequently and instructed him in the use of arms so that he should soon be able to make war on Set, reclaim his inheritance and avenge his father.

When Horus reached manhood, he began a long war to conquer his enemies and succeeded in destroying many of them. But Set could not be vanquished by force of arms alone, for he was too cunning. In order to terminate the endless bloodshed, the other gods called a tribunal and summoned the two adversaries before it. Set pleaded that Horus was illegitimate, conceived after Osiris had been murdered; but Horus victoriously established the legitimacy of his birth. The gods condemned the usurper, restored Horus' heritage and declared him ruler of Egypt.

Horus reigned peacefully over heaven and earth, and, with his father and mother, was worshipped throughout the land. In between the tasks of ruling, he frequently visited his father in the underworld, ushering the deceased into the presence of 'The Good One' and presiding over the weighing of the soul.

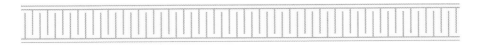

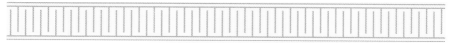

COMMENTARY: No child can redeem the lives of his or her parents. But there is a quality of hope in the future and faith in the innate goodness and innocence of childhood, which can make a dreary or meaningless life worthwhile, and which gives meaning to past suffering. The myth of Osiris, Isis and Horus shows us the deepest core of what makes us seek to create families. It is not only for the continuity of biological life; it is also because the birth of a child augurs a new beginning and the possibility that past pain can be healed. It is the continuity of the spirit as much as the body which we seek in our offspring.

The family of Osiris is archetypal and therefore reflects patterns which exist in every family. The dedication of Isis is an important theme. Despite the obstacles which Set places in her path, she is determined to find and heal her husband's desecrated body. This quality of absolute loyalty is one of the redemptive features of the tale and, in everyday life, it may be expressed by any individual who is willing to give support to his or her partner even in the face of failure and apparent worldly defeat. The wife or husband who is loyal and encouraging when the partner is out of work, or passes through a time of depression or ill-health, may be glimpsed in Isis' dedication. It is in such human ways that we can experience the deeper archetypal theme of redemption presented by this myth.

Another important element in the story is the conception of Horus, which takes place when things are at their worst. Isis conceives her divine child when Osiris is sleeping and awaiting resurrection. What might this mean in terms of ordinary family life? Perhaps it tells us something about the times when we most long to have children; for children often provide a source of hope when circumstances are most difficult. It is not always worldly success and contentment that inspire us to start a family. Sometimes the hard struggle of life makes us seek to establish a foothold in the future and a purpose to our existence.

The childhood of Horus is a precarious one, and he suffers many vicissitudes before he reaches his full strength. This too may tell us something about the pattern of life, for it is out of frail, vulnerable beginnings that our strongest and

The dark god Set, jealous of his brother's power, invited Osiris to a banquet and then murdered him, locking the corpse in a coffer which he flung into the Nile.

DETAIL Death of Osiris, Vatican Borgia Apartment, Benardino Pinturicchio (1454–1513)

most creative efforts are often made. Isis manages to protect her son from Set. Just as we need to protect our vulnerable children, so too do we need to protect that which is most vulnerable and unformed in ourselves, so that it can grow to fruition. Horus understands that he must redeem his father's suffering; Osiris himself no longer wishes to remain on earth to carry on the struggle. At a certain point, we may need to trust our children to deal with the future, for, as we grow older, we may no longer have the energy or courage to do battle with life. Here we can see echoes of other mythic stories: the jealousy which Theseus feels toward Hippolytus (see pages 22–5), for example, reflects his inability to trust his son to take the reins and have his turn at life. Osiris, on the other hand, meets this challenge successfully.

The resolution of the conflict comes not because of any individual conquest, but because the gods as a group decide that Horus deserves the restoration of his inheritance. In the end we, too, may have to allow life to complete what we have left unfinished, and trust whatever we understand as God or the spirit within to fulfill what we are trying to achieve. If what we seek is fair and just, as is the case with Horus, then evil may not be vanquished forever, but it can be rendered powerless to destroy that which is good. Within the family, trusting that time and inner rightness will lead to eventual balance and serenity can help us to accept situations which we cannot change, to forgive those whom we feel have injured us, and to retain our faith in the future.

THE STORY OF POIA

Grandfather and grandson redeem the past

THE FINAL TALE IN THIS CHAPTER COMES TO US FROM THE BLACKFOOT TRIBE OF
THE NORTH AMERICAN PLAINS. IT TEACHES US THAT THE POWER OF LOVE TO HEAL
FAMILIES CAN LEAP A GENERATION FROM GRANDPARENT TO GRANDCHILD,
REDEEMING THE SUFFERING WHICH PARENTS AND CHILDREN MAY EXPERIENCE
WITH EACH OTHER, AND MAKING THE WISDOM OF THE PAST AVAILABLE TO FUTURE
GENERATIONS.

Once upon a time Morning Star looked down from the heavens and noticed on earth Soatsaki, a Blackfoot girl of great beauty. He fell in love with her, married her and took her up to heaven, to the dwelling of his father and mother, the Sun and Moon. There Soatsaki bore him a son, whom they named Little Star.

The Moon, Soatsaki's mother-in-law, made the young woman feel loved and welcome, but warned her not to dig up a magic turnip which grew near their dwelling. But curiosity got the better of Soatsaki. She tore up the forbidden turnip and found that she could see the earth through the hole she had made. Seeing the dwellings of her tribe, she felt violently homesick, and her heart grew deathly sad. To punish her disobedience, her father-in-law turned her out of heaven with her son Little Star and lowered them to earth wrapped in an elk skin. But when the poor girl found herself separated from her beloved husband, she soon died, leaving her son alone and poor.

The child had a scar on his face, so he was nicknamed Poia, or Scarface. When he grew up, Poia fell in love with the chief's daughter, but she rebuffed him because of the scar. In despair, he made up his mind to seek his grandfather the Sun, who could take away the disfigurement. So Poia started out towards the West. When he reached the Pacific Ocean, he halted and passed three days in fasting and prayer. On the morning of the fourth day a luminous trail unrolled before him across the ocean. Poia stepped boldly onto the miraculous path. When he reached the Sun's dwelling place in the sky, he saw his father Morning Star battling with seven monstrous birds. Rushing to the rescue, he slew the monsters. In reward for this deed, his grandfather the Sun took away the scar and, after teaching Poia the ritual of the Sun-dance, made him a gift of ravens' feathers as proof of his kinship with the Sun and a magic flute which would win him the heart of his beloved. Poia returned to earth by another path, called the Milky Way. He taught the Blackfoot tribe the mystery of the Sun-dance and, having married the chief's daughter, took her up to heaven to live with his father Morning Star and his grandparents the Sun and Moon.

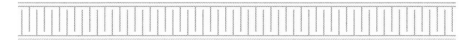

When Poia reached the Pacific Ocean in search of his grandfather, the Sun, a luminous trail unrolled before him; leading to the Sun's dwelling place in the sky.

Sunset, Frederick Childe Hassam (1859–1935)

COMMENTARY: The hero of this charming story is called Scarface — and indeed, many a child suffers the psychological wounding of marital difficulties which result in separation and alienation between the parents. Here the conflict arises because Poia's mother, Soatsaki, cannot abide by the rules of the divine family into which she marries. Through this rebellion against the family, she suffers and is separated from her husband, and Poia is separated from his father.

We may see such a scenario enacted on a regular basis, where an individual marrying into a strongly enmeshed family cannot adapt and is driven out, emotionally and sometimes literally. It often occurs in so-called 'mixed marriages', where a particular economic, religious or racial background forms a powerful edifice into which an 'outsider' cannot fit. And it is the children who bear the scars.

But Poia, the grandchild of the Sun and Moon, refuses to accept this fate. He demands entry into the kingdom of his grandfather, whom he knows can heal his disfigurement. On a psychological level, this tells us that a loving relationship with a grandparent can often heal the damage caused by an unhappy parental marriage. Poia must prove himself – he defends the life of his father, Morning Star, by slaying the vicious birds – and we may sometimes have to take the initiative and approach alienated relatives with courage and compassion, even if we feel they have been responsible for the rift. Because Poia is willing to attempt this, risking his pride in the process, his rewards are great. He is not only healed of his scar, but is able to take the wisdom of the Sun to his wife's people and spread it amongst ordinary humanity, passing the gifts of his ancestors to successive generations.

One profound message embedded in this myth concerns a willingness to swallow pride and make the effort to renew bonds which have been severed by others' mistakes. It is often the case in families that children are alienated from their grandparents because of the parents' disharmony, or because of conflicts between parents and grandparents. Whether because of time, distance or some deeper spark of love which is sustained despite the conflict, the willingness of any child to bridge the past – the magical bridge over which Poia walks to reach his grandfather's kingdom – may bring about a reuniting of the family and a channel through which the wisdom of the past can be transmitted to the generations of the future.

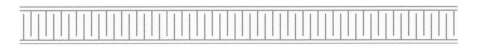

Chapter Two

SIBLINGS

The bonds between brothers and sisters may be as potent, complex and transformative – for good or ill – as those between parents and children. In our siblings we see the mirror of our own undiscovered selves. And the love and antipathy we feel towards them reflect many things, not least how we relate to the lesser-known dimensions of our own hidden depths. Psychology has much to say about sibling rivalry, but myth said it all first. These myths also speak of the healing and redemptive power of sibling love.

CAIN AND ABEL

Who is Father's favorite?

THIS STORY FROM THE OLD TESTAMENT IS KNOWN TO US ALL, BUT PERHAPS WE HAVE NOT REFLECTED SUFFICIENTLY ON HOW A PARENT CAN BE THE SOURCE OF CONFLICT BETWEEN HIS OR HER CHILDREN. THE STORY OF CAIN AND ABEL IS CONCERNED WITH WHAT IS KNOWN AS 'SIBLING RIVALRY' – THE JEALOUSY AND COMPETITION WHICH OCCURS BETWEEN BROTHERS AND SISTERS. SIBLING RIVALRY IS AS NATURAL AND INEVITABLE AS THE SUN'S RISING, AND AS OLD. A LITTLE CAN GENERATE HEALTHY SELF-DEVELOPMENT. A LOT CAN CREATE PAIN AND DESTRUCTIVE BEHAVIOR WITHIN FAMILIES.

Adam and Eve had two sons. Abel, the younger, was a shepherd, while his older brother Cain worked in the fields. There came a time when they both made offerings to God. Cain offered a portion of his crops, the fruit of the fields, while Abel made his offering from the finest and fattest of his flock. God was well pleased with Abel's

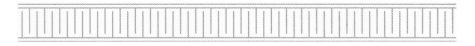

offering, but not with Cain's. And, as Cain could discern no reason for this favoritism, he grew very angry and bitter towards both God and his brother, Abel.

God perceived Cain's anger and said, 'Why are you angry? You will succeed if you work hard. If you do not, the fault will be yours.'

But Cain was not soothed by these words. His anger grew inside him. However, as it is not wise to be angry with God, his anger turned towards his younger brother. He followed Abel into the fields and there attacked and murdered him.

'Cain, where is your brother?' God said to him.

'I do not know,' replied Cain. 'I am not my brother's keeper.'

But God, of course, knew what had happened. 'Why have you done this terrible thing?' God said to Cain. 'Your brother's blood is crying out to me from the ground, like a voice calling for revenge. I am placing you under a curse; you will no longer till the soil. It has soaked up your brother's blood as if it had opened its mouth to receive it when you killed him. If you try to grow crops, the soil will produce nothing. You will be a homeless wanderer on the earth.'

And Cain said to God, 'I cannot bear this punishment. You are driving me off the land and out of your presence. I will be an outcast, and anyone who finds me will kill me.'

But God answered, 'No. If anyone kills you, seven lives will be taken in revenge.' So God put a mark on Cain's forehead to warn anyone who met him not to kill him. And Cain went away from God's presence and went to live in a land called Nod, which means 'Wandering', far east of Eden.

COMMENTARY: *Those who are of an orthodox religious bent will probably not question the dubious morality of this tale. But if we consider the story carefully, we may well wonder why God favors Abel when Cain displays just as much devotion. Indeed, there is no fairness in God's judgement. Each brother gives the best of what he produces; Cain cannot offer sheep because his vocation is tilling the soil. Here we may glimpse echoes of an all-too-common family dynamic: the rivalry between siblings which erupts when a parent favors one child over the*

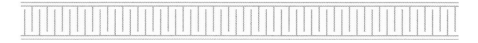

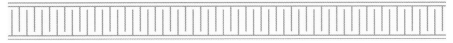

other. Cain can see no reason for being rejected by God, and his anger, viewed objectively, is quite justified. Yet he cannot vent his anger directly on God, any more than a child can vent his or her anger on a powerful parent. Anger exhibited towards God could result in annihilation. Children have a deep and archetypal fear of their parents, not necessarily because the parents merit it, but because a mother and father are godlike figures in a child's psyche, and wield the power of life and death.

Because of this, Cain's anger is directed towards his brother. This is often the result when we are frightened of exhibiting our rage towards someone we love or fear. It is displaced onto the sibling who seems to have won all the parents' love, and although most of the time it leads to a subtler form of killing – coldness and spite – it can sometimes result in physical violence, even in 'normal' families. The key to this story is ultimately not the rivalry between the brothers, but a deity who displays a favoritism based on his personal tastes. God evidently prefers sheep to corn – therefore Cain, rather than Abel, is rejected. A vegetarian might well question this preference! When we look at family dynamics, the reasons for favoritism lie in the individual parent's own psychological outlook. The father who prefers sport to artistic creation may favor an athletic son over a musical one; the mother who is preoccupied with appearances may prefer a pretty daughter to a studious but plain one. Life, like families, is unfair.

In this tale there is no resolution; Cain is made homeless and outcast. Yet God spares him. Perhaps God feels a bit guilty, because the root of this sibling rivalry lies with him. In family life, there may be a resolution to conflict, but this can only come if the warring siblings are honest enough to talk to each other about where the real hurt lies, and if the injured or rejected one can consciously recognize his or her anger towards the offending parent. And perhaps the greatest responsibility of all lies with the parent who, like God in the story, may behave in a distinctly unfair and irrational way, without sufficient inner reflection. God may have the right to such behavior, but parents do not. The sibling rivalry reflected in

Enraged at God's favoritism towards Abel, and unable to understand why his own offerings were refused, Cain brutally murdered his brother in secret.

Cain Slaying Abel, Peter Paul Rubens (1577–1640)

the tale of Cain and Abel does not spring from innate antipathy between the siblings; it is generated by the complex dynamics of the family itself. If we are emotionally generous and honest enough to see to the core, we may be able to eradicate the mark of Cain from our own and our children's brows.

ARES AND HEPHAISTOS

Who gets the girl?

THIS GREEK TALE PORTRAYS THE BATTLE BETWEEN TWO BROTHERS FOR THE SAME WOMAN, AND THE SECRET SOURCE OF THE RIVALRY, WHICH LIES IN PARENTAL MEDDLING. THE RIVALRY BETWEEN ARES AND HEPHAISTOS ERUPTS NOT BECAUSE THEY ARE TEMPERAMENTALLY DOOMED TO HATE EACH OTHER, BUT BECAUSE THEIR PARENTS USE THEM AS PAWNS IN A GAME. IN PSYCHOLOGICAL TERMS, WE MIGHT CALL THIS GAME CONDITIONAL LOVE – THE PROMISE THAT IF A CHILD DOES OR IS A PARTICULAR THING, THEN THE PARENTS WILL OFFER LOVE IN RETURN.

A res and Hephaistos were both the children of Zeus and Hera, king and queen of heaven. We have seen something of Hephaistos' difficult infancy and and his eventual reconciliation with his parents (*see pages 16–18*). Although the story told here is slightly different, we see many similar themes emerging.

The childhood of Ares was quite unlike that of his brother. When he was born a new light shone on Olympus; for unlike Hephaistos, Ares was physically flawless. His father's radiance and his mother's grandeur marked his countenance with beauty and gave strength to his splendid limbs.

Hera demanded what gift Zeus would give to this handsome son as a birthright. But Zeus had already given away the sun and moon, the sea and the underworld. He could not think of anything he could give this child so adored by Hera. Eventually, because his wife nagged him constantly on the matter, he sent his messenger Hermes to roam earth and heaven to find a suitable gift. But Hermes, another son of Zeus, was not fond of his

half-brother Ares. Although the new god was handsome, he was, in Hermes' eyes, dull and surly. A loud voice and a powerful kick seemed to be the scope of his talents. Partly from loyalty to Zeus and partly from mischief, he eventually brought to Olympus Aphrodite, the enchanting goddess of love and desire, just risen from the sea. Her beauty and grace were a fitting tribute to the new child. Her propensity for creating havoc was an equally fitting tribute, although at first only Hermes knew this.

While the birthday party of the young god was being celebrated, Hermes revealed the beautiful Aphrodite to Ares, who, although only a child, responded with the unmistakable signs of naked lust. At the same moment, Hera was suddenly made aware of her first-born son, Hephaistos, who had been living beneath the sea in the kingdom of the sea-goddess Thetis. At the party, Thetis was wearing an exquisite brooch, and Hera, who coveted it, demanded to meet its creator. With some reluctance Thetis summoned Hephaistos to Olympus. Thus mother and son came face to face for the first time since her child had been flung from heaven. Because she desired the treasures which he alone was capable of creating, Hera invited Hephaistos to remain on Olympus. He was then asked what he wished for as a gift to seal this long overdue reunion between injured child and thoughtless mother.

Hephaistos could not think of anything he wanted that he could not make himself. And then he saw the gift which Hermes had brought from the sea to give to Ares, and knew at once what he desired. He demanded Aphrodite as a bride. Although Zeus at first protested at this mismatch, Hera overrode him; her allegiance had shifted from Ares, the handsome war-god, to the crippled artisan-god who could make such beautiful things. Thus Hephaistos was granted Aphrodite as his gift, while his brother Ares was betrayed and left whining with hatred and rage as he crouched on the floor.

OVERLEAF *The ugly Hephaistos received the radiant goddess of love and desire as his bride, even though she had been promised to his brother Ares.*

Venus in the Forge of Vulcan, Jan Bruegel the Elder (1568–1625)

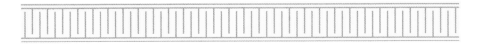

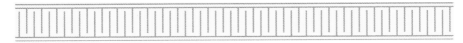

Zeus stared down at this handsome child whose heart, through hurt and disappointment, was becoming as misshapen as his brother's body. In a fit of disgust, Zeus shouted, 'Hatred! Discord! Violence! That will be your birthright! What else are you fit for?' With that he stormed from the hall. Sly Hermes then came to comfort the raging child, who suddenly demanded with a bellow that he wanted the earth for his birthright. Hermes patiently explained that the earth could be the property of no god; it belonged to itself. But Ares would not tolerate yet another disappointment. The young war-god swore by the River Styx that if anyone else was given the earth, he would tear and bite and hack them into bloody pieces. Hermes listened and wondered. To whom would the earth one day belong? For in this dawn-time of the gods' rule, humankind had not yet been created.

COMMENTARY: *Hera demands a gift for her handsome new child because she is proud of his beauty; but this has little to do with the child's own needs. It is vanity rather than love which motivates her. Zeus fobs off the responsibility for choosing the gift – and how many busy parents, too preoccupied with their own concerns, ask someone else to pick a present for their child's birthday, or send a surrogate to the school play because they have no time to go themselves? When Hephaistos is discovered to have talents which can glorify Hera and impress others, then suddenly he is the favored one; and Ares, once adored, is abruptly pushed aside. Is it any wonder, then, that these two brothers find themselves bitter rivals, and that the brother who has been humiliated takes vengeance on the world as a result?*

One of the most striking themes in this myth is the callous indifference which Zeus and Hera show towards both their offspring. Ares may be impetuous and self-willed, but he has positive qualities too – strength, courage, energy – which deserve to be honored. Given a gift suited to his nature and offered with love, he might have turned out altogether different. These Olympian parents do not recognize their children as individuals. They are more concerned with what their children can do for them. Sadly, this indifference is not uncommon in many families, although not perhaps as brutally displayed as here; and it is usually

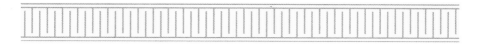

deeply unconscious and not intended to injure. Common too is the theme of love given in exchange for what 'goodies' a child can offer the parent. Unhappily, many well-meaning parents who have been soured by their own early disappointments want their children to shine so that they, the parents, can bask in the reflected glory. 'If you become what I want you to be, I will love you best!' is the unspoken message.

But the anxiety which conditional love provokes is intolerable for any child. While some children manage to perform well to please their parents, others, perhaps a little like Ares, do not have the cleverness or special talents to fulfill parental expectations. They feel humiliated and enraged as a result, later venting this rage on others because, deep inside, they feel worthless. And the clever child who achieves favor may suffer equally. He or she learns to equate self-worth with pleasing others, and may spend a lifetime trying to be what others want. Hephaistos must go on making beautiful objects whether he wants to or not, because, if he stops, he will lose his mother's love.

Aphrodite is the goddess of love, and thus she is a symbol of love itself. It is really love which is the gift first offered to Ares, then snatched away and given to Hephaistos on condition that he pleases his mother. The wise parent does not make love conditional, but offers it freely because every child is lovable as himself or herself. This does not preclude discipline; but it precludes manipulation, which damages children far more than an honest punishment meted out fairly. Whatever our disappointments in life, our children are not obliged to live their lives according to our designs, or to compensate for something we feel we lack. Had Zeus and Hera recognized this simple truth at the outset of the story, then, according to the myth, war would not exist on earth.

ROMULUS AND REMUS

Who is biggest and best?

THERE ARE MANY MYTHS OF RIVAL TWINS, AND MANY OF THESE TALES END BADLY. IN THIS STORY FROM ANCIENT ROME, THE ENMITY IS NOT DUE TO PARENTAL SOURCES; IT ARISES FROM SIMPLE JEALOUSY OVER WHO IS GOING TO BE FIRST AND BEST ON THE WORLD'S STAGE. THE MATTER-OF-FACT WAY IN WHICH THE ROMANS PORTRAYED THE JEALOUSY BETWEEN ROMULUS AND REMUS, AND THE MURDER OF ONE BY THE OTHER, REFLECTS THE TIMELESS AND ARCHETYPAL NATURE OF SIBLING RIVALRY.

One fine afternoon the war-god Mars (known to the Greeks as Ares) took a walk through the woods on one of the seven hills of what would later become the city of Rome. There, in a woodland glade, he found a beautiful young woman asleep. She was Rhea Silvia, daughter of the king of Alba. Although Rhea Silvia was consecrated as a Vestal Virgin, nevertheless Mars raped her. On the orders of her father, the resulting twins were laid in a winnowing basket and set afloat on the Tiber, so that his daughter's shame might not be discovered; for the king did not believe that these children had been fathered by a god.

But the river-god of the Tiber knew the truth; and he made the river overflow, so that the twin boys were carried safely to a grotto beneath a fig tree. The babies were frightened and hungry, and they cried and cried, but no human answered their call. However, a nearby she-wolf heard, and came to suckle the infants.

Eventually the twins were found by a shepherd and his wife, who took pity on the children; so the boys were sheltered and brought up humbly, ignorant of their origins. The shepherd called them Romulus and Remus.

When they were grown, the young men proved to be as strong, courageous and impetuous as their divine father. They decided to found a city, and carefully studied the flight of birds, consulting with local augurs to get the correct auspices. In that section of the sky which the augur's wand

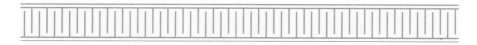

Romulus and Remus, children of the god Mars, abandoned and then succoured by a she-wolf, were finally found by a shepherd and his wife, who took pity on the children.

DETAIL Romulus and Remus, Charles de Lafosse (1636–1716)

had apportioned to Romulus, twelve vultures appeared. But in Remus' section only six could be seen. The augur pronounced Romulus the rightful founder of the new city. Romulus proceeded, with a plough harnessed to a white cow and a white bull, to draw a furrow which should mark the boundary of the new city's walls. Remus jumped over the furrow in derision, for he was jealous and wanted to destroy his brother's confidence. A violent quarrel ensued; Remus first tried to murder Romulus; and in self-defense Romulus, overcome with the frenzy of his father the war-god, killed his brother.

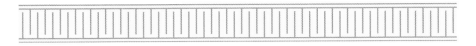

Romulus went on to found his city alone, which was called Rome after him. In order to people the town he founded a place of asylum between the ramparts, where outlaws, villains and homeless wanderers of all kinds began to congregate. Women of the neighbouring tribes refused to marry the men from this settlement of outlaws, so Romulus and his followers abducted the daughters of one of the tribes, and thus the future population of the new Rome was assured. When his work was done and the future of his city secure, Mars called his son home; Romulus vanished mysteriously during a furious thunderstorm and was afterwards worshipped by the Roman people as a god.

COMMENTARY: Although murder is not the usual outcome of sibling rivalry, lasting coldness and enmity in adult life are sometimes the fruit of a childhood in which competition proves stronger than cooperation, and envy more powerful than affection. Material security, in the form of money or property, is the cause of many a quarrel between siblings, especially when it concerns who will inherit how much from the parents when they die. And it is worldly power which fuels the struggle between Romulus and Remus, not a quest for a parent's love.

Is there anything parents can do when confronted with such a demonstration of rivalry between offspring? It is most commonly expressed between two brothers or two sisters; and while in some families such jealousy is balanced by mutual loyalty, in others animosity can corrode the home atmosphere and create lasting scars in one or both children. Perhaps one of the keys to the problem lies in this story. Remus becomes jealous only when he discovers that his augury is not as favorable as his brother's – in other words, that his value is less in others' eyes. The seeds of sibling rivalry of this kind are often sown by comparisons, and it may be important for any parent to recognize how hurtful and dangerous such comparisons can be. 'Why can't you do as well at school as your brother?' says the unthinking father to his son. 'Why can't you dress as nicely as your sister?' says the unconscious mother to her daughter. 'Why do you sit and read a book when the other children are out playing?' says the oblivious teacher. 'Why don't you join in and make friends like other children?' In the story of Romulus and Remus it is the augur who plays this role, revealing a comparison which will

inevitably sow the seeds of discord if it is interpreted as a value judgement. And perhaps the absent father – Mars, after all, does not contribute anything once he has made Rhea Silvia pregnant – has failed his children because he is not present to encourage each one individually.

We may also speculate on how different things might have been if Romulus and Remus had decided to found two different cities, far enough apart so as not to invite comparisons. Their very natures, as children of the war-god, are unsuited to compromise and cooperation. This is a fact of life, not a judgement of character, and it is sometimes wise to recognize that the naturally competitive child needs space to develop his or her own talents without being overshadowed by a sibling. Every child needs to define his or her space and form an individual identity, and everything possible should be done to support this natural and healthy individual development. Then there is room for love, mutual support and friendship to grow. A certain degree of rivalry may always exist between siblings. But a little wisdom and sensitivity, exercised in time, may prevent the spirit of the war-god from entering where it is not welcome.

ANTIGONE

Loyalty over life

THIS GREEK MYTH IS CONCERNED WITH THE DEEP LOVE AND LOYALTY WHICH CAN DEVELOP BETWEEN SIBLINGS. WHILE THERE ARE MANY POTENTIAL PROBLEMS IN SIBLING RELATIONSHIPS, MUCH JOY AND HAPPINESS MAY ALSO BE FOUND. THE STORY OF ANTIGONE POSES US WITH A PROFOUND MORAL DILEMMA: WHICH DO WE CHOOSE, FAMILY LOYALTY OR SOCIAL OPINION?

Antigone was one of the two daughters of King Oedipus of Thebes, born of the dark and tragic union between Oedipus and his mother, Jocasta. But despite this shadowed birth, Antigone's character was loyal and loving, and her actions were entirely blameless. After her father discovered the shame of his marriage and was driven from

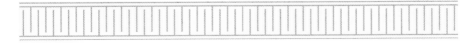

Thebes, blinded and pursued by the avenging Furies, Antigone was his faithful guide as he wandered for years through country after country (*see pages 58–63*).

After Oedipus' banishment, his twin sons, Polyneices and Eteocles, were elected co-kings of the city. They agreed to reign for alternate years. But Eteocles, to whom the first term fell, would not relinquish the throne at the end of the year and banished his brother Polyneices from the city. A terrible war broke out between them for the kingship. Polyneices, to avoid further slaughter, offered to decide the succession of the throne by single combat with his brother. Eteocles accepted the challenge; and in the course of the ensuing bitter struggle, each mortally wounded the other. Their uncle, Creon, then took command of the armies and declared himself king of Thebes, issuing an edict that his dead nephews must not be buried. Without a burial, their shades must wander forever on the shores of the River Styx. Anyone who disobeyed this edict would be buried alive as a punishment.

But Antigone, who had loved her brother Polyneices dearly, knew that the evil which had led to war had come from Eteocles. She crept out secretly at night and built a pyre with Polyneices' corpse upon it, and scattered earth upon the body to release the soul for its passage into the underworld.

Looking out of his palace window, King Creon noticed a distant glow which seemed to proceed from a burning pyre and, going to investigate, surprised Antigone in her act of disobedience. He summoned his son Haemon, to whom Antigone had been betrothed, and ordered him to bury her alive. Haemon feigned readiness to do as he was told, but instead married Antigone secretly and sent her away to live among his shepherds, where she bore him a son. Thus her willingness to die rather than betray her heart created life rather than death.

Antigone, loyal to her dead brother even in the face of her own potential death, is an image of all that is noble, honorable and courageous in the human heart.

DETAIL Antigone, Lord Leighton (1830–96)

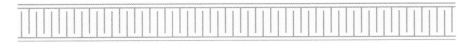

Despite King Creon's edict, Antigone scattered earth over her brother's unburied corpse in order to release his soul for its passage into the underworld.

Antigone from Sophocles' 'Antigone', Marie Spartali Stillman (1844–1927)

COMMENTARY: The figure of Antigone has come down to us as a symbol of absolute loyalty in the face of death. Here is a sister who, far from feeling jealous of her brother, recognizes the injustice of the fate which has been visited upon him and refuses to countenance it, even if this means offering up her own life in the process. She also recognizes the evil of false authority and the horror of gratuitous cruelty, and does what she can to counteract it. Her clear sense of justice is infectious; for, in response to her actions, Haemon, her fiancé, disobeys his father and rescues her.

There are many subtle inferences in this tale, apart from the shining light of Antigone's loyalty to her brother. Creon, self-declared king of Thebes, represents the presiding social rules of the time. While such rules may be rigidly enforced, they reflect the personal values and ambitions of the people who set them, and

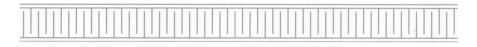

their ultimate rightness may be open to question. Those who slavishly follow what 'The Great They' define as right and wrong may, like Creon, be empty within, propped up only by the power they wield in the outside world. Thus, what is deemed 'socially correct' at any given time may yield to a different interpretation of social correctness later, when the old rule gives way to a new one; and only those like Antigone, with clear sight and a clear heart, can see beyond what is deemed socially appropriate to what is truly right according to the inner voice of the soul.

Although children are rarely called upon to defend their siblings in the face of such a conflagration, nevertheless the decision which Antigone makes reflects the enormous moral and emotional power of a committed heart. It not only redeems the wandering spirit of Polyneices; it also transforms the son of Creon and redeems the evil of his father, which is rendered powerless. This depth of love can be found between many brothers and sisters, and it is one of the great joys and gifts of a strong family life. It can occur even when the rest of the family have gone completely over the edge. The mythic history of the House of Thebes is a dark one, and begins even before Oedipus himself. Sin follows sin in this family, worse than any television soap opera, and the line is plagued by the curses of various offended gods. The House of Thebes is the ultimate 'dysfunctional family'. Yet even in the face of such chaos, a bond of love and loyalty such as that between Antigone and Polyneices can endure. The power of human love within the family can withstand even a psychological inheritance of great destructiveness, redeeming the past and remaking the future.

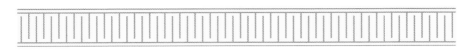

Chapter Three

THE FAMILY INHERITANCE

Myth speaks eloquently and at length about the mystery of inheritance from one generation to another. Unlike today, when we view the matter of family inheritance almost exclusively from either the financial or the genetic point of view, myth presents us with a vivid picture of psychological inheritance – the passing down of unresolved conflicts and dilemmas which face each generation until a family member, sufficiently honest and courageous, deals with the issue consciously and with integrity. Family inheritance in myth may be positive or negative or a mixture of the two; but it is invariably linked with gifts from the gods which are used either constructively or with arrogance and ignorance by each successive generation.

THE CHILDREN OF THE WIND

Intelligence without humility

THIS GREEK TALE IS CONCERNED WITH ONE OF THE GREAT MYSTERIES OF THE FAMILY: WHERE DO OUR GIFTS AND TALENTS COME FROM? THE STORY TELLS US ABOUT A GIFT WHICH IS PASSED DOWN FROM A GOD TO HIS HUMAN DESCENDANTS. IT IMPLIES THAT OUR TALENTS ARE NOT 'OURS', BUT ARE THE PROPERTY OF THE GODS, MADE MANIFEST THROUGH HUMAN BEINGS WHO ARE THE CARETAKERS AND VESSELS FOR DIVINE CREATIVE POWER. IT ALSO SUGGESTS THAT THE MISUSE OF INHERITED GIFTS CAN END IN DISASTER, AND THAT IT IS UP TO US TO USE OUR TALENTS TO SERVE RATHER THAN CONTROL LIFE.

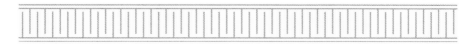

The lord of the winds was called Aeolus. He was clever and ingenious, and it was he who invented ships' sails. But he was also pious and just, and honored the gods; thus his divine father Poseidon, god of the sea, made him guardian of all the winds. Aeolus' son Sisyphos inherited his intelligence, adaptability and ingenuity, but not, unfortunately, his piety. Sisyphos was a cunning rogue and a cattle thief who won a kingdom by treachery; and once in power he proved to be a cruel tyrant. His method of executing his enemies – not to mention rich travellers rash enough to risk his hospitality – was to peg them on the ground and crush them with stones.

In the end, Sisyphos went too far and cheated Zeus, king of heaven. When Zeus stole a girl from her father and hid her, Sisyphos was the only person on earth who knew where she was; and he promised Zeus he would keep the secret. But in return for a bribe, he told the girl's father where to find the lovers. His reward from Zeus was death. But clever Sisyphos tricked the death-god Hades, tied him up and locked him in a dungeon. Now that the lord of the underworld was a prisoner, no mortal in the world could die. This was particularly galling to Ares the war-god, since all over the world men were being killed in battle only to spring back to life and fight again. Eventually Ares freed Hades, and the two of them frog-marched Sisyphos to the underworld.

Refusing to admit defeat, Sisyphos played another cunning trick to escape his fate. When he arrived in the underworld, he went straight to Queen Persephone and complained that he had been dragged down alive and unburied, and that he needed three days in the upper world to arrange his funeral. Suspecting nothing, Persephone agreed, and Sisyphos went back to the mortal world and continued his life exactly as before. In desperation, Zeus sent Hermes, who was cleverer even than Sisyphos, to bring him to his appointed doom. The judges of the dead gave Sisyphos a punishment to suit both his trickery and his cruel method of killing people with stones. They placed a huge rock above him on a steep hillside. The only way he could prevent it rolling back and crushing him was to push it up the hill. Hades promised that if he ever succeeded in pushing it

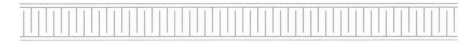

Bellerophon, riding the winged horse Pegasus, thrust a lead-tipped spear into the throat of the fire-breathing monster Chimaera, which choked to death on the molten lead.

Bellerophon, riding Pegasus, slaying the Chimaera, Giovanni-Battista Tiepolo (1696–1770)

over the top and down the other side, his punishment would end. With immense effort, Sisyphos heaved the boulder to the edge of the downward slope, but the huge rock always tricked him, slipping out of his grasp and chasing him all the way back down the hill. This was his doom until the end of time.

Back on earth, Sisyphos had left sons and grandsons, and all of them inherited the sparkling intelligence of the wind-lord Aeolus. But they did not use the gift wisely. Sisyphos' son was called Glaucus. He was a clever horseman but, scorning the power of the goddess Aphrodite, he refused to let his mares breed. He hoped by this means to make them more spirited than other contestants in the chariot races which were his chief interest. But Aphrodite was vexed at this violation of nature by human

machination and led the mares out by night to graze on a special herb. As soon as Glaucus yoked the mares to his chariot the next day, they bolted, overthrew the chariot, dragged him along the ground entangled in the reins and then ate him alive.

The son of Glaucus was called Bellerophon. This handsome young man had inherited his great-grandfather Aeolus' inventiveness and quick wit, his grandfather Sisyphos' fierce temper and his father Glaucus' arrogance. One day Bellerophon had a violent argument with his brother and killed him. Horrified by his crime, he took a vow never to show emotion again and fled from his native land.

He wandered through many countries and eventually arrived at the rock-fortress of Tiryns, where the queen took a fancy to him and invited him to become her lover. Bellerophon, wisely fearing the emotional consequences, declined. But no one had ever refused the queen of Tiryns before. Humiliated and enraged, she went secretly to her husband and accused Bellerophon of attempted rape. The king was reluctant to punish Bellerophon and risk the Furies' vengeance by the direct murder of a suppliant. He therefore sent Bellerophon to the court of his wife's father, the king of Lycia, with a sealed letter which read, 'Pray remove the bearer from this world; he has tried to violate my wife, your daughter.'

The king of Lycia duly sent the young hero on a series of deadly quests. For his first task, Bellerophon had to kill Chimaera, a fire-breathing monster which lived on a nearby mountain, terrorizing the people and scorching the land. Bellerophon was intelligent enough to know that he needed help quickly. He consulted a seer, who gave the hero a bow, a quiver of arrows and a spear tipped with a large block of lead instead of a point. Then Bellerophon was instructed to go to a magical fountain where he would find the winged horse Pegasus drinking. Bellerophon must tame the horse, bridle him, and fly on his back to fight Chimaera.

All this Bellerophon duly did, destroying the fire-breathing monster by hurling the lead-tipped spear into its throat so that the lead melted, ran down into its lungs and choked it. Returning to Lycia, he defeated the enemies the king sent against him by pelting them from the sky with

stones. In the end, the king recognized a champion in Bellerophon, and gave him his daughter and half his kingdom.

Up until now Bellerophon had used his inherited intelligence while curbing his arrogance and impetuousness. But, when he eventually discovered that it was the queen of Tiryns who had been responsible for all his troubles, Bellerophon's rage overcame him and he flew on the winged horse to Tiryns, snatched the queen thousands of feet into the air and dropped her to her death. Then, full of his own hot-headedness and the excitement of flying like the wind – his great-grandfather Aeolus was, after all, lord of the winds – he decided to soar still higher and visit the gods themselves. But mortals cannot enter Olympus unless a god invites them. Zeus sent a fly to sting Pegasus; the winged horse reared, and Bellerophon plunged to his death.

COMMENTARY: There has always been a debate about whether intelligence is something we inherit. All kinds of causes, from environment to education to cultural emphases, are offered to explain why cleverness seems to run in families. However, whether or not intelligence is inherited, the maturity and morality which enable us to use it wisely are not genetic, and remain in the hands of each individual – as well as in the hands of parents who teach their children to value that which is on the side of life.

The Greeks believed in the inheritance of gifts; they assumed that if a god or demi-god, such as Aeolus, stood behind a human line, then his descendants inherited some of his attributes, perhaps diluted over successive generations, but nevertheless present in each family member. Intelligence, in Greek myth, is no less a talent than music, martial prowess or the gift of prophecy. And if the mortals who inherit such talents are foolish enough to forget their mortal limits and offend the gods, then they and they alone – not the gods – are responsible for their bad ends.

Aeolus, part god and part wind-spirit, is pious, and honored accordingly. But his son Sisyphos has neither conscience nor humility and is subjected to a terrible eternal punishment. How do we give our children a framework of values within which they can develop their talents without succumbing to arrogance and

delusions of grandeur? Too rigid a framework stifles talent; the absence of any framework leads to undeveloped potential or the abuse of innate gifts. One significant feature in the story of the descendants of Aeolus is that the fathers do not stay around to help provide such a framework for their children. The gift is inherited, but there is no loving and supportive container in which it can grow alongside a recognition of human limits. Aeolus is too busy ruling the winds to bother with Sisyphos; Sisyphos is too busy cheating travellers to bother with Glaucus; Glaucus is too preoccupied with chariot races to bother with Bellerophon; and Bellerophon, the most attractive of this line and the one most like his ancestor Aeolus, is himself ultimately unable to restrain himself because no one has taught him how to do it. He murders his brother in a rage and, only then, recognizes his great weakness. But by this time he is an adult, and restraint comes hard. He knows what he should do. But when the crunch comes, he can resist the wiles of a woman but not the luxury of his self-aggrandizement.

This story of a clever but arrogant family line tells us many things about choice and responsibility. The heroes of myth, whether male or female, are symbols of the special qualities in each of us which give us a sense of individual meaning and destiny. Because every person has some gift which makes him or her unique, we are all 'descended from gods' in the Greek sense. And we all have the capacity to use our gifts for good or ill. It may be that our talents are the products of an encouraging environment; or it may be that they are inherited along with the color of our eyes and hair. Or perhaps both are true. This story teaches us that intelligence without respect for the value and worth of others can be a double-edged gift which ultimately rebounds on its possessor. Where do we learn what the Greeks understood as respect for the gods? This does not require any specific religious framework, although every great religion offers a code of behavior in accord with the 'will of God'. But piety in the Greek sense demands a recognition of the unity of life and the worth of all things living. The gods are, after all, symbols of the many facets of life itself. We might learn from Bellerophon that, however capable we are, we cannot aspire to Olympus. We can only be human, and must use our gifts with humility.

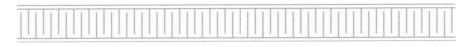

THE HOUSE OF THEBES

Offending the gods

THIS TALE IS CONCERNED WITH WHAT THE GREEKS UNDERSTOOD AS THE FAMILY
CURSE – AN OFFENSE AGAINST A GOD WHICH IS PUNISHED THROUGH SUCCESSIVE
GENERATIONS. IN MODERN PSYCHOLOGICAL TERMS, WE MIGHT UNDERSTAND THIS
AS THE PASSING DOWN OF UNRESOLVED FAMILY CONFLICTS. WHAT OUR PARENTS
HAVE NOT DEALT WITH, WE MAY FIND OURSELVES FACING; AND THESE 'SINS OF
THE FATHERS' WILL IN TURN PASS TO OUR OWN CHILDREN IF WE DO NOT DEAL
WITH THEM. THE MEMBERS OF THIS FAMILY CONSTANTLY OFFEND THE GODS
THROUGH POOR JUDGEMENT, ARROGANCE, INSENSITIVITY AND SHEER BLIND
STUPIDITY. THE CURSE IS ONLY SPENT WHEN THE VERY EXISTENCE OF THE FAMILY
IS ENDED AND THE CITY WHICH SUFFERS UNDER THEIR RULE IS FREED. THERE IS
NO REDEMPTION, LARGELY BECAUSE NO ONE LEARNS THE LESSONS OF THE PAST OR
APPROACHES THE GODS IN A SPIRIT OF HUMILITY.

L aius was the king of Thebes. Grieved by his prolonged child-
lessness, he secretly consulted the Delphic Oracle of the god
Apollo. The oracle informed him that this seeming misfortune
was, in fact, a blessing, because any child born to his wife Jocasta would
become his murderer. The king therefore put Jocasta away, though
without informing her of the reason. Furious, she made Laius drunk and
coaxed him into her arms again as soon as night fell. When, nine months
later, Jocasta bore a son, Laius snatched the child from the nurse's arms,
pierced his feet with a nail and left him exposed on a mountain. This was
the first sin of the House of Thebes against the gods; for Apollo and his
sister Artemis, both protectors of children, took careful note of this
vicious act.

Oedipus, confronted by the riddle of the Sphinx, alone guessed the answer, thus saving the city of Thebes
from the monster's reign of destruction.

DETAIL Oedipus and the Sphinx, Jean-Auguste Dominique Ingres (1780–1867)

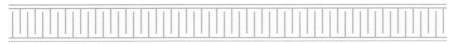

Through their agency, the child did not die on the mountaintop. A Corinthian shepherd found him, named him Oedipus (which means swollen foot) because his feet were deformed by the nail wound, and brought him to Corinth. The king and queen of Corinth took in the boy and raised him as their own, for they were childless and longed for a son. Oedipus grew up thinking himself the heir to the throne of Corinth. But one day, taunted by a Corinthian youth because he did not in the least resemble his supposed parents, Oedipus travelled to Delphi to ask the oracle what future lay in store for him. The god Apollo warned Oedipus that he would murder his father and marry his mother.

Horrified by this prophecy, Oedipus decided that he would not return to Corinth; he was determined to prove the god wrong. This was the second sin of the House of Thebes against the gods; for one does not challenge the will of Apollo with impunity, however cruel and incomprehensible that will might seem. In a narrow defile near Delphi, travelling on foot, Oedipus happened to meet the chariot of King Laius (whom he naturally did not recognize). Laius ordered the unknown young man to step off the road and make way for his betters. Oedipus became incensed and replied that he recognized no betters other than his parents and the gods – oblivious to the irony of his statement. Laius, in retaliation, drove the chariot wheel over Oedipus' foot, reopening an old wound. Transported by rage, Oedipus flung Laius on the road, drove the horses over him, and left the corpse to lie unburied in the dirt.

Meanwhile, Thebes was afflicted by a curse. Laius had, in fact, been on his way to Delphi himself, to inquire how to rid the city of the dreaded Sphinx. This monster had been sent by the goddess Hera to punish Thebes for Laius' abduction and rape of a young boy (this was the third offense of the House of Thebes against the gods, for Hera was the protectress of the family). The monster settled at the city gates and asked every wayfarer a riddle: 'What being, with only one voice, has sometimes two feet, sometimes three, sometimes four, and is weakest when it has the most?' Those who could not solve the riddle were throttled on the spot, and the road was full of half-devoured corpses.

Oedipus, approaching Thebes fresh from Laius' murder, guessed the answer. 'Man,' he replied, 'because he crawls on all fours as an infant, stands firmly on his two feet in youth, and leans upon a staff in his old age.' The mortified Sphinx leaped from the city walls and dashed herself to pieces in the valley below. The grateful Thebans acclaimed Oedipus king of Thebes, and he married Jocasta, unaware that she was his mother.

A god-sent plague then descended upon Thebes, and the Delphic Oracle, when consulted once more, commanded, 'Expel the murderer of Laius!' Oedipus, not knowing whom he had met on the road, pronounced a curse on Laius' killer and sentenced him to exile. Thus he unknowingly cursed himself.

Soon, a blind seer arrived at the court of Thebes and declared that King Oedipus himself was the murderer of Laius. At first no one would believe him, but word finally came from the queen of Corinth confirming Oedipus' true origins. Jocasta hanged herself in grief and shame, and Oedipus blinded himself with a pin taken from her garments. Oedipus was then pursued by the Furies and was banished from Thebes, expelled by Jocasta's brother Creon. Before his banishment he cursed his sons (who were also his brothers), Eteocles and Polyneices. Thus, yet another curse was placed on the House of Thebes. After many years of wandering, with his daughter-sister Antigone guiding him, Oedipus eventually came to Attica, where the Furies released him and he died in peace at last.

However, peace did not come to the House of Thebes. We have seen in the previous chapter (*pages 47–51*) how Antigone, daughter of Oedipus, defied her uncle Creon to release the spirit of her dead brother Polyneices, and was herself sentenced to death. And we have also seen how Oedipus' sons were both destroyed in the war that broke out over the succession to the Theban throne. Even with the death of these two and of King Creon, the conflict did not cease. The son of Polyneices attempted to regain the throne which was his birthright as the grandson of Oedipus. However, in the great battle which ensued, he and his allies lost; Thebes was sacked; and the curse which the gods placed on Laius and his descendants was finally spent.

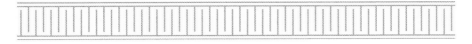

Oedipus, blinded by his own hand when he discovered what he had done, spent many years wandering the earth, with his daughter-sister Antigone guiding him.

Oedipus and Antigone, Charles François Jalabert (1819–1901)

COMMENTARY: What might this tale mean on a psychological level? All families carry unresolved conflicts which pass from one generation to the next; and if one generation refuses to face and work through the conflict, it will be unconsciously imposed on the next generation. We are all individuals, but we also carry the perspectives, attitudes and values of our parents as a legacy. If we remain unaware of our inherited psychological patterns, they will exert a powerful influence on how we treat our own children.

In the myth, the trouble begins with Laius, who reacts to Apollo's warning by repudiating his wife. This is not an offense against the gods; but Laius fails to

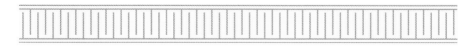

communicate the truth to Jocasta, thereby setting up his own destruction by humiliating her. Lack of communication between partners is a modern as well as an ancient omission. By denying his wife any understanding of why she has been put aside, Laius invokes his own fate. And while we may sympathize with his fear, his cold-hearted attempt to murder his son and his abuse of an innocent young boy are great offenses against the gods. And Laius' destructiveness does not end with his death, for the concealment of Oedipus' birth results in a deadly ignorance on the part of his son.

Oedipus himself has two fatal flaws: he cannot master his anger and he cannot accept the word of the oracle any more gracefully than Laius can. Father and son are alike in that they will not bow to the will of the gods, but place their own safety and importance first. This addiction to power afflicts not only Laius and Oedipus, but also Jocasta's brother Creon and Oedipus' sons and grandson. This is a family in which love, compassion and humility seem to have no place.

The bloody and violent nature of this tale should not deflect us from considering the ways in which we may make mistakes of a psychologically if not materially similar kind. How many husbands or wives fail to share with their partners the reasons for their actions and decisions? How many partners fail to seek the real reason why they are rejected, and inflict vengeance instead? How much deception occurs in every family, where secrets are kept hidden in the hope that we, as parents, will appear important and blameless in the eyes of our children? How many times does the eruption of anger and violent temper wreak havoc on the peace of a family? And how many times do envy and rivalry cause siblings to battle with each other and destroy all traces of a loving family bond?

Fortunately, our offenses are usually milder than those of the House of Thebes, and we may find the honesty and humility to apologize when we have injured someone, or give way gracefully when it is clear that life will not be bent to our will. At any point in the long unfolding of this story, a demonstration of kindness, compassion, patience or willingness to let go – by any family member – could have resolved the curse and freed the family. The fall of the House of Thebes is not really due to angry gods. It is due to human insensitivity and human error repeated generation after generation until the cumulative burden of conflict becomes too great and the family is scattered and irrevocably lost.

THE HOUSE OF ATREUS

A family curse redeemed

WHILE MOST FAMILIES ARE NOT INCLINED TO EAT THEIR OFFSPRING OR MURDER
EACH OTHER AS READILY AS THE CHARACTERS IN THIS GREEK TALE, NEGATIVE
BEHAVIOR PASSED DOWN FROM GRANDPARENT TO PARENT TO CHILD IS A FAMILIAR
CURSE. IT IS WELL KNOWN AMONGST PSYCHOLOGISTS AND SOCIAL WORKERS THAT
VIOLENT PARENTS HAVE CHILDREN WHO, IN TURN, BEHAVE VIOLENTLY TOWARDS
THEIR OWN CHILDREN; AND THOSE WHO ABUSE CHILDREN HAVE USUALLY
THEMSELVES BEEN ABUSED. ULTIMATELY, WE MUST ALL DEAL WITH THE
UNFINISHED PSYCHOLOGICAL BUSINESS LEFT TO US BY OUR FAMILIES. THE STORY
OF ORESTES AND THE HOUSE OF ATREUS TEACHES US ABOUT THE REDEMPTION OF
A FAMILY CURSE THROUGH HUMILITY, HONESTY, THE WILLINGNESS TO CARRY
UNMERITED SUFFERING AND FAITH IN THE GODS AND IN LIFE.

T antalus, king of Lydia, was on friendly terms with the gods and,
in particular, with Zeus, who admitted him to Olympian
banquets of nectar and ambrosia. Anxious to impress, Tantalus
then invited the Olympians to a banquet in his own palace. But he found
that the food in his larder was insufficient for the company. Worried that
his guests would be offended if they did not have enough to eat, he
placed status before love, cut up his son Pelops and added the pieces of
his body to the stew prepared for the gods. But the gods noticed what was
on their platters and recoiled in horror. For his crime, Tantalus was
punished with eternal torment, and his line was cursed. The gods
meanwhile resurrected Pelops, who grew up to have three sons. The two
elder brothers, Atreus and Thyestes, were jealous of their younger brother,

*When Agamemnon returned victorious from the Trojan War, his wife Klytaemnestra, plotting with
her lover, hacked him to pieces.*

*Klytaemnestra kills her husband Agamemnon, Illumination from 'Opus de claris mulieribus' by
Giovanni Boccaccio (15th century)*

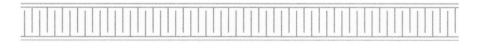

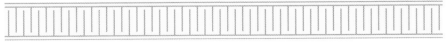

their father's favorite, and murdered him. Pelops discovered the crime and cursed his sons and their line. This was the second curse placed on the descendants of Tantalus.

Atreus married, and then discovered that his wife had slept with his brother Thyestes. He nursed his rage quietly. Then an oracle proclaimed that one of the brothers should become king of Mycenae. Predictably, they quarrelled; and Atreus, still smarting from his wife's infidelity, drove Thyestes out of the city and took the crown. Power did not, however, assuage Atreus' anger towards his brother. He further punished Thyestes by pretending that he wished for a reconciliation and inviting him to a friendly reunion dinner. The main course echoed his grandfather Tantalus' cuisine; for Atreus had murdered Thyestes' sons, cooked them and served them to their unknowing father. When he realized what he had eaten, Thyestes cursed Atreus and his line. This was the third curse placed on the descendants of Tantalus.

Thyestes then received an instruction from the god Apollo to avenge the murders of the children. Thyestes now had only a daughter left, called Pelopia. He raped her in the dark and then went into hiding. Pelopia, ignorant of the real identity of her attacker, was left pregnant and with only a sword which the unknown man had left behind. Pelopia then married Atreus, who had meanwhile divorced his unfaithful wife. Atreus was delighted when Pelopia quickly produced a son, Aegisthus, foolishly believing that the boy was his and would be uncontaminated by the previous family troubles. But the curses of the gods do not vanish through wishful thinking. A drought began to devastate the kingdom, and an oracle proclaimed that it would end only if Thyestes were recalled.

Eventually, Thyestes was found and imprisoned, and Atreus instructed Aegisthus, Pelopia's young son whom he thought was his own, to accomplish his first manly task by raising his mother's sword and killing the prisoner Thyestes (who was the boy's real father). The boy entered Thyestes' cell carrying the sword, which Thyestes at once recognized as his. He sent for his daughter Pelopia. When she was told the truth, she killed herself with the sword. Young Aegisthus, at last discovering the

true history of his parentage and determined on revenge against Atreus, returned to Atreus carrying the bloodstained weapon. The young man then killed Atreus, and Thyestes became king of Mycenae in his brother's place.

Meanwhile, Atreus' son Agamemnon was rescued from slaughter by his nurse and taken away to grow up in exile. When he reached adulthood, he married Klytaemnestra, daughter of the king of Sparta, who helped him to claim the throne of Mycenae. Thyestes and his son Aesgisthus were both driven into exile, and Thyestes soon died.

Klytaemnestra bore Agamemnon one son and three daughters. Agamemnon was one of the Greek warlords involved in the Trojan War; and, in order to secure fair weather for his fleet, he agreed to sacrifice one of his daughters to the goddess Artemis. He lied to his wife, telling her the girl was being sent away to be married, when in fact she was slaughtered in secret. Klytaemnestra discovered his deceit and took a lover – none other than Aegisthus, son of Thyestes, who had appeared at the palace in disguise and wooed the queen while her husband was away at war. Together they plotted the murder of Agamemnon, who was hacked to pieces in his bath upon his return from the Trojan War.

Agamemnon's son, Orestes, who had been sent away while Klytaemnestra and her lover plotted the king's death, was now visited by the god Apollo, who told him the truth of his father's death and demanded that he, Orestes, must avenge it. Orestes protested vigorously, saying that his parents' quarrel was not his concern and he wanted no part in any more killings. But Apollo declared that, like it or not, Orestes was the son of Agamemnon and therefore had a duty to avenge his death; and if Orestes did not obey, the god would ensure that Orestes' life would become very unpleasant indeed. Orestes knew that if he killed his mother, the Furies – the underworld goddesses who champion the rights of a mother – would punish him with madness. Whatever he did, he was doomed. Reluctantly, Orestes decided that ultimately his allegiance must lie with his father because he was a man; so he murdered his mother and her lover.

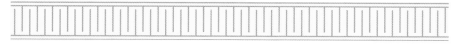

The Furies duly arrived to torment Orestes with madness. After a year of mental anguish and torture he sought sanctuary at the altar of the goddess Athene in Athens, and she, in combination with the first human jury, judged him innocent and freed him from the curse on his line. Eventually he married, took the throne of Sparta and founded a line free of the contamination of his family past.

COMMENTARY: In this dark and bloody tale, the savagery begins with Tantalus, who has no qualms about destroying his son in order to impress and trick the gods. We might think about those parents who place their own ambitions before the welfare and happiness of their children. Given such parenting, it is not surprising that Pelops is insensitive to his own children. We have seen in earlier tales how parental favoritism can provoke great anger and enmity between siblings. In this story, both Atreus and Thyestes are cursed by their father. If corrosive jealousy erupts between siblings, parents who are prepared to look deeply at the sources are in a position to help. Pelops only fans the flames. In everyday life, this is demonstrated by the parent who says to his or her child, 'Because of your bad behavior I will cease to love and want you. I wish you ill-fortune and hope you have a miserable life.'

Throughout this story runs the repeating theme of the willingness to brutalize one's children, either to satisfy emotional compulsions or for material gain. In modern families, this brutalization is sometimes literal; violence and sexual abuse occur now as in ancient Greece. But more often the brutalization is subtle, and can coexist with love and deep parental concern. When we fail to recognize the feelings and individuality of a child, but instead impose our own feelings, wishes and expectations at the expense of that child's identity, then we are far closer to the House of Atreus than we might imagine.

Yet, despite all the horror, this tale does not end in tragedy like the story of the House of Thebes. In Orestes we find an image of the resolution of conflict. Orestes,

Orestes, obeying the command of the god Apollo and avenging his father's death by murdering his mother, was pursued into madness by the Furies.

Orestes and the Furies, Gustave Moreau (1826–98)

like most of us, would rather not be involved with the sins of his family. But he is given no choice. Caught between two divine commands, he will suffer regardless of the choice he makes. What might this mean for our own lives? Often, when parents separate in hatred or live together in continuing enmity, the child feels impelled to take sides. This attempt to resolve the conflict by showing loyalty to one parent and denying feelings of love for the other may be encouraged by parents who try to use the child as a weapon to hurt each other. How many mothers, feeling 'wronged' by an erring spouse, convince their children that their father is a bad person and unworthy of his children's love? How many fathers, unable to meet their wives' emotional needs, create a fantasy world with a beloved daughter which excludes the mother and claims the daughter as a surrogate wife?

Necessity may require that, in early life, we choose between quarrelling parents. But to which parent do we owe allegiance? And how do we live with the guilt of repudiating our love for a parent? We may initially have to take sides in order to emotionally survive the internal and external conflict; but in choosing one side against the other we will inevitably suffer for a time, until we are mature enough to step back and see both parents as human beings trapped in a cycle of mistakes and unconsciousness which has been inherited over many generations.

The brutalization of children in this story is another way of describing a family where love and genuine concern are denied, and where the will to power reigns supreme. Orestes is split in half because he loves both parents and cannot murder one without suffering great inner torment. Like Orestes, we would no doubt all like to ignore the past and avoid the repetition of parental mistakes by removing ourselves from the family orbit. And, like Orestes, we may have to undergo the suffering which comes from recognizing our allegiance to both parents, enduring the tug-of-love which may be imposed upon us, and exhibiting an unshakeable loyalty to our own hearts.

There is another important insight which the myth of the House of Atreus offers us. Redemption comes for Orestes partly through his own patience, suffering and acceptance of the gods' will. But he is also redeemed through the gods themselves – and in particular the goddess Athene, who establishes a human jury and mediates between Apollo and the Furies. What might this mean? Athene is

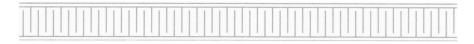

the goddess of wisdom, and she and her human jury embody the capacity of the human mind to detach, reflect and recognize the point of view of each side of any warring faction, internal or external. Athene not only makes it possible to see the problem; she also makes it possible for the participants to express themselves about the problem. In short, she personifies not only consciousness, but also communication and the willingness to listen to both sides. This goddess reminds us that if we can find a way to resist the indulgence of acting out our most compulsive emotions, and can begin the difficult process of honest reflection and communication, even a family such as the House of Atreus can be freed from its curse.

Consciousness must be paid for with suffering – nothing comes for free. Remorse and atonement may be a necessary part of the reparation which we need to enact with our families, and we may also have to do penance for wrongs and mistakes committed long before we were born. Life is not always fair; there is certainly nothing fair in what happens to Orestes. But the process which he undergoes and its ultimate resolution teach us that every one of us has the potential to cleanse the sins of the past and emerge free to love and relate to our families with a whole heart.

PART II

BECOMING AN INDIVIDUAL

There is a mysterious impulse in all of us to become ourselves – unique and defined individuals apart from the family bonds, partnerships and community life which give us a feeling of identity. But, as myth tells us, the process of becoming an individual is a hard and sometimes painful one. It involves not only a willingness to meet the inner and outer challenges that test our strength, but also a capacity to stand alone and endure the envy or hostility of those around us who have not yet begun this journey towards selfhood. Myth presents us with stories about how hard it is to leave home and what kind of dragons we must encounter and fight in our struggle towards autonomy. Not least, mythic tales also reveal the profound importance of a sense of personal purpose and meaning – perhaps the deepest mystery embedded in our efforts to become what we truly are. We may not always recognize the degree to which we have avoided the challenge of individuality and the everyday ways in which we betray our most heartfelt values in order to feel we belong. In these spheres, myths can offer not only insight, but also the reassurance that self-development is not necessarily the same thing as selfishness. We cannot really offer to others what we have not yet developed within ourselves.

The young David's battle with the giant Goliath is an archetypal image of the inner struggle every young person faces in order to move out into life.

DETAIL David and the Head of Goliath, Louis Finson (1617)

Chapter One

LEAVING HOME

Leaving home is as archetypal an experience as that of the family. In order to become ourselves, we must separate psychologically from the matrix from which we have emerged. In order to achieve this, we may also have to separate ourselves physically from our parents and home, so we can discover our own thoughts, feelings, beliefs, values, talents and needs. Leaving home does not imply that family life is 'bad'. It may be that those who fear this journey into life are more likely to have suffered family problems than those who move out into the world with confidence and hope. There is pain in leaving loved ones behind, which can be made worse if those we are leaving are unwilling to let us go; but equally there is joy in discovering that we are capable of making our own decisions and taking responsibility for our own lives.

ADAM AND EVE

Relinquishing paradise

THE BIBLICAL STORY OF ADAM AND EVE IS A TALE OF SEPARATION AND LOSS. WE MAY BELIEVE IT IS LITERALLY TRUE; WE MAY UNDERSTAND IT AS A MORAL PARADIGM; OR WE MAY SEE IN IT AN ALLEGORY OF THE ORIGINAL SEPARATION FROM THE MOTHER AT BIRTH. IT IS TRUE ON MANY LEVELS, BUT ONE OF THE MOST IMPORTANT THINGS IT HAS TO TEACH US IS THAT WE CANNOT REMAIN IN PARADISE FOREVER, BUT MUST TAKE UP THE BURDEN OF EARTHLY LIFE. THE EXPULSION FROM THE GARDEN OF EDEN IS THE QUINTESSENTIAL TALE OF LEAVING HOME.

I n the East, in Eden, God made a Garden and filled it with many kinds of living things. In its center stood two trees: the Tree of Life and the Tree of Knowledge. And God made Adam and put him in the Garden, telling him he could eat of any fruit he liked, except the fruit of the Tree of Knowledge. And God sent all the animals to Adam, who named each of them; and then He sent Adam into a deep sleep. While he slept, God took one of his ribs and used it to make Eve, so that Adam should not be alone. And Adam and Eve walked naked and happy in the Garden of Eden, at peace with God.

But the Serpent, that most devious of all creatures, questioned Eve, asking her if she were allowed to eat any fruit she wished. 'Indeed,' replied Eve, 'we may eat of any fruit except that of the Tree of Knowledge. If we eat that, we will die.'

'On the contrary,' said the Serpent. 'If you eat from the Tree of Knowledge you will discover the difference between good and evil, and so be equal with God. That is why He has forbidden its fruit.'

Eve stared longingly at the Tree and was sorely tempted by the juicy fruit that would make her wise. At last, she could bear it no longer and picked a piece of fruit, which she ate. Then she handed another piece to Adam, which he ate. And, as they looked at each other, they became aware of their nakedness and the differences of their male and female bodies, and they were ashamed. Hastily they gathered some fig leaves, which they used to cover themselves.

In the cool of the dusk, they heard the voice of God as He walked in the Garden, and they hid so He would not see them. But God called to Adam, asking where he was and why he was hiding. Adam replied that he had heard God's voice but was afraid. And God said, 'If you are afraid, you must have eaten the fruit I forbade you to eat.'

Adam promptly pointed at Eve and said, 'It was the Woman who gave me the fruit.'

'Yes,' replied Eve, 'but it was the Serpent that tempted and deceived me.'

So God cursed the Serpent, and banished Adam and Eve from the Garden, saying, 'Now that you know both good and evil, you must leave

Eden. If you stay, you might eat from the Tree of Life and then you would live for ever. And that I will not permit.' And God drove them out into the world and cursed them, saying that henceforth Adam must live by the sweat of his brow, and Eve must suffer the pains of childbirth. And east of Eden God stationed a Cherubim with a flaming sword, to guard the entrance to the Garden and the Tree of Life.

COMMENTARY: *The name 'Adam' means 'earth', and the name Eve means 'life'. Thus we are told from the outset what this tale really concerns: the process by which we enter the earthly world and live our mortal lives. As a punishment for their disobedience, Adam and Eve must suffer the two burdens which all adults face on one level or another: working for a living and becoming a parent.*

On one level, this story describes the first loss that we must face – the separation from mother's womb at the start of existence. In the womb, life is pleasant and without stress or strain. There is no need for clothes, as there is no extreme heat or cold, nor is there any experience of hunger or thirst. Life is peaceful, without loneliness, conflict or suffering. And then comes the shock of birth. Just as Adam and Eve are propelled unceremoniously from Eden, so the baby has its first taste of loneliness as well as physical pain.

But birth is not limited only to the emergence of the baby from the womb. We are also 'born' when we begin to realize that we are independent beings who have thoughts, feelings, dreams and goals different to those of our parents. The family is itself a kind of Eden, in which the child can bask in the love and protection of the parents without the burden of facing worldly challenges and without the pain of adult loneliness, conflict and struggle. We think as we are told, feel as we are asked to feel, and act without question according to rules and values given to us. All is at peace within the family until the child, now reaching puberty and arriving on the threshold of adulthood, seeks his or her own knowledge of the world – the forbidden fruit which will make us like God. In other words, as we

In the beginning, Adam and Eve walked naked and happy in the Garden of Eden, in harmony with all creation and at peace with God.

Creation, Hieronymus Bosch (c.1450–1516)

taste of life's experiences and discover our own physical, emotional and mental power, we earn the right to make decisions and take responsibility, thus becoming the equals of our parents. We must find our own way; and we may feel frightened and ashamed. And many parents – rather like God in the story – feel that this is a terrible challenge and a direct flouting of their authority. The young person is expelled from the unity of the family psyche into the hard, cold world of independent individuality, never again able to re-enter the magical, loving world where child and parent are one.

Sexual feelings and sexual experience are important initiatory processes through which we taste of the fruit and discover our individual natures. But this story does not describe sex alone. Knowledge of good and evil is really about making choices according to our individual values. At core, all our choices, including the sexual ones, reflect who we are as unique individuals. But with this discovery comes the pain of separation, for inevitably we will find areas of conflict even with those whom we love most.

Sooner or later we will have to challenge our parents' assumptions, make our own decisions, and take our own consequences. These choices may involve a particular vocational direction, a decision to go to university or not, a certain relationship we long to pursue despite our parents' warnings, or the expression of ideas and feelings which cause conflict within the family. Whatever they are, at some stage we have to risk the experience of psychological separation and the loneliness of life outside of Eden.

Our emergence into adulthood may involve many feelings of loss, isolation, shame and guilt. This may be one of the reasons why so many university students suffer depressions, breakdowns and suicidal feelings as the time approaches to take exams; for the moment has come to move out into the world, and the pain of leaving childhood and innocence behind can be, in some cases, extreme. For the young person at such a threshold, much depends on how, as parents, we respond to the urge of the Serpent within our children. If we view their need to taste life as a sin against our authority and world-view, we will increase the burden of suffering on them and instill in them a sense of being guilty and outcast. Whatever our personal moral and sexual codes, we may have to recognize that our children must – and will – find a way to develop their own. All we can

do is provide the best example we can and offer love, support and understanding unstintingly. And if we can recognize that the Serpent, too, was created by God and that its injunction to taste of the fruit is that which gives all young adults the impetus to pursue their potentials and take their rightful place in life, we may ultimately be less unkind than the God of Genesis. Thus we can help our children recognize that unity and peace may ultimately be found on the inner, emotional and spiritual level, even outside the walls of Eden.

THE BUDDHA'S DEPARTURE

Life cannot be avoided

THE STORY OF BUDDHA IS AS RELEVANT IN THE WEST AS IT IS IN THE EAST. WHETHER OR NOT WE BELIEVE IN THE BUDDHA'S LIFE AS HISTORICAL FACT, THE FIGURE OF THE BUDDHA IS ALSO MYTHIC, AND THE SEGMENT OF THE STORY WHICH FOLLOWS – AN ACCOUNT OF HIS BIRTH, CHILDHOOD AND THE CALL OF HIS VOCATION – IS A MOVING AND PROFOUND TALE WHICH HAS BEARING ON EVERY COMPASSIONATE INDIVIDUAL SEEKING TO UNDERSTAND THE INNER CALL TO MOVE OUT INTO THE WIDER WORLD.

The Buddha's birth was miraculous. At the moment of his conception the whole universe showed its joy by miracles – musical instruments played without being touched, rivers stopped flowing to contemplate him, and trees and plants were covered with flowers. The child was born into a kingly family without causing his mother any pain; he began at once to walk; and where his foot first touched the earth, a lotus appeared. He received the name Siddhartha. His mother died of joy on the seventh day after he was born, but his mother's sister became a devoted adoptive mother. Thus the childhood of the young prince was spent in love and joy and bounty.

When Prince Siddhartha was twelve years old, the king called a council of Brahmans. They prophesied that if the prince beheld the spectacle of

old age, sickness and death, he would devote himself to asceticism. The king preferred his son to inherit the throne and be a ruling sovereign, rather than becoming a hermit. The sumptuous palaces with their vast and beautiful gardens were therefore surrounded with a well-guarded triple wall. Mention of the words 'death' and 'grief' were forbidden.

When Siddhartha reached manhood, the king decided that the surest way to bind his son was through marriage and family life. Siddhartha was accordingly married to the daughter of one of the king's ministers. Soon the young bride was pregnant. But equally soon, despite his father's efforts, Siddhartha's divine vocation awoke in him. Music and dancing and beautiful girls ceased to move his senses, and instead seemed to show him the vanity and transience of human life. One day the prince called his equerry; he wanted to visit the town. The king ordered that the entire town should be swept and decorated, and that every ugly or depressing sight be kept from his son. But these precautions were useless. As he rode through the streets, Siddhartha beheld a trembling, wrinkled old man, breathless with age and barely able to walk without a staff. With astonishment, Siddhartha learned that decrepitude is the inevitable fate of those who live out their lives. When he got back to the palace, he asked if there was any way of avoiding old age. But no one could answer him. Soon he visited the town again and came upon a woman pain-ridden by an incurable disease. Then he beheld a funeral procession and thus came to know of suffering and death. Finally, Siddhartha encountered a begging ascetic, who told him that he had abandoned the world to pass beyond joy and suffering and attain peace of heart.

These experiences, and his own meditations, convinced Siddhartha that he should abandon his comfortable, self-indulgent life and become an ascetic. He begged his father to let him go. But the king was overwhelmed with grief at the thought of losing the beloved son in whom

When Prince Siddhartha left his home to seek wisdom, he cut off his long hair with one sweep of his sword, and exchanged his royal garments for a hunter's poor rags.

DETAIL *19th century wall painting, Thailand*

all his hopes lay. The guards around the palace walls were doubled, and there were continual amusements devised to prevent the young prince from thinking of leaving. Siddhartha's wife gave birth to a son, but even this did not hinder the prince from his mission. One night his decision became final. He looked one last time on his sleeping wife and baby son, and went out into the night. He mounted his horse and called his equerry to him. The gods, in complicity, ensured that the guards slept and that the horse's hoofs made no sound. At the gates of the town, Siddhartha gave the horse to the equerry and took farewell of both. Henceforth there was no more Prince Siddhartha, for the Buddha had begun on the true journey of his soul.

COMMENTARY: *The journey we make from the home of childhood to the path of our future destiny does not usually require us to give up life's joys in exchange for asceticism — although those with a religious calling may well follow such a path. But in this story, many embedded themes are relevant to us all. Prince Siddhartha, like so many children, is the repository for all the hopes and dreams of his father, who hopes the boy will inherit the throne after him. In just such a way, a father may dream of a son who will inherit his business or take after him in his profession. On the deepest level, Siddhartha's father does not want his child to experience life, for life beyond the orbit of the parental container changes us and awakens inner needs and qualities which are unique to the individual and not necessarily in accord with parental aspirations. In particular, the king does not want Siddhartha to encounter life's suffering, for this means growing up on the most profound level. If the prince can be kept childlike, then he can be molded and shaped by his father and will remain at home. These parental dreams are not negative or evil in themselves. But they are ultimately futile. Every young person is an individual with his or her own unique identity that must be fulfilled if that young man or woman is ever to be at peace within.*

Even the bonds of marriage and parenthood cannot keep Siddhartha from his journey. This is a hard lesson many young people may have to learn. If we establish a family of our own when we are too young to recognize what we are and where we are going — especially if our choice of partner is really our parents'

choice or one we make to please others or ensure security – then life may, sooner rather than later, call us another way. The pain and sadness of separation may accompany the inner commitment to become oneself.

As parents, we can help counteract this all-too-common experience by not pressuring our children to 'settle down' before they know who they are and what they want. The harder we try to make our children stay, the more suffering we may cause them when, eventually, they seek to leave us. And, as children, we may have to endure parental anger and disappointment in order to avoid creating greater hurt and disappointment later through being disloyal to our own souls. Had Siddhartha's father not been so determined to bind his son through marriage, Siddhartha might have, at least, been spared the unhappy separation from his beloved wife and child. But this wife and child are part of his father's world, not the world he feels destined to enter. Sadly, there is no way in which Siddhartha can pursue his inner calling and also remain his father's child, his wife's husband or his child's father.

We often react with derision or anger to a young person's decision to pursue a particular vocation if it is not favored by us – especially if it threatens to take the person from us through distance or exposure to a world which we know nothing about. It is true that many young people change direction later in life, and we cannot expect someone in their late teens or early twenties to know, with any certainty, what they want to do with the rest of their lives. Yet, like Siddhartha, some do indeed know. Whether the vocation is lasting or only appropriate for a period of time, if it springs from the heart, then it is not the place of any family member, teacher, friend or counsellor to deflect that young person because of ulterior motives. Siddhartha's vocation is a spiritual one and demands that he relinquish all worldly bonds and pleasures. The vocation might equally be to play music, to paint or to write, to set up a business, to travel around the world or to become a doctor, an accountant or a farmer. Or it may, indeed, be to marry one's beloved and raise a family. What matters is the call from the heart. This may not arise in every young person, but it is more likely to be heard if the noise of others' disapproval does not drown out its voice. Parents who are able to communicate well with their children and who can recognize the child's individuality, will not have decided in advance, like Siddhartha's father, what the child

Siddhartha, determined to understand the secret of human suffering and death, chose the hard path to enlightenment over the temptations of a comfortable, privileged existence.
DETAIL 18th century, Tibet

must become; nor will they set metaphorical guards around the walls and threaten the child, overtly or covertly, with rejection or punishment if parental wishes are flouted.

There is deep sadness in the tale of the Buddha's departure, because his father, his wife and his child are doomed never to see him again. Yet much of the world's population believe that their ultimate salvation lies in the decision he made, a decision which sacrificed personal happiness for the redemption of millions. Hopefully, encouraging our children to hear and follow the voice of their hearts

will eventually result in the parents' and the child's lives being enriched in the future, with a wider world that can be shared. *The story of Siddhartha teaches us that each individual has a destiny, great or small. If we are prepared to listen and recognize the difference between indulgence and vocation, and let go when we must, then not only our own lives, but those of many others as well, may be enriched.*

PEREDUR THE SON OF EVRAWC

Finding the courage to leave Mother

THE CELTIC MYTH OF PEREDUR IS A LONG TALE WHOSE ROOTS LIE IN THE DARK AGES WHEN PAGANISM AND CHRISTIANITY WERE NOT YET FULLY SEPARATED, AND IT IS ONE OF MANY STORIES WHICH WERE EVENTUALLY WOVEN INTO THE GREAT TAPESTRY OF THE HOLY GRAIL SAGA. PEREDUR, LIKE HIS FRENCH AND GERMAN COUNTERPARTS PERCEVAL AND PARZIVAL, EVENTUALLY FINDS THE GRAIL. BUT IT IS THE FIRST PART OF THE TALE WHICH CONCERNS US NOW – THE CHALLENGES WHICH FIRST FACE THE YOUTHFUL PEREDUR AS HE CLAIMS HIS RIGHT TO MOVE OUT INTO THE WORLD AND BECOME A MAN.

Peredur was one of seven sons of the Earl Evrawc. His father and all his brothers fell in combat, and Peredur was brought up by his mother in the wilderness, where the boy was kept ignorant of wars and knights. He did not even know his father's name, let alone his knightly status. Thus, his mother hoped to keep him by her side, fearing that she would lose him like all the others.

One of Peredur's favorite pastimes was to wander through the woods. One day, three knights rode by and called a greeting to the youth. He was dazzled by their noble, proud faces, the glitter of their armor in the sunlight and the bright colors of their pennants and saddlecloths. When he returned to his mother, he asked her what these creatures were. Frightened, she declared that they were angels, and that it did not befit a mere mortal youth of humble birth to attempt to commune with them.

But such deception could not hold back the tide of life in Peredur. One day, he wandered far and saw a castle on the border of a lake. A venerable, lame old man, clad in velvet, was seated by the lakeside, fishing. The old man invited Peredur to join him at table and asked the youth if he knew how to fight with a sword. 'I know not,' replied Peredur. 'But were I to be taught, doubtless I should.' Whereupon the old man revealed to Peredur that he was in fact Peredur's uncle, his mother's brother.

'Leave the habits and discourse of your mother,' said the old man. 'I will give you a horse and show you how to ride it, and thereby help to raise you to the rank of knight.'

Peredur decided at once that he would become a knight. He received the horse from his uncle the next morning and, with the old man's permission, rode forth. He saw another fair castle, standing in a meadow; and another venerable old man greeted him, invited him to table and asked him if he could fight with a sword. Peredur once again replied, 'Were I to receive instruction, I think I could.' Whereupon the old man gave him a sword and made him test it.

Then the old man said to Peredur, 'Youth, you have arrived at two-thirds of your full strength. When you have achieved your full power, no one will be able to conquer you. I am your uncle, your mother's brother and I am brother to the man who lives in the castle by the lake.' And the old man gave him instruction in wielding the sword which he had given him.

The following morning, with his uncle's permission, Peredur once again rode forth, this time armed with his new sword. He came to a wood and, within the wood, he heard a loud cry. He saw a beautiful woman with auburn hair. Near her stood a horse and, at her side, was a corpse. Each time she tried to lift the corpse into the saddle, it fell to the ground, whereupon she began wailing. When Peredur inquired of her what had happened, she replied, 'Accursed Peredur! Little pity has my ill-fortune ever met with from you.' When Peredur inquired of her why she called him accursed, she said, 'Because you are the cause of your mother's death. For when you rode forth against her will and chose to become a knight

and receive instruction from your uncles, anguish seized upon her heart, so that she died. Therefore you are accursed. This corpse was once my wedded husband, slain by a knight who is in a glade in this wood. Do not go near him, lest you are slain by him likewise.'

'Cease your lamenting,' replied Peredur, 'for I will bury the body of your husband and go in quest of the knight, and see if I can do vengeance upon him. But first I must grieve for my mother, whom I will never see again, and whose death lies heavily on my conscience.'

And when he had grieved and buried the lady's husband, he found the knight and immediately overthrew him. When the knight sought mercy from Peredur, the youth replied:, 'You shall have mercy, but you must take this woman in marriage whose husband you have slain. And you must go to King Arthur's court and tell him that I overthrew you to do him honor and service.' For Peredur's great longing was to join King Arthur's court.

The knight did as he was asked. And, after many other tests and adventures, eventually Peredur was admitted to the court of King Arthur and became his best-loved knight.

COMMENTARY: *The strangely matter-of-fact way in which Peredur decides to leave his mother and become a knight may be attributed to the proverbial 'callousness of youth'. In such a way, many young people fix their sights on the future, rejecting the past and the parents who have tried to do their best to raise the child well. But this tale is about more than the ingratitude of youth. Peredur's mother has suffered grievous losses – her husband and all her other sons have been slain. Not surprisingly, she seeks to claim this last child by keeping him ignorant of the world. Yet, however understandable her attempts to bind her son, the world intrudes, as it always does – here in the form of the three knights who meet Peredur in the wood. What Peredur glimpses in them is an image of the manhood he is seeking and which his mother has attempted to deny him. In the nobility and grandeur of the knights lies his own future, of which he is, as yet, ignorant. These knights are also Peredur's past, his inheritance, for his father was a noble knight. Hidden in this tale is the necessity of every son to find a model of manhood in a father or father-surrogate; and this urgent psychological necessity*

will sooner or later drive the young man to leave his mother behind in pursuit of what he must eventually become.

In the two venerable uncles, Peredur finds the father he was denied in childhood. Both recognize his worth as a fighter and both help him on his way by giving him a horse – a means of moving out into the world – and a sword – a means of carving a place for himself and battling for his rights and status. As a young person leaves home, figures such as uncles and aunts, family friends, teachers and other older mentors become increasingly important, for they are both surrogate parents and also individuals who can lead the young man or woman into an understanding of the broader world. It is vital for any parent to recognize that such wisdom from outside is needed by the child; no parent can be everything to his or her child, and the role of parenting changes as the child begins to make relationships with figures in the outer world who can offer a perspective unavailable within the immediate family framework.

So far so good; Peredur seems to move as though blessed, suffering no grief and no sense of loss. He does not even remember the mother he has left behind – until he meets another bereaved woman who, like his mother, has suffered the loss of her husband. It is often through a young man's first feelings of sexual attraction that he becomes conscious of his real feelings about his mother; and this beautiful, bereaved woman touches his heart as well as pricking his conscience and informing him of his mother's death. This woman, strangely knowledgeable about his mother's death, is, in fact, his mother in another form. Peredur's pursuit of the knight who murdered the lady's husband is an act of vengeance for the death of his own father. His willingness to put his life at risk means he is ready to meet the tests of life; and his championing of the lady is a gesture of loyalty to the mother he has left behind. Through all these actions, he expiates the past, grieves for the loss he has suffered, and achieves his first conquest in battle, which enables him to make himself known at the court of King Arthur, where he longs to gain acceptance in the world of men.

The youthful Peredur, deciding he would become a knight, had to face the grief of losing his mother as well as the challenge of bloody battle, before he was admitted to the ranks of fighting men.

DETAIL *14th century illustration from 'Roman de Fauvel'*

What can these early episodes in Peredur's life teach us about leaving home? On one level, leaving one's parents is like a death; for, although parents do not usually die of heartbreak at our departure, there is still a sense in which something has died. We can never go back to childhood again, and it is this stark emotional reality that the death of Peredur's mother symbolizes. Experiences in the outer world change us and cut the umbilical cord which binds us in psychological fusion with the family. If we are fortunate enough to preserve a good and loving relationship with our parents once we have left home, it is, nevertheless, a changed relationship, for we are now adults and equals, ready to meet our own challenges and even parent our parents if necessary – as Peredur does when he seeks to aid the lady and buries the corpse of her husband. Peredur's grief is a rite of passage which awaits each of us if we are to make the journey successfully from childhood to separate adulthood. With this encounter and its consequences, Peredur loses his innocence. He faces death, feels grief and sheds blood, and he can never again be the innocent child whom his mother sought to shield against life.

Equally, the parent who can recognize the child's right to become an individual with an independent destiny may find, unlike Peredur's mother, that the child-become-adult wishes – voluntarily and without pressure, deception, emotional blackmail or the imposition of guilt – to come home to visit, to share and to continue the building of a rich and rewarding adult relationship. The parent who, like Peredur's mother, wilfully refuses to be honest about her own fears, losses and needs, but instead tries to prevent her child from becoming separate, may suffer heartbreak – not because of the callousness of youth, but because the parting is right and inevitable. There comes a time when we must acknowledge that the outer world may provide our children with what we ourselves cannot give. Peredur cannot become what he is destined to become as his birthright – a knight and a seeker after the spiritual wisdom symbolized by the Grail – if he is kept from life. This story tells us that no parent, however powerful, can prevent life from fulfilling itself; and perhaps no parent has the right to try.

Chapter Two

FIGHTING FOR AUTONOMY

The emergence of individuality involves not only leaving childhood behind, but also facing and battling with those forces in the world and within ourselves that are regressive, destructive, stagnant and unwilling to cope with the limits of earthly life. This battle for autonomy is a rite of passage which every young person faces and it may have to be fought many times on many different levels, from the teens through the thirties, before we feel confident, real and worthwhile enough to express who we are in the most positive, creative way. There is no cheating with this rite of passage. It may be subtle, taking forms which are not immediately recognized as a battleground. But if we try to avoid the challenge of autonomy, we remain forever fragile, immature and vulnerable to having our brittle defenses shattered by the slightest of life's disappointments.

SIEGFRIED

Battling with inertia

THE GREAT FIGURE OF SIEGFRIED IS KNOWN IN MYTH FROM GERMANY TO ICELAND, AND HE IS THE QUINTESSENTIAL NORTHERN EUROPEAN HERO. CALLED SIGURD IN SCANDINAVIAN STORIES, HIS EXPLOITS ARE THE SUBJECT OF SOME OF THE FINEST EPIC POETRY IN THE WORLD. THE PART OF THE TALE THAT IS RELEVANT HERE IS THE BATTLE BETWEEN THE YOUNG SIEGFRIED AND THE DRAGON FAFNIR, GUARDIAN OF THE NIBELUNGS' GOLD.

S iegfried was the child of a forbidden union between Siegmund and his sister Sieglinde. Although both brother and sister met a tragic end, Siegmund left a great and beautiful sword to the son he would never meet. The sword was broken, yet, if mended, it could never be defeated in battle. The orphaned child Siegfried was raised by the Nibelung (dwarf) Mime, who grudgingly looked after him in the hope that one day the powerful, courageous youth would find the strength to kill the dragon Fafnir and capture the great hoard of gold which had, long before, been stolen from the Nibelungs by the god Wotan. Then Mime planned to kill Siegfried and keep the gold for himself.

But the gods favored Siegfried, for one day when the youth was walking through the forest he heard a bird singing and found that he could understand its song. The bird warned him, not only that Mime intended to kill him, but also why. When Siegfried returned to Mime's forge he said nothing of this new-found knowledge; but he bided his time, waited and watched. Soon, Mime asked him to forge his father's sword anew, and Siegfried did as he was bid, turning his strength and endurance to the task. Mime told him of the hoard of gold, hidden deep in a cave and guarded by the sleeping dragon Fafnir. Amidst this gold was the Ring of the Nibelungs, which had many powers, and which Mime coveted above all else. The dwarf then instructed Siegfried to return to him with the gold. But Siegfried had heard enough of the dwarf's treachery; and he killed him with the sword.

The young hero now set off in search of the dragon Fafnir. This dragon had once been a giant, not very intelligent, but extremely large and threatening. Through the power of the Ring, Fafnir had turned himself into a huge, loathsome, scaled creature. This dragon slept all the time, perpetually enchanted by dreams of the gold buried beneath its serpent-like coils. The bird which had first told Siegfried of Mime's treachery now led

Siegfried wandered far into the heart of the forest, where a bird, hidden among the boughs, warned him that the dwarf Mime was plotting his death.

DETAIL In the Forest of Fontainebleau, *Pierre Auguste Renoir (1841–1919)*

the young man to the cave, and Siegfried, brandishing his sword, killed the dragon and found the golden hoard. But so unaffected was Siegfried by the temptations of wealth, that he chose only two things to take with him from the hoard: a helmet that could make him invisible and the Ring of the Nibelungs, whose powers he did not yet understand. And thus he set out on further adventures.

COMMENTARY: *Like so many heroes of myth, Siegfried does not know his parents, nor his true potential. All he has is a broken sword, inherited from a father who died before he was born. Yet this sword, although it must be forged anew, is a legacy of strength and courage which has passed down through the generations. So too do we inherit gifts from our parents and grandparents, which we must shape according to our own values and abilities in order to use them in our own way and in pursuit of our own individual destiny. Also like many heroes of myth, Siegfried is in danger from a treacherous creature who wishes to use the youth's strength for his own purposes. This first conflict with a foe reflects the early realization that not all the world is on our side, and that we must be conscious of the reality of envy, meanness and destructiveness – whether in our families, our school environment, our place of work or within ourselves – if we are to make our way in life.*

Siegfried becomes aware of this need for self-protection by listening to a bird's song. What might this strange image mean to us? The bird is the voice of nature and the instincts warning us that we are in danger and showing us the right path when the time comes to pursue our quest. Perhaps all of us possess this ability to understand the voice of the instincts, if we would only take the time to listen. Because Siegfried stops and listens and opens himself to the wisdom of the bird, he learns not only where the gold is hidden, but also whom he must fight in order to survive.

In killing Mime, he acts in self-defense, for otherwise the dwarf would kill him. We do not usually have to kill anyone in order to achieve autonomy; but the killing of Mime suggests, on the symbolic level, that we must be willing to be ruthless in removing ourselves from those people who wish us ill. This is a hard lesson for any young person to learn; for unless we have grown up embittered by

life, we have ideals which make us believe that all doors will open for us at our command and assume that all people will be kind and love us. This is both the gift and the shortcoming of youth. Sadly, like Siegfried, we may have to learn, early rather than late, that the world is peopled with both love and hatred and that, while some people may be loving, some may not.

The dragon Fafnir is a curious creature, part giant and part dragon. This figure is an image of human greed and inertia. Content with simply possessing the gold, Fafnir has no intention of using it, for good or ill; he just wishes to keep it in his grasp. Unlike many dragons, that are altogether more rampant and dangerous, Fafnir is an image of waste, of unused power and potentials. Gold represents value and energy; and thus the dragon, a symbol of all that is lazy, slothful, greedy and stagnant in human nature, is content to sleep on these precious unused resources, doing nothing, going nowhere and keeping the forces of life in stasis. In destroying the dragon, Siegfried releases these potentials, allowing them to flow into life once again.

But the hero does not want great wealth, nor all the things which the gold could buy him. Because of the trials through which he has already passed, he has learned the wisdom of the instincts, has faced the reality of human malice, and has reclaimed and renewed his inheritance – the sword which gives him the power to conquer. But he has also found something else, which is integrity. Siegfried knows what he values, and that is not the indiscriminate luxury and wordly power which the gold could give him. He chooses only the helmet of invisibility and the Ring. He does not know their history; he chooses them because he finds them beautiful and because his instincts tell him they are of greater value than any coin or golden bauble.

These objects are profoundly important, for they carry magical powers. The helmet of invisibility is an ancient symbol we find also in Greek myth; there it is portrayed as the property of Hades, and it allows its wearer to move through life concealed. It is an image of worldly wisdom, for with it we know when to be still, so that we can observe and learn from life without imposing our own views, wishes and opinions on others. It is also an image of the ability to know and keep secrets, without which we remain children who must blurt out everything we feel and think to anyone who will listen.

And the Ring of the Nibelungs? Entire volumes have been written about its meaning, and the golden Ring of Power appears not only in Teutonic and Norse myth, but also in J. R. R. Tolkien's classic twentieth-century tale, The Lord of the Rings. The Ring of the Nibelungs first comes from the depths of the waters, an image of the natural magic and power in the depths of the human soul. It is stolen first by the dwarf Alberich, who seeks power over the world; and in turn it is stolen by the great god Wotan. This Ring holds the power to both create and enslave others. It is wrested from the depths of the unconscious and forged into a tool which can be used for good or evil – for such is the power of human ingenuity and creative inspiration. Alberich wishes to use it for evil; Mime wants to do the same; Wotan wishes no evil, but feeds his vanity and sets evil in motion unwittingly. Yet Siegfried wants the Ring only because it is beautiful. He does not yet understand what it can do. Eventually it leads him to tragedy; but that is later, and due to his own foolishness. For now, we need to remember that the Ring contains all the human potentials for creativity and leadership which can be discovered by every young person, if the dragon of sloth, inertia and unconsciousness can be conquered.

THE FAIR UNKNOWN

Finding an identity

IN MYTH, THE HERO REPRESENTS THE HUMAN IMPULSE TO LEAVE THE SAFETY OF TAME AND FAMILIAR SURROUNDINGS AND MOVE OUT INTO UNKNOWN, EVEN DANGEROUS, TERRITORY. IN ARTHURIAN MYTHS, THE KNIGHT ERRANT CONFRONTS MANY DANGERS, BUT THE TWO GREATEST PERILS HE MUST FACE ARE DISHONOR AND DEATH. IN OTHER WORDS, HE RISKS HIS LIFE FOR HIS IDEAL OF WHAT HE SHOULD BE. IN THIS TALE, OUR HERO IS GUINGLAIN. IN THE BEGINNING, LIKE PEREDUR AND SIEGFRIED, HE DOES NOT KNOW HIS NAME, NOR WHO HIS FATHER IS. HIS MOTHER HAS BROUGHT HIM UP ALONE AND, ON ACCOUNT OF HIS STUNNING GOOD LOOKS, CALLS HIM FAIR SON.

On reaching manhood, Guinglain left his mother's house and rode off to the court of King Arthur. He boldly entered the great hall, and asked the king to grant him whatever he asked. Arthur, amused by the youth's strange mixture of confidence and naivety, agreed. As the young man had no name but a handsome and pleasing countenance, the king called him the Fair Unknown.

Just then another stranger appeared – a maiden, whose name was Helie. She begged Arthur to send a knight to rescue her mistress, Blonde Esmeree, the queen of Wales. Two wicked sorcerers had turned Esmeree into a dragon, and the poor queen could only be released from her bondage by a kiss. Of course, Guinglain offered his services immediately; and Arthur, bound by his promise to give the youth anything he asked, granted him permission. At first Helie was irritated by being given an inexperienced young man, lacking even a name, to accomplish such an important task. She rode away in a fury, and Guinglain had quite a job to catch up with her.

However, before long, Helie changed her mind, as the Fair Unknown proved a courageous and clever companion. He overcame a fierce knight at the Perilous Ford, saved a girl from two giants, and defeated a further three knights who attacked him. Helie and the Fair Unknown arrived at the Golden Island, which could only be reached by a causeway. It was well defended by a formidable knight who wished to marry the lady of the Golden Island; but this lady did not love him, and promised that she would only consent to marriage if he managed to hold the causeway for seven years. The knight had succeeded in this for the first five years, and a row of severed heads on tall spikes marked his efficiency in combat. Guinglain, however, challenged, fought and killed the knight without further ado.

The lady of the island was a breathtakingly lovely fay called the Maiden of the White Hands. She lived in a castle made of crystal, set in a garden filled with spices and flowers which blossomed all the year round. The fay had long loved Guinglain, although he did not know this. She welcomed him to the island and declared her wish to marry him. Guinglain felt a

strong attraction to her, too; but Helie reminded him of the task in hand, and early next morning they crept away.

That night, they arrived at a castle where the custom was to fight the castellan for a night's lodging. Guinglain won the joust easily, and the castellan gave them a warm welcome. The next day he led them to the Waste City of Senaudon, where Helie's mistress, the Blonde Esmeree, was imprisoned. The castellan warned Guinglain that he should return any welcome he received in the city with a curse.

The city of Senaudon had once been glorious, but now it lay in ruins. Guinglain rode through a broken gate and passed crumbling, deserted towers; and at last he reached a palace. There, pale minstrels played in candlelit windows, calling him welcome. But Guinglain obeyed his orders and cursed them. He entered the great hall, where he was attacked by axes – yet the hands which wielded them were invisible. Then a huge knight appeared on a fire-breathing horse. Guinglain, though powerfully afraid, courageously fought and killed him, and the knight's body miraculously putrefied before his eyes.

The minstrels then fled with their candles, and Guinglain was alone in darkness, keeping his spirits up by thinking of the beautiful Maiden with the White Hands. Then a horrible fire-breathing serpent glided towards him in the darkness and kissed him on the lips. A mysterious voice announced, 'Your name is Guinglain and you are the son of Gawain.' His quest finally achieved, Guinglain fell asleep on the spot, exhausted but overjoyed that he now knew who he was.

When he awoke, the hall was full of light, and next to him stood a beautiful woman, although not quite as beautiful as the Maiden with the White Hands. This lady was Blonde Esmeree, returned to her human form. She told Guinglain that the two enchanters, Mabon and Evrain, had bewitched both her and the city in order to make her marry Mabon; and the spell had driven all the inhabitants of the city away. Mabon was the giant knight on the fire-breathing horse, whom Guinglain had killed the night before; and now that she was free from the spell, Esmeree intended to marry Guinglain.

Guinglain at first agreed, but found himself wishing for his beautiful fay, the Maiden with the White Hands. He returned once more to the Golden Island, where at last he and the fay consummated their love. She told him she had watched over him all his life. She had sent Helie to Arthur's court, knowing that Guinglain would volunteer for the adventure; and it was her voice that pronounced his name and revealed his true identity to him at last.

However, when news arrived that King Arthur had organized a grand tournament, the fay knew she could not hold her lover any longer. And, having slept in her arms, Guinglain awoke alone in a wood, armor-clad and with a horse at his side. He proved his valor over and over at the tournament and was reunited with Blonde Esmeree, who had followed him there. Together they travelled to Senaudon, delighting in the fact that its people had returned. There they were married and crowned king and queen amid great rejoicing.

COMMENTARY: *The story of the Fair Unknown describes the search for identity and tells us that only through enduring danger and difficulty can the true self be discovered. At the beginning of the story, Guinglain, like most other young people, does not know who he is. In order to discover himself, he must face many perils. In everyday life, each individual must leave the safety of home to strike out alone. In many myths, a dragon fight is a requirement in order to conquer evil. Dragons are often symbols of human greed, chaos and destructiveness; they devour whatever crosses their path and destroy everything by fire. But Guinglain's task is not to kill this dragon; it is to kiss the creature to break the spell and restore the city to life. This suggests that compassion and understanding may achieve far more than rage or suppression in the battle against inner destructiveness. The wicked sorcerers, Mabon and Evrain, represent an anti-life-force, promoting stasis and corruption. They numb the city by driving away its people; and the minstrels with their candles, who welcome Guinglain so avidly, are the walking dead, the people who have died within because they have given way to an inner despair and darkness. Mabon, too, is inwardly dead – there is no love, compassion or joy in his heart – which is why he putrefies immediately.*

These images of evil which Guinglain conquers are not only 'out there' in the world, but also within the Fair Unknown himself. They are the dark, destructive, regressive impulses with which all young people must battle if they are to win their place in the light and claim a sense of inner identity and a fulfilling and productive life. In the images of the sorcerers, we may glimpse the bitterness and hopelessness which lie behind so many tragic examples of young people who become drug addicts and criminals. Like the queen and her city, they are bewitched by the belief that there is no hope and that the world is a terrible, barren place. It is not sufficient to blame these anti-life-forces on 'society' or 'government'. They lie within each of us, and the quest for identity involves facing them honestly and surmounting them.

Guinglain brings the Waste City back to life by marrying its queen, and becomes a king of life rather than of death. He also wins the love of the fay, and it is she who tells him his name. It was once believed that the real name of a person contained the essence of that person's being, and receiving the gift of his name means that Guinglain now knows who and what he truly is. He gains the fay's love through his courage and beauty, yet it is ultimately his devotion to duty, reflected in his allegiance to King Arthur, which breaks her spell over him. Instead of dwelling with the fay, he marries a human queen and rules over a human city, not a fairy's domain. This is an important part of the tale; for it is through marrying a real woman, not a creature of fantasy, that Guinglain reaches his full integrity. He must turn away from fantasy loves and lives, for his path lies in the human world, not in a tempting land of ever-blooming flowers. In this way, the fay represents an inner death if Guinglain stays with her too long; the road to her domain is, after all, lined with severed heads. The fay's magical island is the realm of the imagination, separated from life, which can lead us to our potential creativity. She is also an image of the ideals which give us the incentive to move out into life. Ideals inspire us to pursue the good, the true and the beautiful; yet,

As the young knight Guinglain stood alone and frightened in the darkness of the hall of the ruined palace of Senaudon, he kept his spirits high by thinking of the beautiful Maiden with the White Hands and the Blonde Esmeree, whom he must save.

DETAIL Beethoven-Frieze, Gustav Klimt (1862–1918)

by their nature, they can never be entirely achieved, and if we dwell too long in the realm of the imagination we may ignore the outer world which requires our efforts and attention. We need both ideals and a sense of reality, for each individual must come to terms with living life here and now, and must find his or her own identity within the framework of being human.

GILGAMESH AND THE TREE OF LIFE

Accepting mortality

THE BABYLONIAN EPIC OF GILGAMESH IS A LENGTHY FOUR-THOUSAND-YEAR-OLD TALE DESCRIBING THE EXPLOITS OF THE FIRST OF THE GREAT MYTHIC HEROES. GILGAMESH, LIKE HIS LATER COUNTERPARTS, IS AN IMAGE OF THE HEROIC ASPECT OF EACH ONE OF US, STRIVING TO BE AN INDIVIDUAL, ENTERING THE BATTLE OF LIFE AND DEFINING A PLACE IN THE WORLD. THE PART OF THE TALE WHICH CONCERNS US HERE DESCRIBES HOW GILGAMESH DECIDED HE WANTED TO BE IMMORTAL, AND SET OFF IN QUEST OF THE TREE OF IMMORTALITY BENEATH THE SEA. NEEDLESS TO SAY, HE LEARNED WHAT WE ALL MUST LEARN SOONER OR LATER, AS OUR YOUTHFUL HOPES AND ASPIRATIONS COLLIDE WITH THE REALITY OF LIFE IN THE EARTHLY WORLD.

Young Gilgamesh and his friend Enkidu fought many hard battles against monsters and demons, and always returned victorious. But Enkidu incurred the wrath of the great goddess Ishtar, who persuaded the other gods that Enkidu must die. When Gilgamesh found out about the unexpected and unfair death of this bravest and most beloved of comrades, the hero mourned deeply. He mourned not only because he missed his friend, but also because Enkidu's death reminded him that he too was mortal and would one day die.

Being a hero, Gilgamesh could not sit about pondering the ultimate fate of all humanity. He decided to go in search of immortality. He knew that his ancestor Utnapishtim, the survivor of the Great Flood sent by the

gods to punish humankind, was the only earthly creature ever to have achieved immortality. He was determined to find this man and learn from him the secrets of life and death.

At the outset of his journey, he came to the foot of a great range of mountains guarded by a scorpion-man and his wife. The scorpion-man told Gilgamesh that no mortal had ever crossed the mountains and braved their dangers. But Gilgamesh told him the purpose of his quest, and the scorpion-man, full of admiration, let the hero pass. Gilgamesh travelled for twelve leagues in darkness and, eventually, arrived at the abode of the sun-god. The sun-god warned the hero that his quest was in vain, but Gilgamesh would not be dissuaded and went on his way.

At last, he arrived at the shores of the sea of the waters of death. There he met a guardian, a woman with a jug of ale, who, like the scorpion-man and the sun-god, endeavored to dissuade him from his quest. The ale-woman reminded him that life was to be enjoyed:

'Gilgamesh, where do you wander?
You shall not find what you seek.
When the gods created human beings,
Death is what they allotted to mortals,
Retaining the secret of life in their own hands.
Let your belly be full, Gilgamesh,
And make a feast of rejoicing each day.
Day and night, dance and play.
Bathe yourself, and pay heed to the child who holds your hand,
And let your wife delight in you.
For this is the task of humankind.'

But Gilgamesh could not forget Enkidu or his own eventual end. He pushed on to the end of his perilous journey. By the shore he met the ancient boatman who had been the steersman of Utnapishtim's boat when the Great Flood destroyed most of the world, and he commanded this old man to ferry him across the waters of death. But the boatman told

Gilgamesh, after long, hard travelling, at last reached the shores of the waters of death, which he knew he must cross to find the Tree at the bottom of the sea which had the power to make the old young again.

DETAIL *The Sea, Gustave Courbet (1819–77)*

him to make a boat himself and never to touch a drop of the waters of death as he rowed across the sea. Gilgamesh did as he was instructed and, finally, arrived on an island where dwelt the survivor of the Great Flood.

But Utnapishtim only repeated what all the others had told the hero: the gods have declared immortality for themselves and have assigned death as the lot of humankind. Gilgamesh, abandoning hope at last, prepared to depart. But Utnapishtim took pity on him and told him of a secret Tree that grew at the bottom of the sea, which had the power to

make the old young again. Gilgamesh rowed out to the middle of the sea, dived into the waters of death and found the Tree, bringing a branch back to his boat. He crossed safely to land again and began to make his way home with his treasure concealed in a sack. On his way home, he stopped by a pool to bathe and change his clothes. But a serpent, creeping near, smelled the heavenly scent of the Tree of Immortality and carried the branch off and ate the leaves. This is why the serpent is able to renew itself by shedding its skin.

Gilgamesh the hero knelt down by the pool, put his face in his hands and wept. He understood now that what he had been told was true: even the mightiest and most courageous of heroes is human and must learn to live with joy in the moment and acceptance of the inevitable end.

COMMENTARY: This tale really needs no interpretation; its message is clear and its relevance no less today than it was four thousand years ago. Gilgamesh, the young hero who has already made many conquests, comes face to face with a characteristic manifestation of life's unfairness. He loses his friend, and the only explanation is that it was the will of the gods. In such a way, do we all, sooner or later, encounter the first glimpse of life's cruel face through the loss of a loved one. Often this is a parent or a much-loved grandparent, but it may also be a school friend or a work colleague who is struck down. Or it may not be death that reminds us of the lot of humankind; it may be a realization of the hardship in which so many people live, a confrontation with illness oneself, or difficult circumstances which disrupt one's life and throw one's plans and dreams awry.

Gilgamesh, like the youthful part of all of us, refuses, at first, to accept his fate. After all, he is special; he is a hero; he has conquered monsters and is making his mark on the world. When we hear of others' misfortune, we all say to ourselves, 'How sad; but it won't happen to me!' The pursuit of one's destiny in youth is full of confidence and a profound sense of specialness. This is one of the gifts of the first half of life, and, if we are fortunate, we may retain it – perhaps in subtler, more tempered forms – in later life as well. But this firm belief in one's ability to conquer anything will one day collide with reality. Gilgamesh is warned by both guardians, as well as by his ancestor Utnapishtim, that immor-

tality is reserved for the gods alone. He ignores their good advice and, at great risk, steals a branch from the Tree of Immortality. The story of Gilgamesh is older than that of Genesis, and the Babylonian hero is not punished by the gods as are Adam and Eve. It is Nature itself, in the form of the serpent, which gently brings the message home.

There is a deep paradox embedded in this ancient tale. We, like Gilgamesh, need to challenge life when we are young and test our strength against life's limits; and, like Gilgamesh, we may often win and achieve many of our goals. To display cowardice in youth is to ignore the purpose of life, and to try to avoid conflict through clinging to childhood is to avoid one's ultimate destiny as a human being. But, while it is right that the young person challenges life's unfairness and tests what appears to be fate, we may be reminded, in the end, that there are some boundaries we cannot cross. Whatever our religious or spiritual persuasion, and whether we call those boundaries the will of God, human limits or simply 'the way life is', we cannot claim to be more than human. We must take our share of grief as well as joy, and failure as well as success. The Tree which renews life and transforms old age into youth may beckon in every health farm or cosmetic surgery clinic, and many of us tend, by the time we reach thirty, to start seeking ways to prolong youth. Perhaps this is fitting and necessary. But Gilgamesh's discovery is one of the great watersheds of arrival at maturity. The individual who can recognize his or her potentials and can take up worldly challenges is indeed heroic, and each of us has this capability, within the limits of our individual gifts and personalities. The young man or woman who can do this, while also remembering that limits must be respected and that life is to be lived here and now, however unfair it may sometimes seem, has truly become adult.

Chapter Three

THE QUEST FOR MEANING

The quest for meaning bears a different face for the young than for the old.
In the flower of youth, we seek to define who and what we are, and search
for a sense of uniqueness which can reflect an individual purpose and
destiny. Meaning may be sought in what we achieve in the world, in love
or in whatever gives us joy. But more often than not, meaning arises, not
from the conscious pursuit of a deeper understanding of life, but from
experiences which reveal dimensions of life we had not known existed. In
other words, meaning for the young is often the result of an encounter with
experience, rather than the goal of a conscious quest. Later in life, we are
more aware of the greater whole of which we are a part and the continuity
of generations in which we partake only for a short span. Meaning, for the
old, may lie in voluntarily exploring life's deeper mysteries and in that
sense of unity which generates compassion, detachment and an awareness
of spiritual realities. Meaning is usually pursued as a conscious goal when
the attractions of the outer world have faded. But meaning for youth is
often a highly egocentric business, just as it should be – a vague but
beckoning light which gives our lives magic, passion, impetus and
direction.

VAINAMOINEN AND THE TALISMAN

The compromise of ideals

VAINAMOINEN, THE HERO OF THE GREAT FINNISH EPIC, THE KALEVALA, IS A
SEMI-HUMAN, SEMI-MAGICAL FIGURE, BUT CAPABLE OF SUFFERING LIKE ANY
MORTAL. HERE WE SEE HIS ATTEMPT TO MAKE A MAGICAL TALISMAN TO WIN
HIMSELF THE WOMAN OF HIS CHOICE. IN THE END, IT IS NOT THE WOMAN, BUT
THE TALISMAN ITSELF, WHICH PROVES TO BE MORE IMPORTANT. VAINAMOINEN'S
MISTAKES AS WELL AS HIS COURAGE SHOW US THAT, WHILE WE MAY THINK WE
WANT ONE THING, WE MAY FIND WE ARE MEANT TO SEEK ANOTHER.

V ainamoinen, son of the Virgin of the Air, wished to marry a beautiful woman of the Lapps, but she threw herself into the sea rather than marry him. Weary and sad, the hero left his home and wandered for a time. He then decided to take a wife among the people of a faraway land. Louhi, the protectress of that land, promised Vainamoinen the hand of her own daughter, a peerlessly beautiful maiden, if he could forge a sampo, a talisman which could bring eternal prosperity to the land. Spurred on by the promised reward of a beautiful young wife, Vainamoinen set about making the talisman. But he quickly grew bored with all the planning, preparation and hard work, so he asked his friend, the smith Ilmarinen, to make the sampo for him. This Ilmarinen did. But the daughter of Louhi, seeing the magic object and the great art and ingenuity of its creator, decided she preferred the smith. Thus, Vainamoinen was once more rejected and without a wife.

But his friend's marriage soon ended in grief, for Ilmarinen's wife, who should have been Vainamoinen's, was devoured by bears. The smith then asked to marry Louhi's second daughter, and carried the girl off

Vainamoinen set about forging the magic talisman called the sampo, but he soon grew bored and tired, and asked his friend, the smith Ilmarinen, to finish the work for him.

DETAIL The Forging of the Sampo, Akseli Gallen-Kallela (1893)

forcibly when he was refused. But she crept away, when his back was turned, and gave herself to another man. Humiliated and ashamed, Ilmarinen told his friend Vainamoinen about the prosperity which their sampo had brought to the land and declared that Vainamoinen should have made it for himself and his own people rather than leading his friend into such unhappiness. Feeling angry and ashamed himself, Vainamoinen hatched a plan to steal the sampo, which was now hidden on a secret island.

Vainamoinen sailed towards the island, but the ship ran into an enormous fish and nearly sank. The fish was killed and, from its bones, Vainamoinen made a wondrous musical instrument, a five-stringed dulcimer with magical powers. With this instrument, Vainamoinen lulled the guardians of the sampo to sleep. He then stole the talisman and sailed away. But the guardians woke up too soon, and Louhi, the protectress of the land, roused a horrifying tempest, in the course of which Vainamoinen's magical instrument was carried away by the waves and the sampo was broken in pieces. Vainamoinen was able to rescue only its scattered fragments from the waters. Yet even these poor fragments were sufficient, when he reached home again, to ensure a reasonable degree of prosperity for his own land and people. Although the enraged Louhi unleashed a series of scourges against Vainamoinen's people, and even shut up the sun and moon in a cavern, Vainamoinen triumphed, and the land was safe.

COMMENTARY: *This strange tale, full of magical feats, presents us with some of the typical dilemmas of youth. What are we seeking in life, and what do we believe will make us happy? For most young people, as for Vainamoinen, finding the right partner is initially the dominant drive, and it seems as though all our problems will be solved and we can find our place in the sun if only we can discover the perfect love.*

Vainamoinen is rejected by the woman he first loves. Then he decides to leave his homeland and resolves to take a wife amongst strangers. So far, meaning, for our hero as for so many, is embodied in a beautiful face and the promise of

sensual delights. In just such a way are we impelled by what we believe to be our destiny, when what really drives us is our disappointed dreams and the need for our own emotional and physical gratification. Vainamoinen does not truly know or love the woman who is promised to him by her mother Louhi. But she looks good, and her family is important. He is asked to make a talisman – a task which, as he possesses magical powers, he can easily achieve. Yet he cannot be bothered to discharge this task himself, and passes it over to his friend. As a result, Louhi's daughter falls in love with the talisman's maker, and Vainamoinen is rejected once again.

This characteristic emotional blundering, which so many people experience in the first part of life, is presented in the Kalevala in a spare, no-nonsense way. Vainamoinen is young, self-centered and irresponsible, and he gets slapped in the face, metaphorically if not literally. If he wishes to find meaning and purpose, and to become the true hero that he is destined to be, he will have to look further than the 'right' wife, and do more than expecting his friend to provide the answers. It is this friend, the embittered smith Ilmarinen, who provides Vainamoinen with a more important goal: stealing the talisman (which, after all, was designed by the hero) and bringing it home to create prosperity in his own land. Vainamoinen has now begun to recognize that he belongs to a wider world and that others besides himself are important – namely, his own people. Ilmarinen is, on one level, the dark side of the hero himself – his youthful bitterness, his disappointment at having his desires thwarted and his recognition that high dreams and ideals wind up being at best compromised and at worst shattered. And on a deeper level, Ilmarinen's sad marriage and loss remind us that, when we create only in order to win love and approval, our creations may end up giving us no joy and may be used by others as selfishly as we have used them ourselves.

Once Vainamoinen decides to steal the sampo (the Kalevala never tells us exactly what it is), things suddenly begin to go right for him. The huge fish that he accidentally kills, itself magical, provides the substance for a magical instrument that can lull his enemies to sleep. This is a strange mythic image, suggesting that, if we can seize opportunities as they present themselves – even in apparently unfortunate or dangerous situations – and create something

individual out of those opportunities, we may progress further in our quest for meaning and purpose.

The vengeance of Louhi is predictable; even a magical hero cannot hope to have everything go his own way, and the terrible storm which nearly destroys the ship also smashes the talisman. If Vainamoinen were less than a hero, he would, at this point, no doubt give up and go home in despair. But the hero is a hero because he (and potentially, each of us) does not give up. Vainamoinen combs the waves for the pieces of the sampo and manages to salvage just enough to bring reasonable – not total or perfect – prosperity to his people. Thus the hero's ideals are compromised, and his effectiveness shown to be less than complete; yet he has found a deeper and truer meaning than the one which originally drove him from home. The foreign bride is not, in the end, where Vainamoinen finds meaning. It is in the magic which he starts to create, fobs off and then reclaims for his own, fighting for it in the face of danger and affirming its value, even when it has been irrevocably damaged. In this way, each young person may find a sense of inner purpose and destiny, even in the midst of emotional disappointment, disillusionment and apparently shattered dreams.

PARSIFAL AND THE GRAIL

Asking the right questions

THE GRAIL STORY SYNTHESIZES THE MYTHS AND IMAGES OF SEVERAL DIFFERENT CULTURES – CELTIC, TEUTONIC AND MEDIEVAL FRENCH – INTO ONE MOVING TALE OF DISCOVERY, LOSS, STRUGGLE, COMPASSION AND REDEMPTION. THE GRAIL HAS BEEN INTERPRETED AS MANY DIFFERENT THINGS, FROM A PAGAN IMAGE OF FERTILITY TO A CHRISTIAN SYMBOL OF SPIRITUAL REDEMPTION. IN ALL ITS DIFFERENT FORMS, THE GRAIL IS A SYMBOL OF LIFE'S DEEPER MEANING. HERE WE MEET PARSIFAL AS A YOUNG MAN, SEARCHING FOR MEANING – BUT THE QUEST IS UNCONSCIOUS AND THE DISCOVERY BUNGLED. WE SEE HERE THE DIFFICULTY OF FINDING SOMETHING WHEN WE DO NOT REALLY KNOW WHAT WE ARE LOOKING FOR.

As a boy, Parsifal was kept from the world by his mother. His father had died in battle before Parsifal's birth, and his mother had nothing left but the youth whom she was determined not to lose. She kept him hidden in the depths of a forest and denied him knowledge of his noble birthright to be a knight like his father at King Arthur's court.

But Parsifal's mother did teach him about God, assuring him that the love of God helps all those who live on earth. Thus, when one day he met a handsome, gentle knight who had been chased deep into the forest, Parsifal could only suppose that this superior creature was God Himself. Although the youth was duly disillusioned, the meeting with the knight aroused his natural instinct to pursue his own destiny, and he begged his mother to let him go out into the world.

His mother at last gave her consent, and Parsifal set off, dressed in a fool's clothing. His mother hoped that this attire would attract such derision that the youth would return home to her. But Parsifal persevered in his quest despite the mockery which followed him and, in due course, arrived at the castle of Gurnemanz. This nobleman was prepared to act as a mentor to the youth and taught him the rules of chivalry. The fool's clothing was taken away, as were Parsifal's foolish ways, and Gurnemanz instructed the youth in courtesy and, perhaps more importantly, in the ethics behind courtesy. 'Never lose your sense of shame,' Gurnemanz told the fledgling knight, 'and do not importune others with foolish questions. Always remember to show compassion to those who suffer.' Although Parsifal carefully memorized these fine words, he did not, however, truly understand them. He learned the outer forms, but not the inner meaning.

In due course, Parsifal's travels took him to a far-off land where the country was desolate and barren. In the midst of this Waste Land stood a castle where he faced his first true test of manhood. It was, however, a task he was not yet ready for. In the castle lay an ailing king, thrashing on his bed in great agony. He was the Grail King, who had transgressed the laws of the Grail community by pursuing earthly love without permission. In punishment, he was wounded in the groin until such time as an unknown knight should ask two questions. 'Lord, what ails thee?' the knight must first inquire of the sick king. There were also great marvels in the castle, and the Grail itself could appear to those who wandered in from the outside world; but the king could not be healed until the unknown knight should ask, 'Lord, whom does the Grail serve?' In these two questions lay the redemption, not only of the sick king, but also of the Waste Land.

But when Parsifal saw the sick king on his bed, he only remembered the outer form of Gurnemanz's advice – that curiosity was rude and that he must not importune with foolish questions. He forgot about showing compassion to those who suffer. So he said nothing. And when the Grail itself appeared, accompanied by the sweet sounds of celestial music, carried in slow procession by the Grail Knights, guarded by maidens and revealed in a burst of heavenly light, the young knight stared and stared, but clamped his lips shut because he feared looking foolish. So he said nothing. Then there was a great clap of thunder and the castle vanished, and a voice pronounced, 'Foolish youth. You have not asked the questions you should have asked. Had you asked them, the king would have been healed and his limbs made strong again, and all the land would have been restored. Now you will wander in the wilderness for many years, until you have learned compassion.' And Parsifal, realizing his foolishness too late, rode off into the wilderness in a cold, grey dawn, determined that one day he should earn the right to be vouchsafed the vision of the Grail again.

COMMENTARY: Parsifal could be any young person setting out into life. In his upbringing and character we can see echoes of the story of Peredur, another myth with roots in the same Celtic tradition. Parsifal's mother is anxious because she knows that life does not always prove sweet, and she is scarred by her own loss. Rather than speaking to Parsifal of the trials, tribulations and rewards that life holds, she keeps life's potential sorrows as well as joys firmly from him. Many parents prefer not to worry their children with difficult truths about life and try to gloss over the challenging aspects. They might refuse to recognize that their child could become interested in sex, drugs and alcohol, and they provide no education

on such matters or impose rules without explanation or discussion; then they are horrified to learn of a child's addiction or unwanted pregnancy. However, the Serpent comes to us all in some form, and Parsifal, meeting the knight in the forest, discovers that there is life beyond his mother's sheltered domain.

Parsifal is prepared to be taught by Gurnemanz, and this is a familiar theme in adolescence. We seek role models outside the family who can help us to separate from the family matrix and form an individuality of our own. But Parsifal merely parrots Gurnemanz. He is still too young and inexperienced to understand

The noble knight Gurnemanz was prepared to act as mentor to the youthful and foolish Parsifal, exchanging the boy's old clothes for finer ones and teaching him the rules of chivalry, courtesy and ethics.

Parsifal's education from Gurnemanz, Edward Jakob von Steinle (1810–86)

the significance of the older man's instruction. This is, in part, because his mother has not provided any sound ground in which Gurnamanz's words could take root. The knowledge we acquire in youth and early adulthood can only contribute to building a solid sense of self if the soil is fertile and first prepared by parents who are themselves willing to share their own experience with honesty. Thus Parsifal departs from Gurnemanz's castle with information but no wisdom. He knows the rules of conduct but has no comprehension of their meaning or purpose. He has, as yet, suffered no disappointments or losses, and has not passed through any hard lessons from which he might learn compassion. Therefore, when faced with an ailing man writhing in agony, all he can think of is not appearing foolish; and when he is received a vision of the Grail, he can only bite his tongue and avoid saying anything that might sound stupid. In other words, he is preoccupied with how he appears to others, and therefore unable to respond to the actual situation before him. Thus, he fails to ask the important questions and is driven out with only the realization of his failure and the dawning of a determination to one day redeem what he has lost.

The two questions Parsifal fails to ask are themselves deeply symbolic and tell us about the kind of attitudes we need to carry as we move out into life. They also tell us what kind of questions we need to encourage our children to ask in order to equip them for life.

'Lord, what ails thee?' is the question Parsifal must address to the sick king, and it embodies a genuine interest in and compassion for others. Behind all human actions and conditions there lie reasons which may be very different from the appearance we meet; and in questioning them, we may discover that much of what we deem bad or unacceptable in life is the product of human weakness and ignorance, not human evil or inferiority. The less we know, the more we judge others, often unfairly and mistakenly, because we do not understand how they wound up as they are. Nor do we understand our own difficulties until we can ask ourselves what we have done to put ourselves there. Questioning is one of the great paths to compassion; when we encounter human misfortune, it does not become us to feel morally superior and virtuous if we know that we ourselves, given the same circumstances, might be capable of many of the actions for which we condemn others.

The second question is, 'Whom does the Grail serve?' This question has puzzled and intrigued scholars since the first Grail stories were written. When we are confronted with any good fortune – whether it is early success, the gift of a loving relationship or a spiritual experience of great value and import – we need to ask what higher purpose this good fortune serves. This is, in effect, a religious attitude, although it is not limited to any specific religious persuasion or doctrine. It is a way of viewing life in which we perceive some deeper pattern and purpose. When life appears to offer us free rewards, we need to look beyond our self-congratulation and ask what higher purpose our gift might serve. This transforms any life experience into something meaningful, removing it from the clutches of the ego and allowing us to share our wisdom, vision, creativity, talents and good fortune – not at our own expense, but equally not entirely for our own benefit either. Such an attitude sanctifies life – the word 'sanctify' comes from a Latin root which means 'to make sacred', and in asking this most fundamental of questions, we enlarge our vision and connect with a deeper and greater whole. This is what Parsifal, the young fool, fails to do, and this is what, so often, we all fail to do in youth – especially if we are given no wisdom or instruction in such attitudes when we are children. Parsifal must wander in the wilderness for many years until, through suffering, he learns the compassion and humility that allow him to find the castle again and ask the questions he should have asked all those years before. We too may need to wander for a long time until we learn these lessons. But perhaps, with a little more wisdom – both as parents and as young people beginning our quest in life – we may be able to make that time shorter and less painful.

PERSEUS

Meaning lies in service

THE STORY OF PERSEUS IS A TALE OF LOVE AND COURAGE CONQUERING HATE AND
FEAR, AND REFLECTS THE WAY IN WHICH THE DIVINE IS PRESENT IN ALL ITS
PROGENY. STRUGGLE AND SACRIFICE ON BEHALF OF LOVED ONES LEAD TO THE
ENDING OF CONFLICT AND THE FOUNDING OF AN ENDURING FAMILY LINE. BUT
THE HERO DOES NOT PURSUE THIS QUEST WITH CONSCIOUSNESS. VERY FEW
YOUNG PEOPLE ARE ACTUALLY AWARE OF A NEED TO FIND MEANING IN LIFE; WHAT
THEY ARE AWARE OF IS THE NEED TO MAKE THINGS BETTER. PERSEUS STARTS OUT
TO SAVE HIS UNHAPPY MOTHER, YET ENDS WITH FAR MORE THAN HE HAD
ORIGINALLY SET OUT FOR.

Perseus was the son of a mortal woman, Danaë, and the great god
Zeus, king of heaven. Danaë's father, King Acrisius, had been told
by an oracle that he would one day be killed by his grandson and,
in terror, he imprisoned his daughter and drove all her suitors away. But
Zeus was a god and he wanted Danaë. He entered her prison disguised as
a shower of golden rain, and the result of their union was Perseus.
Acrisius, on discovering that he had a grandson despite his precautions,
bundled Danaë and her baby into a wooden chest and cast them out to
sea, hoping that they would drown.

But Zeus sent fair winds to blow mother and son across the sea and
gently to shore. The chest landed on an island where it was found by a
fisherman. The ruling king of the island took Danaë and Perseus in and
gave them shelter. Perseus grew up strong and brave and, when his
mother was troubled by the unwanted advances of the king, the youth
accepted a challenge thrown down by this unwelcome suitor to bring him

Armed with the deadly Gorgon's head and mounted on the winged steed Pegasus, the hero Perseus risked
his life to rescue the princess Andromeda from the clutches of a terrible sea-monster.

DETAIL *Perseus Rescuing Andromeda, Guiseppe Cesari (1568–1640)*

the head of the Gorgon Medusa. Perseus accepted this dangerous task, not because he wanted to acquire personal glory, but because he loved his mother and was willing to risk his life to protect her.

The Gorgon Medusa was so hideous that one glance at her face turned the observer to stone. Perseus needed assistance from the gods to conquer her; and Zeus, his father, made sure that this assistance was offered. Hades, king of the underworld, lent him a helmet that rendered its wearer invisible; Hermes, the Divine Messenger, provided him with winged sandals; and Athene gave him a sword and a special shield polished so brightly that it served as a mirror. With this shield Perseus could see Medusa's reflection, and thus severed her head without looking directly at her hideous face.

With the monstrous head safely concealed in a bag, he headed home. On the voyage, he spied a beautiful maiden chained to a rock on the seashore, awaiting death at the hands of a terrifying sea-monster. He learned that her name was Andromeda and that she was being sacrificed to the monster because her mother had offended the gods. Touched by her plight and her beauty, Perseus fell in love with her and set her free by turning the sea-monster to stone with the Gorgon's head. He then brought Andromeda back to meet his mother who, in his absence, had been so tormented by the advances of the wicked king that in desperation she had taken refuge in Athene's temple.

Once more, Perseus held the head of the Medusa aloft, thus turning his mother's enemies to stone. He then gave the head to Athene, who mounted it on her shield, where it became her emblem forever after. He also returned the other gifts to the gods who had provided them. He and Andromeda lived in peace and harmony thereafter and had many children. His only sorrow was that, one day while attending some athletic games, he threw a quoit which was carried exceptionally far by a gust of wind. It accidentally struck and killed an old man. This man was Perseus' grandfather Acrisius, and thus the oracle which the old man had once sought to cheat was finally fulfilled. But Perseus had no spirit of spite or vengeance in him and, because of this accidental death, he no longer wished to rule his rightful kingdom. Instead, he exchanged kingdoms with his neighbour, the king of Argos, and built for himself a mighty city, Mycenae, where he lived long with his family in love and honor.

COMMENTARY: The tale of Perseus begins with fear. Acrisius is afraid of the oracle's prophecy and tries to do away with his own daughter and infant grandson. The theme of age fearing youth is a familiar one in myth, and Acrisius embodies the negative attitude that the old can sometimes have towards the young. Perseus' name, which means 'destroyer', describes his role as slayer of the Medusa; but Acrisius sees the destruction only in relation to himself. The god Zeus in this story plays the part of a good father who watches over his child, invisibly guiding and protecting both mother and son so that their lives can be preserved.

Danaë is loved and cherished by Zeus and, in turn, she loves and cherishes her son, despite her own father's destructive character. Perseus responds to this love by gladly risking his life for his mother. When his mother is distressed by the aggressive pursuit of the king, Perseus decides to leave home and conquer any monsters which might threaten her safety. He is impelled out into the world by his desire to protect someone precious to him, rather than seeking to learn the meaning of life. Although he is helped by the gods, he uses their help wisely and modestly. He is ingenious and courageous in disposing of the Medusa and, when he falls in love, he is fearless in defending his beloved's enemies. Although he leaves his mother, he draws on his positive relationship with her to perform courageous deeds – unlike Peredur, Parsifal and Guinglain, who sever their ties with home rather abruptly in order to find themselves.

Perseus is always decent and gentlemanly – an image of something within each of us which can achieve goals without making the blameless suffer. He punishes only those who deserve punishment and he always honors and respects the gods. He gives back their gifts, because he knows that he is mortal and has no right to claim divine attributes. To the very end of the story, he behaves sensitively, giving up his rightful kingdom because of the unhappy death of his grandfather. He can forgive Acrisius for the old man's corrosive fear and does not feel obliged to seek revenge. Perhaps that is why he lives long and happily with his mother, his wife and his children – an unusual occurrence in Greek myth!

PART III

LOVE AND RELATIONSHIPS

Love, as they say, makes the world go round. The number of myths which tell of passion and repulsion, marriage and separation, love and rivalry, sexual fidelity and infidelity, and the transcendent power of compassion underlines the central importance of love in our lives. No variation exists on the theme of relationships which cannot be found in the world's mythology. And, because human relationships are so complex, the morality which myth presents is equally multifaceted. There is no greater puzzle than the mystery of why people are attracted or repelled by each other, and we often seek simple answers to questions which require a stretching of the soul to even formulate properly. The loves and sorrows of myths come in many shapes and colors, and some are distinctly exotic. But, despite the fact that some of these stories may challenge many of our moral assumptions about relationships, myths about love can also offer solace in our unhappiness, guidance for our dilemmas, and sorely needed insights into why we sometimes create the dilemmas we do in our personal lives.

The mythic marriage of Eros and Psyche is full of profound symbolism, for the name Psyche means 'soul', and the union between these two portrays the transformation of the human soul through the power of love.

DETAIL Cupid and Psyche, Baron François Gerard (1770–1837)

Chapter One

PASSION AND REJECTION

Sexual passion is portrayed in myth as a force more powerful than any other, capable of driving humans and gods alike into actions against their will, often ending in tragedy. The Greeks attributed it to the workings of the goddess Aphrodite, who, through afflicting men and women with uncontrollable passions, could bring madness and destruction on those who had offended her. Yet, passion is not, in itself, portrayed as a negative or immoral force. It is allied with strength, courage, sexual potency and the soul's response to beauty; it reflects the power and tenacity of the life-force itself; and because it is god-inspired, it is sacred. Myth teaches us that it is the manner in which mortals pursue their passions, and the degree to which passion overwhelms consciousness, that are the real sources of hurt, rejection and even catastrophe.

ECHO AND NARCISSUS

The tragedy of narcissistic love

THIS SAD MYTH FROM GREECE TELLS OF PASSION AND REJECTION, AND SHOWS HOW RETALIATION AND REVENGE, FAR FROM BRINGING RELIEF, ONLY INCREASE THE AGONY. MORE IMPORTANTLY, IT IMPLIES THAT IF WE DO NOT KNOW OURSELVES, WE MAY SPEND OUR LIVES SEEKING THIS KNOWLEDGE THROUGH SELF-OBSESSION – WHICH MEANS THAT WE ARE NOT ABLE TO OFFER LOVE TO OTHERS.

There was once a young man called Narcissus. His mother, anxious to know her son's fate, consulted the blind prophet Tiresias. 'Will he live to old age?' she demanded.

'As long as he does not know himself,' he replied. So she ensured that the child never saw his own reflection in a mirror. The boy grew up to be extraordinarily beautiful and was loved by everyone he met. Although he had never seen his own face, he guessed from their reactions that he was beautiful; but he could never be sure, so he depended on others telling him how beautiful he was in order to feel confident and assured. Thus, he became a very self-absorbed young man.

Narcissus took to walking alone in the woods. By this time, he had elicited so many compliments that he began to think that no one was worthy enough to look at him. In the woods lived a nymph called Echo. She had displeased the mighty goddess Hera by chattering too much and, in exasperation, Hera had taken away her power of speech except in answer to another's voice. And even then, she could only repeat the last words spoken. Echo had long loved Narcissus and followed him through the woods, hoping he would say something to her; for otherwise she could not speak. But he was so wrapped up in thoughts of himself that he did not notice her trailing behind him. At last, he stopped at a woodland pool to have a drink, and she took the opportunity to rustle some branches to attract his attention.

'Who's there?' he cried.

'There!' came back Echo's reply.

'Come here!' said Narcissus, becoming irritated.

'Here!' she echoed, and glided from the trees, holding out her arms to embrace him.

'Begone!' he shouted angrily. 'There can be nothing between the likes of you and the fair Narcissus!'

OVERLEAF Echo tried desperately to gain the attention of the beautiful youth, but Narcissus had fallen in love with his own reflection, obsessed by the image in the water which he could never possess.

Echo and Narcissus, John William Waterhouse (1849–1917)

'Narcissus!' sighed Echo sadly, and crept away in shame, whispering a silent prayer to the gods that this proud young man might one day know what it is like to love in vain. And the gods heard.

Narcissus turned back to the pool to drink and was presented with the most beautiful face he had ever seen. He instantly fell in love with the stunning youth before him. He smiled, and the beautiful face smiled back. He leaned into the water and kissed the rosy lips, but his touch broke the clear surface and the beautiful youth vanished like a dream. As soon as he withdrew and was still, the image returned.

'Don't despise me in this way!' Narcissus pleaded with the image. 'I am the one that everyone else loves in vain.'

'Vain!' cried Echo sorrowfully from the woods.

Again and again Narcissus reached into the pool to embrace the lovely youth, and every time, as if in mockery, the image disappeared. Narcissus spent hours, days and weeks staring into the water, neither eating nor sleeping, only murmuring, 'Alas!' But his words only came back to him from the unhappy Echo. At last, his heavy heart stopped beating, and he lay cold and still amid the water lilies. The gods were touched by the sight of such a beautiful corpse and transformed him into the flower which now bears his name.

As for poor Echo, who had invoked such punishment on his cold heart, she gained nothing but grief from her answered prayer. She pined away until nothing was left of her except her voice; and even to this day she is still allowed the last word.

COMMENTARY: *There are many profound themes embedded in this well-known myth. Narcissus is a dearly beloved son, and his mother, anxious to know his future, consults a prophet when he is still very young. The prophet advises that, if he is to reach old age, he should not know himself. So his mother, attempting to cheat fate (which is always a bad idea), keeps him sheltered and unaware, oblivious to the fact that, in doing so, she architects his fate herself. Narcissus grows up inconsiderate and self-absorbed, because all his energy is given to affirming his identity through the eyes of others. Because he is so beautiful,*

everyone forgives him his arrogant behavior. He has never actually seen himself; he only knows that everyone around him makes a great fuss of him and, therefore, he assumes he is better and more important than others, treating them with disdain. Beneath this disdain is deep dependency and corrosive self-doubt; for how can we value ourselves if we do not know who or what we are?

Then Echo falls in love with him. Her inability to communicate has rendered her naive and vulnerable; for only through communication can we come to know others' thoughts and feelings. We may surmise that Hera punished her because she talked too much and listened too little; so she never truly communicated. Echo falls in love with a beautiful face; she knows nothing of his real nature. When Narcissus rejects her, it evokes cruelty and anger in her. She prays for vengeance, and Narcissus is doomed to end his life as tragically as hers. In the end, both suffer – Narcissus through his self-obsession, and Echo through her mute rage.

One important lesson that can be drawn from this myth is that love can only flourish in an atmosphere of giving rather than taking; and this can only occur when both individuals are aware of themselves and able and willing to communicate. The term 'narcissism' is used in psychology to describe a person who is unable to relate to anyone other than himself or herself. This is usually the result of an upbringing in which the child is spoiled and cosseted but never really seen as an individual, and, therefore, never learns to see himself or herself. If we do not value ourselves as real people, we can never trust another's love, let alone offer our own. This myth warns us that such self-obsession can lead to cruelty, stagnation and the loss of all future growth and creative potential – a psychological death.

A child's natural self-absorption, tempered by a growing awareness of limits and the honest communication of the family, will eventually develop into healthy self-esteem. We all need to feel special and loved, but we need to feel it in relation to who we really are, not in relation to an idealized fantasy of perfection. Many relationships fail or generate great cruelty and unhappiness because both parties have never been loved as themselves. They have been 'divine' children, meant to fulfill a parent's dream, and adored because of what they can offer the parent rather than what they are in themselves. Thus, in childhood, they have not experienced genuine recognition as individuals, and, in adulthood, are constantly seeking to fill a terrible inner sense of emptiness through eliciting the love of others

– and then rejecting it when they remember, deep down, that they are worthless. Echo and Narcissus are really two sides of the same coin, each mirroring the other's unreality.

The unhappy love lives of many public 'icons' bear testimony to this voracious hunger for love which is meant to replace what was missing early in life – a sense of being real as oneself. It may be that we all have a little narcissism in us, and this can impel us to make the best of our gifts. But a little goes a long way; and when self-absorption as a defense against emptiness enters a relationship, love flies out the window. When we become Narcissus, we do not see the lover; we are in love with the intoxicating experience of someone being in love with us. Then we may treat people cruelly when the old familiar emptiness creeps in, despite the lover's declarations, for we may fear their discovery of the thing we fear in ourselves. When we become Echo, we fall in love with an idealized image of what we wish we could be – and we may be treated cruelly if we have so little self-value that we can only echo the beloved. And Echo's revenge only causes her more grief. She too does not grow, but remains permanently frozen in unrequited love and anger which eats away at her until there is nothing left. Sadly, it is likely that every divorce lawyer has heard the tale of Echo and Narcissus many times.

CYBELE AND ATTIS

The dangers of possessiveness

THIS IS A STARK AND SAVAGE VISION OF JEALOUS PASSION CARRIED TO EXCESS.
THE TALE IS OLD: IN CENTRAL TURKEY, CYBELE'S WORSHIP DATES BACK AT LEAST
SIX-THOUSAND YEARS. YET THE THEME IS ALSO UTTERLY CONTEMPORARY, FOR IT
SPEAKS OF THE TRAGIC CONSEQUENCES OF POSSESSIVE LOVE. ALTHOUGH THE
JEALOUS LOVER IS ALSO THE MOTHER IN THIS TALE, MANY ADULT RELATIONSHIPS
INVOLVE UNCONSCIOUS FEELINGS OF INFANTILE DEPENDENCY AND PARENTAL
POSSESSIVENESS. AND IT MAY BE THAT WE BRING UNRESOLVED ISSUES WITH OUR
PARENTS INTO OUR ADULT LIVES AND ENACT THE THEMES PRESENTED BY THIS
STORY – IN SUBTLER BUT PSYCHOLOGICALLY SIMILAR WAYS.

T he great Anatolian earth-goddess Cybele, creator of all the kingdoms of nature, bore one child, whom she called Attis. From the moment he was born, she was entranced by his beauty and grace, and there was nothing she would not do to make him happy. As he grew from infant to toddler to youth, her love deepened on every level and, as he came into manhood, she appropriated this manhood to herself and became his lover. She also made him the priest of her mysteries and bound him with a vow of absolute fidelity. Thus the two lived, locked into a sealed paradise-world, where nothing could mar the perfection of the bond.

But Attis could not be kept from the world outside forever, and one of his chief pleasures was roaming the hills. One day, as he was resting beneath the boughs of a huge pine tree, he looked up and saw a beautiful nymph; and he instantly fell in love with her and lay with her. But nothing could be hidden from his mother Cybele, and, when she realized her son-lover had been unfaithful, she fell into a terrible jealous rage. She struck Attis with a frenzied delirium and, in his madness, he castrated himself to ensure that he never broke his vow of fidelity again. When he recovered from his delirium, he was mortally wounded and bled to death in Cybele's arms beneath the pine tree where he had once lain with his beloved nymph. But, because Attis was a god, his death was not final. Each spring, the youth is reborn to his mother and spends the rich and fruitful time of summer with her; and each winter, when the sun reaches its lowest ebb, he dies once again and the earth-goddess grieves until the next spring comes at last.

COMMENTARY: *The incest between Cybele and Attis need not be taken literally. The intense bond between mother and child is wrought of many feelings – sensuous, emotional and spiritual – and it is neither unusual nor pathological for a mother to look into the face of her newborn baby and find the child beautiful. Nor is it unusual or pathological for the bond between mother and child to be echoed in later life, when a young man or woman may seek, in the arms of a beloved, qualities and emotional responses similar to those experienced in early life. Most loving relationships contain elements of nurturing and dependency; it*

is, in the end, a question of whether there is also room in the relationship for equality and separateness, too. The tragedy of this myth lies in the absolute possession Cybele seeks to maintain over her beloved. While this, too, is not uncommon, in adult relationships as well as in mother–child bonds, the psychological consequences can be deeply destructive if the possessiveness is not acknowledged and contained.

Cybele cannot allow Attis to be an equal partner. She wishes him to be bound to her alone, utterly dependent on her and unable to have his own life apart from her. We may see echoes of this pattern in any relationship where one partner – male or female – resents the other's independent friends and interests. There may be jealousy of a partner's commitment to work or creative endeavors; there may even be resentment of the partner's withdrawal into his or her own thoughts. This is not relationship, but rather, ownership. Such absolute possessiveness invariably arises from deep insecurity which makes the individual feel threatened by any separateness existing within the bond. And such profound insecurity can invoke intensely destructive feelings – especially if the insecure person, like Cybele, has nothing else in life except the beloved.

Cybele's revenge on Attis' infidelity – which is, in essence, an attempt on his part to establish an independent male identity – is to drive him into self-castration. This is a frightening and brutal image and, fortunately, it is generally limited to the world of myth. But there are subtler levels of self-castration which may occur in everyday life. If anyone seeks to undermine the partner's independence through the power of emotional blackmail, that man or woman has, in effect, attempted to castrate the partner's potency in life; and if the partner colludes, because of the fear of losing the relationship, then Attis' self-castration has been accomplished on a psychological level.

The madness of Attis may be glimpsed in the emotional confusion that psychological manipulation can create when it is imposed on any individual who is not sufficiently conscious or emotionally mature to see what is being done. Imposing feelings of guilt, criticizing, emotional and sexual withholding as a power-ploy, and isolating the partner through subtly interfering with friendships and outside interests – these are all methods through which present-day Cybeles, male or female, may drive their partners into a state of uncertainty and self-doubt.

Intense passion and insecurity make a bad mix, for out of this mix arises the kind of possessive love this dark myth illustrates so graphically. Perhaps the insecurity must exist on both sides, for otherwise Attis would break free and make a new life. Cybele has the power to drive him mad because he needs her so absolutely; he is still a psychological infant and cannot bear to be separated from her. The dependency which he feels is that of a child for a parent. When we bring such intensely dependent feelings into our adult relationships, we may open the door to a great deal of suffering. Unless we can cope with being separate, we cannot withstand another person's attempts to manipulate and bind us; nor can we refrain from attempting to manipulate and bind others in order to keep them close to us. Caught in such a net, we cannot fully live our lives, but must give away the power to shape our own destiny because we are frightened of being alone. Neither Cybele nor Attis can bear the fundamental human challenge of independent emotional existence. Thus, they cannot become lovers who truly respect and appreciate each other's 'otherness'. They doom themselves to a psychological state of fusion which results in the cyclical repetition of betrayal, hurt, confusion and self-destructiveness. This myth teaches us that it is not passion alone which unleashes tragedy, but the unwholesome mix of passion and the inability to stand as a separate human being.

SAMSON AND DELILAH

Succumbing to temptation

THE BIBLICAL MYTH OF SAMSON PRESENTS US WITH THE TRAGIC RESULTS OF MISPLACED PASSION AND MAY BE INTERPRETED, ON ONE LEVEL, AS A MORAL INJUNCTION AGAINST SUCCUMBING TO TEMPTATION. BUT THE MYSTERIOUS RELATIONSHIP BETWEEN SAMSON'S STRENGTH AND HIS HAIR, AND HIS BLINDING AT THE HANDS OF THE PHILISTINES, REVEAL DEEPER MEANINGS WHICH MAY TEACH US MORE ABOUT THE ROLE PASSION PLAYS IN SELF-DISCOVERY THAN ABOUT THE MORAL RULES BY WHICH SOCIETY DEEMS WE SHOULD LIVE OUR OUTER LIVES.

Manoah the Israelite suffered because his wife was barren and they could not have a son. So Manoah prayed to the Lord. The Lord heard and answered, and Samson was born.

Samson grew tall and strong, and the spirit of the Lord began to move him to great anger as well as great feats of strength. One day, he saw a Philistine woman and wanted her for his wife. But, at that time, the Philistines had dominion over the Israelites, and his mother and father asked him why he could find no woman among his own people. But Samson was determined, and his anger was a source of fear; so, in the end, he took the woman as his wife. Later he tired of her, and she was given to one of his companions. But it came to pass that Samson visited her, and her father would not permit him to see her. In his anger, Samson set fire to the standing corn of the Philistines. When the Philistines found that he had done this, they burned his wife and her father to death in revenge. In retaliation, Samson slew many of them, and they tried to defeat and capture him. But the Philistines could not conquer him. And, thus, the ground was laid for bitter and unending hatred between Samson and his wife's people.

One day, Samson went up to Gaza and saw a harlot. He lay with her, and the Philistines waited to kill him as he left; but again they could not conquer him. Then he saw and loved a woman whose name was Delilah. The rulers of the Philistines approached her and asked her to entice him and discover for them where the secret of his great strength lay, so that they could prevail against him. And they offered her eleven hundred pieces of silver.

Delilah tried and tried to get Samson to tell her his secret. It came to pass that he became so vexed and sore from all this importuning that he told her all his heart. He told her that if his head were shaven, all his strength would go from him. And Delilah sent for the lords of the Philistines and told them Samson's secret, and they gave her the pieces of silver as agreed. Then, while Samson was asleep in her arms, a man came who shaved off the seven locks of his head; and Samson's strength went from him.

Samson, lured by Delilah's charms into revealing the secret of his great strength, fell asleep in her arms and awoke to find that he had been betrayed, and his long locks shorn by his enemies while he slept.

Samson and Delilah, *Gustav Moreau (1826–98)*

When Samson awoke, the Philistines took him and bound him with fetters and put out his eyes. He was put in the prison house, and all the Philistines rejoiced because their great enemy was conquered. He languished in prison for a long time, and then he was brought before the people for sport. But, in that time, Samson's hair had grown again. He was set, bound in chains, between the pillars of the palace, where three thousand Philistines had gathered to mock and laugh at him. Samson called upon the Lord and he took hold of the pillars on which the palace stood. Bowing himself with all his might, the whole building fell down upon the Philistines. Although Samson was killed, his enemy was vanquished.

COMMENTARY: The obvious moral implications of this tale need no elaboration: Samson errs, first by choosing an unsuitable wife, second by aggravating the enmity between the Israelites and the Philistines, third through his passion for Delilah (another unsuitable lover), and fourth through foolishly revealing his secret to her. He pays for his sins and, in the end, is redeemed through the destruction of his enemies. But we need to look more closely at both the details of this story and the character of Samson himself, if we are to understand the insights it offers about the nature of passion.

From the outset, Samson is an angry man. The 'spirit of the Lord' which moves him to excesses is an ambiguous spirit, because it makes him violent and self-willed. Like many Greek heroes, Samson is afflicted with hubris – in other words, he does not understand self-restraint and, therefore, does not seek to contain what drives him from within. When he wants something, he must have it, and this includes choosing a wife from amongst his enemies. Love is not the issue here. What we see is a passion fuelled by physical attraction which Samson, driven by his instinctual needs, must fulfill. When he tires of his wife, he puts her aside. When her father, understandably, will not allow him to see her afterwards, he wreaks havoc on the Philistine cornfields – and tragedy ensues. In short, Samson is not a likable character. He is violent, self-willed and unfeeling. He is the architect of his own tragedy.

For Samson, temptation is bound to succeed, as he has no capacity for reflection. He is not suspicious of Delilah's persistence, because his emotions and instincts drive him. In the end, he reveals all and thus loses his strength.

Hair – short, long, dark or pale – appears in the symbolism of many of the world's myths. Even historically, its symbolic importance is clear: the Merovingian kings of France, for example, did not cut their hair because they believed it was a mark of their God-given royalty. Freud associated hair in dreams with sexual potency and strength; to have one's hair cut in dreams can be an image of impotence. But Freud notwithstanding, we should remember that Samson's strength-producing hair grows on his head, and this is the seat of mind. Hair may be linked with one's thoughts; it is a symbol of the individual's power of reflection, which shapes and directs one's will and world-view. Our strength, in other words, lies in our capacity to think, to perceive the world and process it

through our own consciousness. Only in this way can we contain our destructive impulses and avoid sinking into blind emotion. In allowing himself to be driven by physical passion, Samson gives away his independent consciousness. His hair is symbolically lost long before it is physically cut, because he ignores the power of reflection in order to feed his passions. His undoing lies not in feeling attracted to women, nor even in pursuing that attraction in unsuitable places. It lies in the way in which he freely abandons all capacity for reflection.

As a result, Samson is imprisoned and blinded. Blindness in myth is often linked with inner vision and with the understanding which comes from turning one's eyes away from the outer world. The blind prophet Tiresias in Greek myth — whom we met in the story of Narcissus (see page 125) — is an example of the wisdom which results from turning one's focus inwards; the self-blinding of Oedipus (see page 61) is also an image of self-discovery. In prison, Samson learns to look inward; and what does he find? His hair grows again; he gains a capacity for thought and reflection; he prays to the god he had forgotten; and his strength returns. We may surmise that, on the psychological level, this powerful man, accustomed to brutally claiming what he wants, is forced by life's limits and his own failure to recognize who and what he really is and to remember what ideal he really serves.

What can this teach us about passion in everyday human life? We need to balance its blind power with inner sight, with reflection and with a recollection of what ideals really drive us in life. Through the mistakes, messes and hurts we inflict and receive through pursuing our passions without reflection, we are humbled and forced to turn inwards. In this way, we may regain our strength and recover our individuality. Samson's death may also be taken symbolically, for in such a humbling recognition we, too, undergo a kind of death. We must let go of our arrogance and self-will, and recognize life's limits. The story of Samson reveals the transformative effects of passion, which can lead us into suffering, but also into self-revelation and a new understanding of ourselves and life.

THE ENCHANTMENT OF MERLIN

Deception attracts a deceiver

RATIONALITY, AND EVEN INTELLECTUAL BRILLIANCE, MAY NOT BE AN ANTIDOTE TO
PASSIONATE LOVE. ALTHOUGH WE MAY NEED TO REFLECT, WE CANNOT SILENCE
OUR HEARTS – OR OUR BODIES – THROUGH THE POWER OF REASON ALONE. IN
FACT, ATTEMPTING TO USE THE RATIONAL MIND AS A DEFENSE AGAINST PASSION
MAY MAKE ANY INDIVIDUAL PARTICULARLY VULNERABLE TO BLINDNESS IN
RELATIONSHIPS. EVEN MERLIN, THE GREAT MAGICIAN OF CELTIC MYTH, WAS
HELPLESS IN THE FACE OF HIS PASSION FOR A CERTAIN WOMAN.

Merlin was King Arthur's advisor and friend, and his magical powers were awesome. Not only was he wise in all herbal lore, he could also foresee the future and was a shape-shifter, able to appear in many different forms, such as an old man with a sickle, a young boy, a beggar and a shadow. He guarded his powers jealously and was never known to share either his wisdom or his bed with any woman.

But perhaps because he did not allow himself to know women, he did not truly know himself. In the end, this wise and skilled enchanter met his undoing through the honey-trap of love and sexual desire. One day, Merlin met a beautiful maiden. Her name was Nyneve and, although Merlin was by this time an old man, he fell desperately in love with her the moment he saw her. In order to impress her, he took the form of a handsome young man and boasted of his prowess as a powerful magician. He conjured fabulous illusions out of the air, hoping to win her admiration: knights and ladies courting, minstrels playing, young knights jousting and fantastic gardens filled with fountains and flowers. And the young woman simply stood and watched, but said nothing.

The unhappy Merlin followed Nyneve everywhere, trying to win her love by revealing the secrets of his magic; but in the end she imprisoned him with the very spells which he himself had taught her.

DETAIL *The Beguiling of Merlin, Sir Edward Burne-Jones (1833–98)*

Merlin was so preoccupied with making an impression, that he failed to notice that Nyneve did not return his feelings. Yet she promised to become his lover if he shared with her the secrets of his magic. He eagerly agreed, believing he had found a devoted disciple as well as a lover. Nyneve proceeded to coax more and more knowledge from him, learning all his spells and magical recipes, yet forever withholding herself and frustrating his desire. Merlin, in his wisdom, gradually understood what was happening, and knew that he was being tricked and deceived. Yet he could not help himself.

Seeing clearly what the future held for him, Merlin then went to King Arthur, warning the king that the end was near for his trusted advisor and enchanter. The king was baffled and demanded to know why Merlin, with all his wisdom, could do nothing to save himself. Merlin replied sadly, 'It is true that I know many things. Yet in the battle between knowledge and passion, knowledge never wins.'

The unhappy enchanter, burning with unrequited passion, followed Nyneve everywhere, like a lovesick adolescent. But Nyneve never granted him his desire; she always promised and tempted, elicited yet more secrets, and withdrew again. Finally, he committed the folly of teaching her the secrets of those spells which can never be broken. In order to please her, he created a magical chamber hollowed into the great Cornish cliffs high above the sea and filled it with unbelievable wonders. He intended it to be a glorious setting in which they might finally consummate their love. Together, they walked through a secret passage in the rock and approached the chamber, hung with gold and lit by hundreds of scented candles. Merlin entered, but Nyneve lingered outside. Then she pronounced the words of a terrible spell that could never be broken, a spell she had learned from him. The door to the chamber closed, and Merlin was trapped inside forever. As Nyneve moved away down the passage, she could hear his voice faintly through the rock, begging for release. But she took no notice and continued on her way. They say that Merlin is there in his gold-hung chamber even to this day, just as he knew he would be.

COMMENTARY: This well-known myth of the enchantment of the great enchanter can be seen, re-enacted in everyday life. Look at those relationships where one individual, man or woman, has managed to avoid the pain, joy and transformative power of passion for many years, only to finally succumb to a passion which proves unrequited or destructive. 'There's no fool like an old fool,' the saying goes, but this truism does not apply to everyone who has reached the latter part of life. It is applicable only to those who have managed, throughout their youth and early adulthood, to avoid getting their hands and hearts stained with the confusion and ambiguity of powerful emotional and sexual needs. Such individuals, ultimately, cannot cheat nature or their own natures, and often fall for unsuitable love objects when it is too late to learn the wisdom that only direct emotional experience can bring.

In Merlin's jealous guarding of his secrets lies the seeds of his undoing. The enchanter is frightened of vulnerability and depends on power to sustain himself in life; and where there is a craving for power, there is little room for genuine relationship. Merlin has used his impressive intellect and knowledge to control life, rather than allowing himself to experience it and be changed by it. We, too, may attempt to control our passions in this way, because passion makes us vulnerable. When we need another person intensely, we are no longer in control, and are at the mercy of whatever life brings us. For those who have been wounded in childhood and have learned to mistrust love at an early age, knowledge and power may be the favored means by which they protect themselves from being hurt. Yet, such a hard defensive shell can leave us childlike and naive underneath. We cannot grow up because we will not permit ourselves to go through those experiences of frustration and separation which might mature us. And then, like Merlin, we are deeply vulnerable to exploitation.

We may often read about powerful older men who parade beautiful young women on their arms, boasting to the world through these 'trophy' wives and lovers that they are still virile and lovable; yet inwardly such men may live with the constant fear that they are wanted for their power and wealth, and not for themselves. As social attitudes become less rigid and puritanical, famous older women may also be observed, struggling to retain the illusion of youth through cosmetic surgery and stringent exercise and dietary regimes, parading handsome

'toy boys' on their arms. Without doubt, there are relationships between an older man and a younger woman, or between an older woman and a younger man, which are rich, loving and totally sincere. But there are also many such relationships in which position and power are the currency with which an illusory love is purchased.

If we look at Merlin's story through psychological eyes, we may see a man riddled with deep insecurity, confident only in the power of his wisdom and magic. His quest for power compensates for loneliness and self-doubt, and he is so lacking in feelings of self-worth that, when he meets the object of his passion, he can only think of impressing her with power rather than revealing a real and vulnerable person. This, too, can be observed in everyday life; for when we are unsure of ourselves, we may seek to impress with our power, money, talents or knowledge, never realizing that, in such betrayal of our real selves, we may be opening the door to rejection and hurt. In presenting ourselves as something we are not, we deceive, consciously or unconsciously; and in doing so, we may attract a deceiver. The story of Merlin has much to teach us about the sad outcome of passion when the passionate individual has no real belief in his or her worth and avoids the deep and truthful meeting of equals, which any enduring love ultimately requires. Samson, the Biblical hero whom we met earlier in this chapter (see pages 133–7), is in touch only with his physical desires, and has no capacity for intellectual reflection. Merlin, on the other hand, is frightened of his physical desires and only trusts his mind. Only a balance between the two can provide psychological health and the potential of a fulfilling relationship.

Chapter Two

THE ETERNAL TRIANGLE

The eternal triangle, by its very name, indicates that humans have always had difficulty in loving one person exclusively. Triangles are the essential stuff of the world's great poetry, drama and fiction, as well as of many lawyers' incomes. Infidelity hurts and demeans us; yet it also fascinates us, perhaps because we know its sufferings and enchantments all too well. The eternal triangle is an archetypal experience, and psychology is full of explanations about why we stray. We know, sometimes from bitter experience, that loss of trust corrodes marriages and destroys family life; and deceit makes us feel humiliated. Some of the greatest human suffering arises from betrayal. Yet we are really no closer to understanding why we seek monogamy and enact polygamy than we were millennia ago when the great myths of sexual and emotional betrayal were first written down.

THE MARRIAGE OF ZEUS AND HERA

Commitment versus freedom

ONE OF THE MOST FAMOUS MYTHIC PORTRAYALS OF INFIDELITY IS THE MARRIAGE OF ZEUS AND HERA, CLASSICAL KING AND QUEEN OF THE GODS. HERE WE FIND NOT JUST ONE TRIANGLE, BUT AN SEQUENCE OF THEM, FOR ZEUS IS THE ARCHETYPAL SERIAL ADULTERER, WITH HERA THE JEALOUS WIFE. THEIR MARRIED LIFE IS A CATALOGUE OF AFFAIRS, SEASONED WITH JEALOUSY, REVENGE AND ILLEGITIMATE CHILDREN; YET SOMEHOW THEIR MARRIAGE SURVIVES.

Zeus was king of heaven, and it was he who organized and governed the smooth and orderly workings of the cosmos. He married his sister Hera after a highly romantic courtship, and it seemed he was besotted with her. But, from the very beginning of the marriage, he was unfaithful to her, and she was hurt and furiously jealous. They bickered constantly, and Zeus was not averse to occasionally beating her to silence her accusations and protests. Hera was enraged by his constant pursuit of other loves – goddesses and mortals, women and boys. The constantly changing objects of his desires always required great inventiveness and effort to pursue. In fact, the more difficult the challenge, the more powerful his passion; and he often had to shape-shift – in various disguises and animal forms – in order to slip past angry husbands and possessive fathers. For Leda, he transformed himself into a swan; for Europa, a bull; for Demeter, a stallion; and for Danaë, a shower of gold. Yet, the moment he had achieved his desire, the object of his love would no longer appeal to him, and he would be off in search of a new one.

Hera, on the other hand, spent most of her time feeling wounded and rejected. She concentrated all her energies on seeking out proof of Zeus' adultery and then working out some cunning plan to humiliate him and take revenge on his lovers. It sometimes seemed as if this gave her life meaning, since she did little else. Zeus' illegitimate children – who were as myriad as the stars in the sky – were especially in danger of Hera's wrath, and she always persecuted those whom she feared Zeus loved more than her or the legitimate children of their marriage. She drove Dionysus mad and contrived to have his mother Semele burned to death; she tormented Herakles, the son of Alcmene, with impossible tasks. She even bound her husband with thongs and threatened to depose him, although he was, conveniently and inevitably, rescued by the other gods. Yet, through it all, their relationship continued, and their passion periodically

While Zeus courted one lover after another, Hera watched and waited, conceiving cunning plans by which she could humiliate her erring husband and take revenge on her rivals.

DETAIL God Jupiter falling for Io while Juno watches, Jacopo Amiconi (1682–1752)

resuscitated itself. Hera was also quite capable of borrowing Aphrodite's golden girdle to enchant and excite Zeus' desire to suit her own ends. During the Trojan War, Hera (who held a particularly strong grudge against the Trojans) used this magic girdle to seduce Zeus and distract him from offering his protection to Troy.

Zeus was every bit as jealous as Hera and he adhered firmly to a double standard. Once, a mortal called Ixion wanted to seduce her; but Zeus read his mind and shaped a false Hera out of a cloud, upon which Ixion proceeded to take his pleasure. Zeus then bound him to a fiery wheel which rolled through the heavens for eternity. On another occasion, Hera decided she had had enough, so she left her husband and went into hiding. Without his mighty wife at his side arguing and berating him, great Zeus felt destitute and lost. His other loves suddenly seemed less interesting. He searched everywhere for Hera. Finally, taking the wise advice of a mortal experienced in marriage matters, Zeus gave out word that he was going to marry someone else. He fashioned a statue of a beautiful girl, draped it in veils like a bride, and paraded it through the streets. On hearing the rumours which Zeus had carefully spread, Hera hurried out of hiding, rushed to the statue, and tore the veils off her imagined rival – only to discover the rival was made of stone. When she realized she had been duped, she burst out laughing, and the couple were reconciled for a time. And for all we know, they may still be quarrelling and reconciling, hurting, deceiving and loving each other on Mount Olympus to this day.

COMMENTARY: *The marriage of Zeus and Hera is certainly not a harmonious one, and the moral climate of our present society is quick to condemn any latter-day Zeus who behaves as the ancient Greek god was said to have done. Yet, there is passion and excitement in this marriage, and each partner is lost without the other. On the surface, we may take a conventional moral stance and condemn Zeus' adultery. However, there are deeper levels to this marriage, which may surprise us with their insights into the nature of what binds people together.*

Why should these two powerful deities, each quite capable of divorcing and

choosing a less stressful partner, remain together? Zeus is the epitome of creative power and ingenuity. His shape-shifting and ceaseless pursuit of the ideal tell us that he is a symbol of the mysterious, fluid, fertile and potent power of the imagination, which cannot be bound or contained within conventional worldly structures and rules. Hera, on the other hand, is the goddess of home and family, and symbolizes those bonds and social structures which involve continuity, responsibility, rules and respect for tradition. In fact, these deities are two sides of the same coin and reflect two dimensions of the human psyche which are forever at war, yet forever dependent on each other for their fulfillment. In most relationships, one individual tends to lean towards the imaginative dimension of life, while the other leans more towards containing and structuring life. But we all possess both these capacities, and need both in our lives.

If we understand Zeus' infidelities on a psychological level, they reflect a ceaseless quest for beauty and magic, and a desire for self-expression which is the essence of any artist's creative power. If we understand Hera's jealousy also on a psychological level, we may glimpse the difficulty – and the great strength – of remaining committed in life, and the anger we inevitably feel when our freedom is curtailed by our own choice, while someone else appears to get away with self-indulgence without consequences. Each of us, man or woman, may identify with either Zeus or Hera. Yet this mythic marriage really tells us that both Zeus and Hera exist within each of us, and, if we wish to avoid having their marriage enacted in painful and concrete ways in our own lives, we might be wise to find a balance within ourselves.

Zeus and Hera can also laugh together. This is the magic ingredient which reconciles them when they have quarrelled. And each stands up to the other. Although Hera is jealous, she is not made of the stuff of martyrs. She fights back with spirit and wit rather than dissolving into a puddle of abject self-pity. Thus, they respect each other, although they also hurt and anger each other. This myth describes something fundamental about human nature: the grass, as they say, is always greener in the next pasture, and greener still if it is forbidden. Zeus pursues love objects in part because he is forbidden them; when Hera leaves him, he pursues her with as much passion as he does his illicit loves. And Hera pursues Zeus because she cannot ever wholly possess him. The deepest secret of this

No matter how often he himself strayed, Zeus could not bear the thought that his wife too might be unfaithful, and when he thought he had lost her, he was overjoyed to be united with her again.

Jupiter beguiled by Juno, James Barry (1741–1806)

Olympian marriage is that enduring love springs from never being entirely able to own the other. Painful though it may be, when we are confronted with a straying partner, we might do well to ask ourselves whether we have given away possession of ourselves and have therefore become wholly obtainable and owned. And, when we are confronted with our own propensity to stray, we might ask ourselves whether our pursuit of perfection masks a fear of becoming wholly obtainable and owned. Recognition of this quest for the unobtainable which lies deep in human nature can lead us to an awareness of the necessity for compromise if we are to make any relationship work in real life. Compromise is an imperfect

solution in which both people get something of what they want but nobody gets it all his or her own way. In order to have a workable human relationship, we must give up the ideal of perfection; yet equally, we must never give up our own souls.

There is no 'resolution' in the marriage of Zeus and Hera; and perhaps there is no resolution to the problem of infidelity, literal or fantasized, in human relationships. So much depends on the personal morality, ethics, honesty, self-control and psychological insight of the individuals involved. Unless we have discovered Zeus' and Hera's secret, we may continue to be baffled by marriages in which these mythic antics are enacted, while both partners continue to love and inspire each other. But the more we understand the struggle between commitment and freedom, the better able we are to cope with this tension within ourselves. It is then less likely that we will polarize into a rampant Zeus or a complaining Hera.

ARTHUR AND GUINEVERE

Redemption through suffering

THE TALE OF KING ARTHUR AND QUEEN GUINEVERE, AND OF HER LOVE FOR THE KING'S BEST FRIEND, LANCELOT, IS ONE OF THE BEST-KNOWN OF ALL MYTHS ABOUT THE PAIN OF BETRAYAL. IT IS ALSO VIRTUALLY UNIQUE IN THAT NONE OF THE PARTICIPANTS IN THIS TRIANGLE ATTEMPT TO DESTROY EACH OTHER, BUT INSTEAD FIND RECONCILIATION AND INNER PEACE THROUGH INTEGRITY, LOYALTY TO FRIENDSHIP AND A RECOGNITION OF THE ESSENTIALLY SACRED NATURE OF DEEP AND HEARTFELT LOVE.

After many years of wars and battles, having achieved victory over the invading Saxon hordes, King Arthur said to his wise advisor Merlin, 'The time has come for me to take a wife.' Merlin inquired whether the king had already made a choice; and it seemed he had, for he had been told of a wondrously beautiful princess called Guinevere, the daughter of King Leodegrance of Cameliard, and was inflamed with love even before he had met the lady.

But Merlin was a prophet and he could foresee that this choice would end in tragedy. 'If I should advise you that Guinevere is an unfortunate choice, would that change you?' asked Merlin.

'No,' replied Arthur.

'Well, then, if I should tell you that Guinevere will be unfaithful to you with your dearest and most trusted friend ...' said Merlin.

'I would not believe you,' said Arthur.

'Of course not,' said Merlin sadly. 'Every man who has ever lived holds tight to the belief that, for him alone, the laws of probability are cancelled out by love. Even I, who know beyond doubt that my death will be caused by a silly girl, will not hesitate when that girl passes by. Therefore you will marry Guinevere. You do not want advice – only agreement.'

And so Arthur sent Lancelot, the chief of his knights and his most trusted friend, to bring her from her father's house to the king's court. On the journey, Merlin's prophecy came to pass, and Lancelot and Guinevere fell in love with each other. But neither would consent to break their promise to the king.

Soon after the wedding, King Arthur had to attend to business elsewhere in the kingdom. In his absence, King Meleagant laid a trap for the queen, and seized her and carried her off into his kingdom. No one knew what had become of her. The only way into the moated prison in which Meleagant had incarcerated her was by a perilous bridge which had never been crossed by anyone, as it was made of sharp swords laid end to end. No one dared go after Guinevere but Lancelot, who made his way through unknown country until he discovered where Guinevere was hidden. He crossed the sword bridge and sustained grievous wounds, but he rescued the queen and fought and killed Meleagant. And when they returned to the court, she took pity on Lancelot and nursed his wounds herself. As he lay healing, the two at last consummated their secret love.

When Arthur returned, Merlin told him that he had seen the queen and Lancelot in a vision and that Guinevere had betrayed her husband. And other members of the court also told Arthur that the queen and Lancelot were known to secretly love each other. But Arthur refrained from

violence or accusation, and held his own counsel, because he knew that both his friend and the queen suffered greatly because of their love, and that both struggled against it as best they could. Because he loved them both, he was loathe to destroy either of them through public exposure of the betrayal. So he waited, and all three were made wretched because of the love which each bore the other two.

But the knights of the court were angry at the shame the queen and Lancelot had brought to the king, and also they saw a chance for grasping power and ousting the king's best friend from his side. So they plotted to catch Lancelot and Guinevere together, in order to bring the king proof of the betrayal and make public the queen's misdeeds. Among these knights was Mordred, who was the king's illegitimate son and who secretly sought the throne for himself.

That night these self-seeking men lay in wait for the lovers and burst into the chamber where they lay. But Lancelot escaped, and the knights took the queen prisoner and brought her before the king with proof of her betrayal. So Arthur was forced against his will to accuse her publicly and made her stand trial. Guinevere was judged guilty and sentenced to the fire. But as she was dragged to the stake, Lancelot, who had received news of her fate while he lay in hiding, rode forth to rescue her. There was a great battle, and many knights were slain before Lancelot carried the queen off to his castle called Joyous Gard.

Now Arthur could no longer be forgiving, for Lancelot had killed many of his best knights. So the king set off with his army to besiege the castle of Joyous Gard. But Lancelot refused to ride forth from the castle, for he would not do battle with Arthur. And then Arthur and Lancelot spoke to each other, and each remembered the love and loyalty they held for each other. Lancelot repented and swore he would give up the queen's love, so Arthur and Lancelot were reconciled.

OVERLEAF *From the moment that they met, Lancelot and Guinevere fell deeply and irrevocably in love, but at first neither would consent to break their promise of loyalty to King Arthur.*

Lancelot and Guinevere, Herbert James Draper (1864–1920)

Arthur would have taken back his queen, but the other knights would not countenance such a spirit of forgiveness. They demanded vengeance, so Lancelot had to come forth to do battle with these knights, lest he be thought a coward. And a great battle followed. During this battle Arthur and Lancelot met, and there were tears in both men's eyes. But they could not undo what had been done, and the battle went on around them, although these two had made peace with each other.

At length, both sides were exhausted. A parley ensued, and there was a truce. Arthur returned to court with Guinevere and offered Lancelot his old place at the Round Table. But Mordred, who saw power slipping from his grasp, plotted the downfall of all three. He led a great host against the king and, in this battle, the king was mortally wounded. Although Lancelot fought on the side of Arthur and killed Mordred, when all was over he could not bear his guilt, and told the widowed queen that he must depart forever. So he rode off and entered a monastery, and spent his days repenting his misdeeds. And the queen, too, could bear neither her guilt nor the loss of both the men she loved, and she took herself to a nunnery.

Many years passed, and one night Lancelot had a vision in which he was told to go to see the queen. When he had found the nunnery in which she had spent her days, he was told that she had died half an hour before, and he was faced with her corpse. And then Lancelot took neither meat nor drink, and sickened more and more. Eventually, he pined away and died.

Both Lancelot and Guinevere were placed on the same bier and brought to Lancelot's castle of Joyous Gard, and all the surviving knights who had sought their destruction in life came to honor them in death, for they had expiated their sins and now all knew of their great love for each other and for the king. So all three were forgiven in death, who were not forgiven in life.

COMMENTARY: *The tragic triangle of Arthur, Guinevere and Lancelot is a shining vision of the nobility of the human heart. It portrays a potential of which all of us are capable but which, sadly, is rarely met in real life. This triangle is not based, as so many are, on self-indulgence, mere sexual attraction,*

boredom or an attempt to escape commitment. It is rooted in deep love on all sides, and it teaches us that love is not always exclusive; we may love different people deeply in different ways. This is a hard thing for the modern person to swallow, for we are brought up to believe that if we love our partners, we cannot possibly love anyone else; we take marriage vows which demand exclusivity; and, in our attempts to understand why we get involved in triangles, we persist in believing that those who betray must be shallow and unfeeling. In many triangles, shallower reasons, conscious or unconscious, may indeed motivate the betrayal. But the myth of Arthur and Guinevere tells us that this is not always so, and that sometimes life is simply unfair; and so, too, may be the human heart.

Arthur's refusal to retaliate, despite his hurt, reflects a generosity of spirit and a capacity for self-control which we may well envy. Unfortunately, these qualities are not shared by his knights, who, like so many, are loud and obvious in their condemnation of something they cannot understand, because they have never loved deeply themselves. And these knights also have their own secret agendas which blind them to the profound rightness of what Arthur tries to do. In popular opinion, a modern-day Arthur, faced with such a situation, may well be thought a 'wimp', a weak man who tolerates a shameful situation because he is not manly enough to do anything about it. Yet Arthur is the opposite – his loyalty to both his friendship with Lancelot and his love for his wife causes him deep suffering, yet he refuses to betray his own heart and, thus, he proves himself more manly than any of the knights who bay for revenge.

None of the characters in this story finds romantic happiness in the ordinary sense. But perhaps more important than living happily ever after is the absolute loyalty all three show towards the deepest demands of their souls, even though it costs them nothing less than everything. If the love between Guinevere and Lancelot were anything less than a love of the soul, neither would have given way to temptation. If Arthur's love for both his friend and his queen were anything less than a love of the soul, he would have indulged himself in revenge, with the complete approval of everyone around him. There may be times when such a love enters our lives; and if it does, we may understand why the ancients thought it the visitation of a god, against which human will is powerless. Often simple lust, or the secret desire to punish a partner, is disguised by declarations of grand

Mordred, King Arthur's illegitimate son, plotted the downfall of both Arthur and Lancelot. He led a
great host against the king, who was mortally wounded and lay dying as the battle raged on.
La Mort d'Arthur by James Archer (1829–1904)

passion. But the real nature of such desire is revealed when we are faced with the
kind of choices that are forced on these three mythic figures. Perhaps we may
consider ourselves fortunate if such cauterizing fires do not enter our lives. If they
do, great suffering inevitably ensues for all three people. Yet, if life does impose
such a challenge on us, we might do well to remember the story of Arthur and
Guinevere, which tells us that betrayal may be the deepest and most profound
means by which we come to know ourselves and what we truly believe in.

Chapter Three

MARRIAGE

There are many myths about marriage; but none describe the 'happy marriage' so many people long for. It is, perhaps, ironic that the commonly quoted 'myth' of a happy marriage never appears in mythology. Myth presents us with how things really are psychologically, rather than how we would like them to be. The images they offer about marriage describe the archetypal ebbs, flows and conflicts of human emotions, and the difficulties and trials that are endemic to any effort at genuine relationship. The stories that follow offer us insight and wisdom into the dynamics of two people trying to relate to each other. But we will find no recipe for effortless permanent bliss. In real life, a happy marriage is the product of human effort and consciousness, and perhaps a bit of good luck as well; but it is not a guaranteed part of the archetypal backdrop of the human psyche.

GERDA AND FREY

The importance of courtship

THE NORSE STORY OF THE GOD FREY'S COURTSHIP OF GERDA IS TESTIMONY TO THE REWARDS OF PERSEVERANCE IN LOVE AND THE IMPORTANCE OF COURTSHIP RITUALS IN ENSURING THAT A RELATIONSHIP BLOSSOMS INTO A HAPPY MARRIAGE. WHILE WE MAY NOT HAVE TO RESORT TO SPELLS, WE MIGHT NEVERTHELESS LEARN FROM THE DETERMINATION AND PASSION WITH WHICH FREY – OR, IN TRUTH, HIS BEST FRIEND SKIRNIR, WHO DOES ALL THE REAL WORK – PURSUES THE CHOSEN BRIDE; FOR AN ENDURING AND FULFILLING BOND IS NOT LIKELY TO FALL FROM HEAVEN WITHOUT EFFORT AND TENACITY.

F rey's wife, like his mother, belonged to the race of giants. He was drawn to her by irresistible love. One day, while sitting on Odin's throne, he amused himself by observing what was taking place on earth. In the kingdom of the giants he saw a maiden of incomparable beauty coming from her father's house. The gleam of her white arms filled the sky and sea with light. Her name was Gerda. Frey's heart was at once inflamed with vehement love. But profound melancholy soon followed, for he did not know how to win his beloved. When his parents saw the change that had come over him, they sent for Frey's friend and servant Skirnir, and asked him to discover the secret of their son's unhappiness.

Skirnir quickly elicited the source of the trouble and offered to ask for the young maiden's hand on his friend's behalf. He asked Frey to loan him a famous sword which moved through the air of its own accord and a horse which could ride through fire. Skirnir rode through the night until he reached the land of the giants. At the door of Gerda's father's house, ferocious dogs were chained, and the house was surrounded by the fiery flames of enchantment. But Skirnir was not frightened. He rode the horse through the magic flames and arrived at the door of the house.

Gerda approached, attracted by the commotion the dogs made. Skirnir gave her Frey's message of love and courtship. At the same time, he offered her eleven apples made of pure gold and a beautiful magic ring which had once belonged to Odin. But Gerda was not impressed. Then Skirnir brandished the famous sword which moved through the air of its own accord, and looked as though he would kill both Gerda and her father. The threat was in vain; Gerda remained unimpressed. Despairing of success, Skirnir then resorted to spells and conjurations. He told Gerda that he had a magic wand with terrifying power, and that he would carve threatening and deadly runes on it if she did not agree to the marriage with Frey. He insisted that, by means of these runes, he would ensure she lived a solitary existence, far from men, at the opposite end of the world where, in the icy depths, she would dry up like a thistle.

Now Gerda became truly afraid. No threat could be greater than a life of loneliness, and Frey began to seem a very attractive alternative. As a

sign of conciliation, she offered Skirnir the cup of welcome, filled with mead. Skirnir pressed her to make a rendezvous with Frey then and there, for Frey was consumed with impatience to claim his bride. This Gerda refused to do; but she promised to meet Frey after nine nights had elapsed, in a sacred grove which she named.

Frey, meanwhile, waited in agony for news. When Skirnir brought him Gerda's reply his heart was again filled with joy. Only the delay imposed by her caused him pain. 'A night is long,' he said to Skirnir, 'but how much longer are two nights! How can I be patient for three nights? And how can I possibly survive nine?'

But he did, indeed, survive the nine nights, although he drove both Skirnir and his parents nearly demented with his complaining. In the end, he married Gerda and they enjoyed a blissful and fruitful union.

COMMENTARY: *This Norse tale, unlike so many myths of courtship and marriage, has a happy ending. But the happy outcome is dependent on the courtship itself, which may seem to us a strange one. Gerda is only persuaded to marry Frey through fear, and there is only one thing she truly fears, which is loneliness. Only when Skirnir threatens her with a lonely future does she agree to the marriage. This tells us about one of the dominant forces behind our efforts to make binding relationships with other human beings, for loneliness is one of our greatest sources of fear and suffering. Perhaps the reason why the threat succeeds is that Gerda is honest with herself. We may not wish to admit that we want a partner because it is preferable to being alone; and we may not wish to face the fact that we are more likely to work at a marriage if we face the fear of growing older without one. We prefer to talk about meeting the 'right' person or 'soulmate'. Much is made, in the present social climate, of the joys of being single and freewheeling. There is profound truth in the importance of being able to exist as an independent entity, for relationships based on fear alone, devoid of mutual respect and communication, often do not survive. Yet perhaps Gerda is more honest – and therefore more successful in her marriage – than many who pretend that the single state is preferable largely because they are frightened of the challenges and compromises required of any close bond with another human being.*

Frey does not do his own courting. This too may seem strange to us. But Skirnir, the friend and servant, is really an aspect of Frey himself, as is the case in most myths where a 'double' performs the hard work. Frey is a god, but Skirnir the servant is humble, without pretensions and possessing no pride to lose. Although he wields magical implements, he is merely a spokesman. This suggests that, if we are to succeed in establishing the relationships we seek, we may need to present ourselves not as important, lordly beings, but as ordinary people. Skirnir is also an image of communication; he has the right instruments, the right weapons, the right horse and the right language. He tries several different approaches and then, finally, hits on the right one. This ability to be flexible, inventive and communicative in creating bonds with others is an important insight offered by this myth. Moreover, Skirnir is persistent. He does not give up, even in the face of Gerda's stubborn resistance. His master Frey might have gone off in a sulk, hurt and rejected; but Skirnir's emotions are not involved, so he can be objective in his efforts. Thus, he is not only an image of good communication skills, but also of detachment; he has no pride to lose, no sensitive feelings to be hurt. We too may need to cultivate such detachment in order to find the right message for those we love and seek to get closer to.

The magic weapon, golden apples and beautiful ring that are offered as bribes, ultimately have no effect on Gerda. It is the conjuration of her fear of loneliness which succeeds. Skirnir only recognizes this when his initial threats and bribes fail. Efforts to impress do not work in this strange courtship between god and giantess; and perhaps they do not work in human courtships either. It is a profound yet disturbing truth which the story of Frey and Gerda offers us. When we seek to impress with our powers and talents, we may fail in our efforts to win love. In the end, our capacity to recognize and speak to another's fears – which can only come through recognition of our own – may ultimately be the truest channel through which defenses are breached and the beginnings of an enduring relationship established.

The goddess Freia provided the magic golden apples by which Frey, through his friend and messenger Skirnir, attempted to woo the beautiful giantess Gerda; but Gerda was not impressed.

Freia, the fair one, Arthur Rackham (1867–1939)

NYNEVE'S TRANSFORMATION

Compassion unlocks the power to love

WE HAVE ALREADY MET NYNEVE IN THE STORY OF MERLIN'S ENCHANTMENT (SEE
PAGES 138–42). IN THAT EARLIER TALE, SHE WAS YOUNG, CALLOUS AND SELF-
SEEKING; AND SHE ARCHITECTED THE ENCHANTER'S DOWNFALL IN ORDER TO
GAIN POWER. IN THIS STORY, SHE LEARNS WISDOM AND COMPASSION THROUGH
TIME, EXPERIENCE AND SUFFERING; AND ONLY THROUGH THIS TRANSFORMATION
CAN SHE ENTER A TRUE MARRIAGE IN WHICH SHE FINDS HAPPINESS AND
FULFILLMENT.

I n the Forest of Adventure, Nyneve journeyed restlessly. She had
changed since that time when, as an impatient and ambitious girl,
she had robbed Merlin of his secrets and his life. Then she had
wanted power and eminence, without understanding the price that life
requires for such boons. But in the years since, her power had imprisoned
her own heart as surely as she had once imprisoned Merlin's. Because of
her magic, she could do things ordinary people could not and, rather than
making her free, this made her a slave to the helpless. Her gift of healing
made her the servant of the sick, and her power over fortune tied her to
the unfortunate. And her knowledge of the secrets of other human beings,
which exposed evil no matter what its mask, enlisted her in constant war
against the ambitious plots of greed and treason that went on in the world
around her. More than this, she sadly realized that, while her strength
bound her to the weak and troubled, it did not bind them to her. For they
could not offer friendship as payment of their debt. Thus, Nyneve found
herself alone and lonely, praised but desolate, and often she longed for
the old times when love and kindliness were cast equally in a coffer by all.
For there is no loneliness like that of one who can only give, and no anger
like that of those who only receive and hate the weight of debt. She stayed
little in one place, for gladness for her services invariably changed to
uneasiness in the face of her power.

As she travelled through the forest, she passed a young squire; and she saw that he was weeping. When questioned, he revealed that his beloved master had been betrayed by his lady; and now his master's heart was broken and he lay with arms open for death.

'Take me to your lord,' Nyneve said. 'He shall not die for love of an unworthy woman. If she is merciless in love, the proper punishment is to love and yet be unloved.'

So the squire escorted her to the bed of his master, Sir Pelleas, who lay with hollow cheeks and fevered brow. Nyneve thought she had never seen so goodly and handsome a man.

'Why does good throw itself under the feet of evil?' she said, and soothed his throbbing forehead with her cool hand. She sang to him, and her magic brought him peace and the enchantment of dreamless sleep. Then she sought out the treacherous lady, who was called Ettarde, and brought her to the bed of the sleeping Pelleas.

'How do you dare bring death to such a man?' Nyneve demanded, for she could not forget what she had once done to Merlin, and lived constantly with her own bitter remorse. 'What are you, that you could not be kind? I offer you the pain you have inflicted on another. Already you feel my spell, and you are beginning to love this man. You love him more than anything in the world. You would die for him, so deeply do you love him.'

And Ettarde, caught in the spell, repeated: 'I love him. Oh God! I love him. How can I love what earlier I so despised?'

'It is a little parcel of the hell you were wont to offer others,' said Nyneve. 'And now you will see the other side.'

Nyneve whispered long into the ear of the sleeping knight, and then awakened him, stepping back to watch. When Pelleas caught sight of Ettarde he was filled with loathing for her, and, when her loving hand moved towards him, he shrank away in disgust. 'Go away!' he cried. 'I cannot stand the sight of you. You are treacherous and cold. Leave me and never let me see you again.' And Ettarde sank to the ground weeping.

And Nyneve said, 'Now you know the pain. This is what he felt for you.'

'I love him!' Ettarde screamed.

'You will always love him,' Nyneve said. 'And you will die with your love unwanted; and that is a dry, shrivelling death. Go now to your dusty death.'

Then Nyneve returned to Pelleas, and said, 'Rise up and begin to live again. One day you will find your true love, and she will find you.'

'I have worn out my capacity to love,' said the knight sadly. 'That is over.'

'Not so,' said Nyneve. 'Take my hand. I will help you find your love.'

'Will you stay with me until I do?' he asked.

'Yes,' she said, 'I promise to stay beside you until you find your love.'

And they lived together happily for the rest of their lives.

COMMENTARY: *The story of Nyneve's transformation has many insights to offer us about the capacity to love and the potential for creating an enduring bond. Not least, it teaches us that we must live with the inner consequences of our actions, and that this profound justice, although not always visible in outer life, may change us from callous, self-centered creatures to individuals capable of understanding and compassion. It may be that, while we are all born with the potential to love, we can only fulfill that potential through the suffering born of real self-knowledge.*

Nyneve discovers first that power and position never come without a price, and the price is often isolation from our fellow humans. Whether our power is derived from wealth, knowledge, worldly status, special artistic or healing gifts, or unusual beauty or sexual charisma, nevertheless we must accept the burden of aloneness if we define ourselves by our specialness. And we cannot expect our service to others to earn us love either, for — as Nyneve learns to her cost — obligation and love make poor bedfellows.

Nyneve also discovers that regret for hurts inflicted on others cannot be shed simply through forgetting or through performing good deeds in expiation. When

Although Nyneve had both magical powers and beauty, she was miserable, because her gifts alienated her from her fellow humans and drove her into intolerable isolation.

Morgan le Fay: Queen of Avalon, Anthony Frederick Augustus Sandys (1829–1904)

we injure our fellows through callousness or the urge for power, somewhere deep down we know what we have done; and we must live with this knowledge all our lives. Ordinary guilt is generally a useless mechanism because it is so often merely an intellectual recognition of our culpability, devoid of real feeling. But remorse, which is deeper, arises when we recognize with our whole hearts that we have caused pain unjustifiably. Remorse, deeply felt, can transform us. What Nyneve has done to Merlin cannot be undone and, as she grows older and experiences loneliness, she carries this knowledge within her; and it humbles her.

Nyneve's desire to help Sir Pelleas arises, not because she thinks she can get him for herself, but because she sees, in what his lady Ettarde has done to him, a mirror of what she herself once did to Merlin. She recognizes that Pelleas is a good man, and that a woman not unlike the young Nyneve has nearly destroyed him with her callousness and faithlessness. Nyneve's anger at Ettarde is really an expression of her anger at herself, and it is herself whom she is really punishing. She sees all too clearly that the handsome knight deserves something better in life than the kind of woman she herself once was. And when he declares that he can no longer love, her compassion and pity for him make her vow to help him find another love – never realizing that she herself will be that love.

Nyneve's actions on behalf of Pelleas are entirely free of self-interest and are, therefore, unlike anything she has ever done before. Her urge to right the wrong Ettarde has done springs from her remorse and her painful realization of the wrongness of displaying unkindness to those who genuinely love us. This is a profound change and a release of the poisons of the past; and her reward, which she never set out to claim, is an enduring love. Human beings have filled volumes attempting to understand the nature of lasting love and the secret of making a marriage work. This story may not answer all our questions on the matter, but it contains profoundly important messages about the mysterious relationship between love and self-knowledge, and about the link between humility and real compassion. The story of Nyneve also reveals the difference between 'doing good' as a means of claiming power and assuaging loneliness, and offering service to others as the reflection of an empathy born of self-understanding.

ALCESTIS AND ADMETUS

Loving another more than oneself

THE GREEK TALE OF ALCESTIS' WILLINGNESS TO OFFER HER OWN LIFE TO SAVE THE
LIFE OF HER HUSBAND HAS COME DOWN TO US AS A SYMBOL OF THE NOBLEST
KIND OF SELF-SACRIFICE IN MARRIAGE. HUMAN BEINGS OFTEN INDULGE IN
SOMETHING WHICH LOOKS LIKE SELF-SACRIFICE, BUT WHICH IS REALLY A SECRET
MEANS OF ENSURING ANOTHER PERSON'S LOYALTY. SELF-SACRIFICE IN MARRIAGE
IS OFTEN A KIND OF UNCONSCIOUS 'DEAL' MEANT TO PURCHASE THE PARTNER'S
DEVOTION. THIS MYTH GIVES US A PICTURE OF A LOVE WHICH PUTS THE LOVED
ONE FIRST, NOT BECAUSE OF ANY SECRET HOPE OF FUTURE REWARD, BUT BECAUSE
THERE IS SIMPLY NO OTHER CHOICE OPEN TO THE HEART.

Alcestis, the most beautiful of King Pelias' daughters, was asked in marriage by many kings and princes. Not wishing to endanger his position by refusing any of them, and yet clearly unable to satisfy more than one, Pelias let it be known that he would offer Alcestis to any man who could yoke a wild boar and a lion to his chariot and drive them around the race-course. This news eventually reached the ears of King Admetus of Pherae. Admetus immediately summoned the sun-god Apollo, whom Zeus, king of heaven, had bound to him for one year as a herdsman.

'Have I treated you with the respect due to your godhead?' Admetus asked the sun-god.

'You have indeed,' Apollo replied, 'and I have shown my gratitude by making all your ewes drop twins.'

'As a final favor,' Admetus said, 'help me to win Alcestis, by enabling me to fulfill Pelias' conditions.'

'I shall be pleased to do so,' answered Apollo. And presently Admetus was driving his chariot around the race-course, drawn by the savage team of lion and boar.

All might have been well. But at the wedding, Admetus, in his great joy,

forgot to make the customary sacrifice to the moon-goddess Artemis. Artemis was quick to punish him. When, flushed with wine and garlanded with flowers, he entered the bridal chamber that night, he recoiled in horror. No lovely naked bride awaited him on the marriage bed, but a tangled knot of hissing serpents. Admetus ran shouting for Apollo, who kindly intervened with Artemis on his friend's behalf. The neglected sacrifice was offered at once. And Apollo even obtained Artemis' promise that, when the day of Admetus' death came, he should be spared on condition that a member of his family died voluntarily for love of him.

This fatal day came sooner than Admetus expected, although it had been appointed from the beginning by the Fates. Hermes, the divine messenger, flew into the palace one morning and summoned Admetus to the underworld. General consternation prevailed. But Apollo gained a little time for Admetus by making the three Fates drunk, and thus delayed the final cutting of Admetus' life-thread. Admetus ran in haste to his old parents, clasped their knees and begged each of them in turn to surrender their final days on his behalf. But both refused, saying that they still derived too much enjoyment from life and that he should be content with his appointed lot like everyone else.

Then, for love of Admetus, Alcestis took poison, and her ghost descended to the underworld, fulfilling the bargain between Apollo and Artemis to grant Admetus a longer life. But Persephone, goddess of the underworld, considered it an evil thing that no one but his loving wife would make such a sacrifice. As a fellow woman, she understood Alcestis' great love and decided to reward it. So she sent Alcestis back to the world of the living, and husband and wife lived long in great happiness.

COMMENTARY: *On the surface, the message of this moving tale is clear enough — no greater love can a woman feel than that which impels her to sacrifice her own life on behalf of her loved ones. But there are other themes embedded in the myth which tell us something more about the nature of marriage, and perhaps even about the mystery of life itself. From the very beginning, this marriage is linked to divine figures who are responsible for much of the action in the story. Apollo is*

Admetus' appointed end could only be forestalled if a member of his family died voluntarily for love of him; so his wife Alcestis took poison, and her ghost descended to the underworld in his place.

Alcestis sacrifices herself to save her husband Admetus, king of Pherae,
Jean François Pierre Peyron (1744–1814)

a great and powerful god, yet he acts as Admetus' servant and friend, providing the necessary assistance whenever it is required. Who is this god, and what might he symbolize in the story? As lord of the sun, he is an image of the light – the

light of the spirit and also the light of consciousness. Admetus is a man who is both conscious and spiritually alive, and thus he can meet the challenge which Alcestis' father presents to her suitors. Yoking a lion and a boar together as a chariot team is an image of controlling the instincts and directing raw power to civilized ends. In other words, Admetus has made the effort to contain his instinctual nature and has made an enduring relationship with his inner spirit. He is, in short, on the side of life and of the light; and because of this he is fortunate in choosing a bride.

Admetus is forgiven his first transgression, which is his neglect of the moon-goddess Artemis. Artemis is a deity connected with wild nature; she is a symbol of raw instinct, and therefore Admetus' self-control and consciousness make her angry. But Apollo sorts this problem out, and Admetus is offered a longer lifespan – provided there is someone who loves him sufficiently to take his place in the underworld. Apollo then deals with the problem of the Fates by getting them drunk – a unique image in Greek myth, since even the gods had to obey fate. Perhaps this story is telling us that consciousness and spiritual commitment provide the possibility of freeing oneself from the kind of blind compulsions which the Fates symbolize. And perhaps even death – at least on a psychological level – may be kept at bay for a time through such inner awareness.

Admetus asks his ageing parents if they will offer themselves to spare his life. Their response is quite the opposite of what we might expect: they categorically refuse. The love of parents for children, and children for parents, may sometimes be a rather precarious thing if we take the message of this mythic image seriously. What passes for love in families is often a bond rooted in mutual need, dependency and fear of separateness, rather than a genuine love arising from mutual respect and emotional generosity. For this reason, we may often be let down by our families when we most need their validation of our individuality. Only Alcestis is prepared to sacrifice herself for Admetus; she values him enough to make this offering without question. While we may never have to make such a total sacrifice for a loved one, there are many occasions in every relationship when our affirmation of another's value may make us put that person first, without thinking of the consequences to ourselves. This is a sacrifice based not on some hope of future return, nor motivated by any secret attempt to bind the other with

obligation. It erupts spontaneously from a mysterious core of the heart and soul which cannot do otherwise than give.

Because of this act of total generosity, Persephone, queen of the underworld, refuses to countenance Alcestis' death, and sends her back to the realm of the living. Persephone is an image of the mysterious hidden dimensions of life and, amongst other things, symbolizes the cycles of nature and time which are veiled from rational consciousness. She does not represent the judgement of society; she reflects a deeper law of nature which deals in psychological consequences. We may understand her to symbolize the laws by which the unconscious psyche itself operates. Alcestis is rewarded because she has never sought a reward; she achieves happiness because she does not try to claim it; and she lives her life loving and loved because she has put love before her own gain. It would be unrealistic to expect any human being to live in such a state of total open-heartedness all the time. But we may glimpse the magic of Alcestis' reward when we step beyond our personal motives and agendas, and value someone else so much that we forget, for a little while, our own needs and wishes. However brief the episode, this is a profoundly healing experience which renews life. Without it we cannot hope to achieve the essential core of what marriage is all about.

ODYSSEUS AND PENELOPE

Believing in each other against all odds

THE MARRIAGE OF ODYSSEUS AND PENELOPE IS ONLY A SMALL PART OF THE GREAT SAGA OF THE TROJAN WAR. BUT IT IS A REMARKABLE MYTHIC PORTRAYAL OF THE LOYALTY AND FAITH THAT CAN EXIST IN A MARRIAGE, DESPITE THE TRIALS AND TEMPTATIONS WHICH MAY BESET BOTH PEOPLE.

O dysseus and Penelope, rulers of the island kingdom of Ithaca, rejoiced at the birth of Telemachus, their only son. When Odysseus was called to fight in the Trojan War, he was reluctant to leave his loving young wife and baby for a war he foresaw would be

long and arduous; so he feigned madness. Thus, when the warlords Agamemnon and Palamedes arrived on the rocky island to ask Odysseus to join them, they found him busy sowing salt into fields he was ploughing with an ass and an ox yoked together. Wily Odysseus hoped this would persuade them he was too crazy to fight. But Palamedes was wily too and, catching up the baby Telemachus, he placed the child in the path of the plough. Odysseus' quick reaction to save his son proved that he was not mad after all, and reluctantly he joined the fleet sailing to Troy.

Many trials befell Odysseus as he tried to return home to his wife and son after the Trojan War, among which were the treacherous charms of the Sirens whose sweet singing lured sailors to their deaths.

Ulysses and the Sirens, Herbert James Draper (1864–1920)

The bloody Trojan War dragged on for ten years. When, at last, Odysseus was able to return home, yet more obstacles lay ahead of him on the homeward journey. He inadvertently offended Poseidon, and the god of the ocean sent many storms to blow Odysseus' ship off course. Trials and temptations befell him, and the charms of the sorceress Circe, the beautiful nymph Calypso and the princess Nausicaa seduced him for a time. But foremost in his mind lay his wife and son; and though it took another ten years, he finally made the journey home.

Despite the terrible hardships which both Penelope and Odysseus had to withstand, their loyalty and love endured, and they were happily and triumphantly reunited after twenty years.

Ulysses leaving Sparta with Penelope, Jean-Jacques-François Le Barbier (1738–1826)

Meanwhile, Penelope waited, hoping her beloved husband would find his way back to her and Telemachus. In his absence, many suitors arrived on Ithaca, trying to persuade her to give up hope of Odysseus and marry one of them instead. They all coveted the island kingdom; and Penelope was still very beautiful. She had to find a way of repulsing the suitors (some say no less than one hundred and twelve), so she promised that, once she had finished weaving a funeral shroud for her father-in-law, she would choose one of them. However, although she worked long and hard on her weaving by day, she secretly unpicked her day's work each night, thus never completing her task. Although it was hard to keep believing in the safe return of Odysseus after twenty years, Penelope managed to maintain her faith and loyalty, and was rewarded by his eventual homecoming and their joyous reunion.

COMMENTARY: *The myth of Odysseus and Penelope shows a relationship which endures time, temptation and long separation. But this is only because both people keep their faith in each other, refusing to let go of their joint ideals. Both are sorely tested and both, on occasion, make mistakes; in some versions of the myth, Penelope as well as Odysseus indulges in other loves, which is perhaps understandable given a separation of twenty years. Yet their love and care for each other and for their son binds them absolutely, and sustains them both through the most difficult times. In Homer's great epic, The Odyssey, Odysseus pulls his thoughts back to Penelope and Telemachus whenever he is in danger of remaining with the various women who tempt him along the way. They succeed in seducing him, but they cannot truly touch his heart, for it is already given.*

The image of Penelope's weaving has caught the imagination of readers for over two thousand years. It is a funeral shroud, which she weaves by day and unpicks by night. What might this mean as an image of that which sustains her loyalty, even when companionship is offered which might ease her loneliness? The funeral shroud reflects the motif of death – the death of love, the letting go of the past, the ending of past ties and attachments. Although, when in full view, she goes on with her work, when alone she dismantles it, refusing to relinquish love, memory and the woven past which she shares with her absent husband.

Weaving is also an archetypal image of life itself, a cloth of many different strands, experiences, feelings and events. Each of us has our own unique story which we begin weaving at birth and complete at death. Penelope refuses to accept that the woven cloth of her previous life is complete; she looks to neither past nor future; she lives here and now, loyal to her instincts and feelings, refusing to be bullied into giving up hope, yet equally refusing to fall prey to fruitless fantasies. She is, in effect, living wholly and utterly in the moment, and the pretense of the funeral shroud is only a means of protection against the importuning of the suitors. This ability to take each moment as it comes, and remain loyal to one's heart regardless of what others insist is reality, may be the real key to the endurance of this mythic marriage. For Odysseus, the thought of his wife and son keeps him aligned with his deepest values and desires. For Penelope, the capacity to remain still and serene in the moment, refusing to say to herself, 'Love is finished', is something we may have to work long and hard to find. The nature of love defies time, distance and physical loss, and, along with great art and moments of mystical vision, is perhaps the only thing we mortals can experience which can give us a glimpse of the eternal. If we can find it, even in brief moments in the framework of a close relationship, we may have discovered one of the great secrets of immortality.

It is interesting, too, to speculate that it could be the space between these two mythic figures which makes their loyalty possible. Would the love between Odysseus and Penelope have survived daily mundane life on Ithaca for twenty years, or did their ideals of each other, nourished by absence and longing, help to keep their romance alive? In The Prophet, Kahlil Gibran (1883–1931) says on the subject of marriage:

'Let there be spaces in your togetherness ...
And stand together yet not too near together.
For the pillars of the temple stand apart,
And the oak tree and the cypress grow not in each other's shadow.'

PART IV

POSITION AND POWER

The challenge of finding one's way in the world is exciting to some and
daunting to others. Success and failure occupy us all on one level or
another, and self-sufficiency is a quality not always easy to develop while
retaining compassion for one's fellow humans. Money, position and power
are not merely things to be had 'out there in the world', however; they are
also profoundly symbolic, reflecting our deepest values. Myth has many
stories about ambition and greed, power and failure, and responsibility
and irresponsibility towards others. It reveals our most fundamental
attitudes towards money, and the ways it often symbolizes or replaces self-
worth and the craving for love. Mythic stories can also teach us about the
discovery of one's right place in the world, and what is meant by vocation.
They can give us profound insights into the way we interact in society. We
have many collective assumptions about what is 'right' and 'wrong'. But
myth can sometimes surprise us as it gently reveals our strengths and
weaknesses, our truths and our hypocrisies, our mistaken value systems,
our lack of understanding of our worldly motives, and our often ambivalent
attitudes towards those we feel to be better or worse placed than ourselves.

*Achieving power may be far easier than exercising it wisely and humanely, as the Biblical story of the
Judgement of Solomon portrays.*
DETAIL The Judgement of Solomon, *Sebastiano del Piombo (c.1485–1547)*

Chapter One

FINDING A VOCATION

The word 'vocation' comes from a Latin root which means 'to call', and it reflects the sense of an inner calling or meaningful task which must be accomplished in the world. Although vocation does not necessarily involve a recognized profession or the accruing of money, it needs to involve the heart in order for us to feel we have really found our place in life. It also needs to be manifested outwardly for us to feel we have achieved what we were put on earth for. For some, vocation might involve climbing to the top of one's profession; for others it might involve the quiet but equally committed act of raising a child, or making one's garden beautiful. We all need some sense of vocation, whether it is expressed through a job or pursued quietly outside ordinary working life. Yet we are often bewildered about how to find our vocation and, if we do, how to make it concrete. Vocation may arise from inner inspiration, or it may evolve from external necessity which drives us onto a path which we discover only later is absolutely the right one. Myth offers us examples of both, as well as what to do and what not to do as we make our way in the world.

LUGH

Never give up trying

THE CELTIC TALE OF LUGH'S ENTRY INTO THE HALLS OF THE TUATHA DÉ DANANN IS A DELIGHTFUL LESSON IN THE IMPORTANCE OF PERSEVERANCE IF WE ARE TO FIND OUR RIGHT PLACE IN THE WORLD. VOCATION MAY BE A CALLING FROM WITHIN, BUT IT REQUIRES ADAPTABILITY TO THE OUTER WORLD AS WELL AS INNER COMMITMENT. LUGH IS A MERCURIAL FIGURE – PART DIVINITY AND PART TRICKSTER – AND IN THIS STORY HIS CHAMELEON-LIKE VERSATILITY REFLECTS A MOST IMPORTANT QUALITY FOR THOSE INTENT ON FINDING THEIR PATH IN LIFE.

One day, a great assembly was held at Tara, where the Tuatha Dé Danann, the people of the goddess Danu, were wont to meet. King Nuada was celebrating his return to the throne by a feast. While the feast was at its height, a stranger, clothed like a king, came to the palace gate. The porter asked him his name and errand.

'I am Lugh,' the stranger replied. 'I am the grandson of Diancecht by Cian, my father, and the grandson of Balor by Ethniu, my mother.'

'Yes, yes,' said the porter impatiently, 'but I did not ask your genealogy. What is your profession? For no one is admitted here unless he is a master of some craft.'

'I am a carpenter,' said Lugh.

'We have no need of a carpenter. We already have a very good one; his name is Luchtainé,' said the porter.

'I am an excellent smith,' said Lugh.

'We do not want a smith. We have a very good one; his name is Goibniu,' said the porter.

'I am a professional warrior,' said Lugh.

'We have no need of one. Ogma is our champion,' said the porter.

'I am a harpist,' said Lugh.

'We have an excellent harpist already,' said the porter.

'I am a warrior renowned for skillfulness rather than for mere strength,' said Lugh.

'We already have a man like that,' said the porter.

'I am a poet and tale-teller,' said Lugh.

'We have no need of such,' said the porter. 'We have a most accomplished poet and tale-teller.'

'I am a sorcerer,' said Lugh.

'We do not want one. We have numberless sorcerers and druids,' said the porter.

'I am a physician,' said Lugh.

'Diancecht is our physician,' said the porter.

'I am a cup-bearer,' said Lugh.

'We already have nine of them,' said the porter.

'I am a worker in bronze,' said Lugh.

'We have no need of you. We already have a worker in bronze. His name is Credné,' said the porter.

'Then ask the king,' said Lugh, 'if he has with him a man who is master of all these crafts at once, for if he has, then there is no need for me to come to Tara.'

So the porter went inside, and told the king that a man had come who called himself Lugh *Ioldanach*, which means 'The Master of all Arts', and that he claimed to know everything. The king sent out his best chess-player to play against the stranger. Lugh won, inventing a new move called 'Lugh's enclosure'. Then the king invited him in. Lugh entered, and sat down upon the chair called the 'sage's seat', kept for the wisest man.

The champion, Ogma, was showing off his strength by pushing a flag-stone so large that four-score yokes of oxen would have been needed to move it. The stone, huge as it was, was only a portion broken from a still greater rock. Lugh picked it up in his hands and put it back in its place. Then the king asked him to play the harp. Lugh played the 'sleep-tune', and the king and all his court fell asleep and did not wake until the same hour the following day. Next Lugh played a plaintive air, and they all wept. And then he played a measure which sent them into transports of joy.

When the king saw all these numerous talents, he realized that one so gifted could be of great help to his people against their enemies. So he took counsel with the others and lent the throne to Lugh for thirteen days. And Lugh became the war leader for the Tuatha Dé Danann.

COMMENTARY: 'Master of all Arts' may be too vast a collection of talents for any human to aspire to, and usually such total mastery is not required when we apply for a job. But the story of Lugh tells us that we may need to acquire a variety of skills if we are to find a place in our constantly changing world. This ancient Celtic tale is strangely practical and up-to-date, because it presents us with the importance of acquiring knowledge of many related subjects – even if we aspire to work at only one. The idea of specializing and becoming good at just one thing may have been appropriate decades ago; the job market then was different, and the computer age had not begun. Now the world is changing with incredible rapidity, and we may need the Mercurial all-roundedness of Lugh if we are to beat the competition and make our way towards our worldly goals.

Lugh is also persistent, and this quality is vital if we are to make our aspirations real. He does not go away in a hurt sulk when first rejected, nor does he get angry or arrogant; he simply counters each refusal with another offer. He knows that he must convince the king, not that he is the best harpist or warrior or carpenter, but that he is capable of doing any of these jobs and is therefore worth several other people in terms of the resources he has to offer. His confidence lies in his knowledge of himself and his training in many different arts. In short, he can convince everyone of his worth, including the king, because he believes in himself; and this belief is based not on some self-aggrandizing vision, but on solid practical experience. In this most pragmatic of myths, we are presented with a vivid description of what we need to arm ourselves in the world outside and how we need to present ourselves to those from whom we seek favor. One can almost hear the king weighing up the cost-effectiveness of hiring one man who is capable of doing the jobs of six. Lugh is a thoroughly modern deity, well aware of market forces. There are many deeper and more profound issues concerning the pursuit of a vocation, which we will explore through other myths; but the story of Lugh can teach us that our journey must begin with our feet firmly on the ground.

A Myth of Two Brothers

A lesson in how to prosper

THIS TALE FROM EAST AFRICA HAS MUCH TO TEACH US ABOUT THE INVISIBLE LAWS
WHICH MUST BE HONORED IF WE ARE TO FIND WHAT WE ARE SEEKING IN THE
WORLD. ONE BROTHER GETS IT WRONG, WHILE THE OTHER GETS IT RIGHT – NOT
BECAUSE HE IS CLEVERER OR STRONGER, BUT BECAUSE HE RESPONDS TO THE
NEEDS OF THOSE HE MEETS ALONG THE WAY.

There was a man who had two sons. The elder was called Mkunare, and the younger Kanyanga. They were so poor that they did not own a single cow. Eventually Mkunare proposed that he should go up to Kibo, one of the two peaks of Mount Kilimanjaro, because he had heard it said that a king ruled up there who was generous to the poor. Thus he hoped to fulfill what he felt to be his vocation, which was the salvation of his family and his people.

Mkunare took a supply of food – all that could be spared – and set off up the mountain. After a while he met an old woman who was sitting beside the path. Her eyes were so sore that she could not see. Mkunare greeted her.

'Why have you come to this place?' said the old woman in reply.

'I am looking for the king who lives at the top of the mountain,' said Mkunare.

'Lick my eyes clean,' said the old woman, 'and I will tell you how to get there.'

But Mkunare was too revolted by her sore eyes to lick them, and he went on his way. Further up, he arrived at the country of the Konyingo (the Little People or Wee Folk), and saw a group of men sitting in their king's cattle compound. These men were very small, the size of young boys, and Mkunare mistakenly assumed that they were children.

'Hello!' he called. 'Where will I find your fathers and big brothers?'

The Konyingo replied, 'Just wait here until they arrive.'

Mkunare waited until evening, but no one came. Before nightfall the Konyingo herded their cattle into the compound and slaughtered an animal for the evening meal; but they did not give Mkunare any of the meat. They said that he must wait until their fathers and big brothers arrived. Tired, hungry and disappointed, Mkunare set off again down the mountain, and again passed the old woman sitting beside the path. But, even though he tried to persuade her, she would tell him nothing about what had happened to him. On his way back, he lost his way in uninhabited country and did not get home for a month. Thus, he failed in his quest and told his kinsmen that there were people on the top of Kibo with large herds of cattle, but being mean, they gave nothing to strangers.

Then Kanyanga, the younger brother, decided to go up the mountain in a second attempt to ease his family's poverty. After a while he, too, met the old woman sitting beside a path. He greeted her and, when she asked why he had come up there, he told her he was looking for the king who lived on top of the mountain.

'Lick my eyes clean,' said the old woman to Kanyanga, 'and I will tell you how to get there.'

Kanyanga took pity on her and licked her eyes thoroughly.

'Keep climbing,' the old woman told Kanyanga, 'and you will come to the settlement of the king. The men you will see there are no bigger than boys, but don't jump to the conclusion that they are children. Address them as members of the king's council and greet them respectfully.'

Further up, Kanyanga arrived at the cattle compound of the Konyingo king, and greeted the little men there respectfully. They took him to the king, who listened to his plea for help and ordered that he be given a meal and a place to sleep that night. As a return for their hospitality, Kanyanga taught the Konyingo the incantations and medicines which protect the growing crops against insects and other pests, and also those which invisibly bar the paths against invading enemies. The Little People were so pleased with these new methods that they each gave Kanyanga an animal out of their herds; and he set off down the mountain, driving his cattle in front of him and singing the Herding-song. And so Kanyanga prospered,

as did his kinsmen; but people composed a song about his elder brother Mkunare which is still sung:

'O Mkunare, wait till the fathers come.
What right have you to despise the Little Folk?'

COMMENTARY: Mkunare, like many people, knows what he wants. He wishes to prosper and help his family and kinsmen, and to do so he needs the favor of someone who is in a position to help him. Also, like many people, he is so preoccupied with achieving his goal that he fails to notice what is really going on around him, and does not respond with compassion to someone less fortunate than himself whom he meets along the way. Because he is repelled by the old woman and does not look carefully at the little Konyingo to discover whether they are really boys or men, he receives no help and must return home with empty hands. Thus we, too, may be so focused on what we want as we set out in life that we lose our capacity to remain aware of what confronts us in the immediate present. And in failing to live here and now, we may risk the loss of the goals we so long to achieve.

The old woman whom Mkunare meets is one of life's unfortunates, but she also possesses some very important information, without which Mkunare cannot hope to get what he seeks. We might interpret her as an image of those less well off than ourselves, who, through bitter experience, have acquired wisdom we need. Or we may see her as a symbol of the painful and unfair side of life, which must be faced if we are to understand the world we live in. However we interpret her, the message is clear: refusal to respond to her request results in a fatal ignorance of the real facts, and thus in failure. Figures such as this old woman are common in myth. Sometimes they are portrayed as poor, sick or elderly people seeking a favor, sometimes as animals needing help; and when they appear, they invariably reward whomever responds to their plea with some vital knowledge or implement which ensures future success. It is possible that we all meet such situations as we move through life, yet so often we fail to recognize the importance of what we are facing, and cannot show the necessary compassion.

Mkunare's second mistake, arising inevitably from his first mistake, is that he addresses the Little People with disrespect because he thinks they are children.

When he heard that a generous king lived there, Mkunare decided to seek prosperity and good fortune at the peak of Mount Kibo. But his ambition obscured his respect for those he met along the way.

Mountain Sunrise, Thomas Cole (1801–48)

Because they do not match up to Mkunare's image of what a king's councillors should look like, he 'talks down' to them. In much the same way, we, too, may find ourselves judging others solely by their appearance and treating them with disrespect, never realizing that they may, in fact, hold the key to the goals we are so avidly pursuing. And even if these Little People were children, children too merit respect as individuals; if they are wise enough to know how to herd cattle, they are worthy enough for Mkunare to speak to them with civility. Instead, he dismisses them, and they make him pay for his lack of courtesy. In return, Mkunare learns nothing from all this, but afterwards tells everyone that the Konyingo are too mean to share anything with him. Such a negative and

cynical view of other people is often the result not of others' meanness, but of our own stupidity.

Kanyanga, unlike his older brother, is not blinded by either callousness or superficiality. He pities the old woman and gives her what she needs; if he is revolted, nevertheless his compassion proves stronger. Licking the sore eyes of a nearly blind old woman is a striking image which suggests giving unstinting comfort to someone else's pain and disillusionment. Thus Kanyanga is warned about the Little People, and does not mistake them for children. But he goes further than merely following good advice; he responds to the generosity of the Konyingo with generosity of his own, teaching them everything he knows. This act is not calculated to gain a reward; it is given from the heart. Thus he succeeds in bringing home wealth in the form of cattle. The message here is clear.

PHAËTHON AND THE SUN-CHARIOT

Going too far too fast

THE SAD GREEK MYTH OF PHAËTHON REVEALS MANY OF THE ASPIRATIONS AND DIFFICULTIES OF THE YOUNG PERSON SEEKING TO FIND HIS OR HER PLACE IN THE WORLD; AND IT ISSUES A STARK WARNING AGAINST TRYING TO GO TOO FAR TOO FAST. PERHAPS MORE IMPORTANTLY, IT ALSO TEACHES US THAT ATTEMPTING TO COPY AN ADMIRED PARENT IS NOT ALWAYS A WISE WAY TO DISCOVER ONE'S VOCATION.

B orne by shining pillars, the palace of Apollo the sun-god rose glittering and brilliant in the heavens. To this beautiful place came Phaëthon, Apollo's son by a mortal woman. Phaëthon saw his divine father seated on a vast golden throne, surrounded by his retinue: the Days, the Months, the Years, the Centuries, the Seasons and, moving gracefully to and fro, the Muses making sweet music. Apollo noticed with surprise the beautiful youth who stood gazing at the glory around him in silent amazement.

'Why have you come here, my son?' Apollo asked.

'On earth, men are making mock of me and slandering my mother Clymene,' replied Phaëthon. 'They say that I only pretend to be of heavenly origin and that, in reality, I am only the son of an ordinary, unknown man. So I have come to beg of you some token which will prove to the world that my father is indeed Apollo the sun-god.'

Apollo rose and embraced his son tenderly. 'I shall never disown you in the face of the world,' he told the young man. 'But if you need more than my word, I swear by the River Styx that your wish shall be granted no matter what it may be.'

'Then make my wildest dream come true!' said Phaëthon. 'For one whole day let me guide the winged chariot of the sun!'

Fear and sorrow shadowed the god's shining face. 'You have beguiled me into speaking rash words,' he said sadly. 'If only I could retract my promise! For you have asked something of me which is beyond your strength. You are young, you are mortal, but what you crave is granted only to the gods, and not to all of them, for only I am permitted to do what you are so eager to try. My chariot must travel a steep path. It is a difficult climb for the horses, even when they are fresh at dawn. The middle of the course lies at the zenith of the sky. I myself am often shaken with dread when, at such a height, I stand upright in my chariot. My head spins when I look down on the earth so far beneath me. And the last stretch of the way descends sharply and requires a sure hand on the reins. Even if I gave you my chariot, how could you control it? Do not insist that I keep my word to you; mend your wish while there is still time. Choose anything else that earth and heaven have to offer. But do not ask this dangerous thing!'

But Phaëthon pleaded and pleaded, and Apollo had, after all, given his sacred oath. So he took his son by the hand and led him to the sun-chariot. The pole, axle and the rims of the wheels were all of gold, the spokes of silver, and the yoke glittered with precious stones. While Phaëthon stood marvelling, dawn wakened in the east. Apollo ordered the Hours to yoke the horses and he salved the face of his son with a magic ointment to enable him to withstand the heat of the flames.

'My son, spare the goad and use the reins, for the horses will run of themselves,' he said. 'Your labour will lie in slowing their flight. Keep away from both the South and North Poles. Do not drive too slow, lest the earth catch fire, nor too high, lest you burn up the sky.'

The young man scarcely heard his father's advice. He leaped into the chariot, and the horses bounded up the course, breaking through the mists of morning. But soon they felt their burden was lighter than usual, and the chariot reeled and floundered through the air and swerved aimlessly while the horses wheeled from the beaten paths of the sky and jostled each other in savage haste. Phaëthon became frightened; he did not know which way to pull the reins, nor where he was, nor could he curb the animals. When he looked down at the earth, his knees shook with terror. He wanted to call the horses but he did not know their names. Chill with despair, he dropped the reins, and instantly the horses leaped sideways into unfamiliar regions of air. They grazed against drifts of cloud, which kindled and began to smoulder. They rushed towards the fixed stars, and the earth grew chill and cold and the rivers turned to ice.

Then the horses plunged downwards towards the earth. The sap was dried out of plants, and the leaves of the forest trees shrivelled and burst into flame. The world was afire, and Phaëthon began to suffer from the intolerable heat. He was tortured with fumes and blasts of ashes cast up by the burning earth. Smoke as black as pitch surged around him. And then his hair caught fire. He fell from the chariot and whirled through space like a shooting star until, far below, the arms of the ocean swallowed him up at last.

His father Apollo, who had feared and then witnessed this sight of destruction, veiled his radiant head and brooded in sorrow. It is said that this day brought no light to the world; only the great conflagration shone far and wide.

The sun-chariot which Phaëthon drove hurtled out of control, for he had ignored his father's advice, and the horses would not obey such a youthful and inexperienced driver.

The Fall of Phaëthon, Gustave Moreau (1826–98)

COMMENTARY: Phaëthon, like many an energetic and unreflective youth, wants to be somebody important in the world. He is hurt by others' mockery; they claim he is the son of nobody, not the child of the radiant sun-god. How often do we hear young people boasting about who their parents are, hoping to borrow some of their elders' success and position before they have earned it themselves? And equally often we may hear the children of those who have achieved little in terms of material success, ashamed of their humble origins, boasting of an imaginary lineage in order to claim the admiration of those around them. Phaëthon is neither malicious nor a fool; but he is not mature enough to take his time and work towards the day when success and recognition can be the fruits of his own efforts and abilities. He is seeking his place in the world, searching for a true vocation or calling; but he is impatient to reap the rewards before he understands his abilities and limits.

Apollo, who in this story is a loving and concerned father, wants to do all he can to help the young man find his feet. So he rashly promises anything the youth might desire, perhaps partly to compensate for neglect. This is the mythic equivalent of letting one's son borrow the Porsche before he has got his driving licence, or allowing him to become a partner in the family business before he has demonstrated any knowledge or skill. Many fathers feel deeply guilty because they spend so much time away from their families and, when faced with their children's hurt, they try to make things right again by offering material rewards beyond the child's capabilities. When Phaëthon asks for the sun-chariot, Apollo, the god of foresight and prophecy, can see well enough the tragic outcome. He warns Phaëthon that he is not strong enough for the task, nor is the task one to which any mortal is entitled. Yet he cannot renege on his sacred oath. He must pay dearly for his mistake, made partly from love and partly from an effort to assuage guilt.

Phaëthon, like so many figures in Greek myth, is afflicted with hubris. He wants to be godlike and will not accept his mortal limits. So too may we aspire in the world, wanting to be great and famous, wanting to be wealthy and powerful, oblivious of our human limits and stubbornly refusing to reflect coolly and realistically on just what we are good at and what we may be unfit to do. The challenge of finding a vocation tests us on many levels, whether we face this

challenge in youth or in mid-life when we may seek to change paths and move in a more fulfilling direction. One of the greatest of these tests is the fraught issue of recognizing where our talents lie and finding the humility to see when we will simply not make the grade. Some people do not aspire high enough and fail to develop real abilities, sometimes because of insecurity or restrictive circumstances beyond their control. Some aim too low because of laziness. Others, like Phaëthon, want to emulate someone else because they wish to shine and be seen as special; yet they may not possess the particular combination of qualities necessary to achieve the goal. And if they fail to understand this, they may subject themselves to a great deal of sorrow and humiliation.

We are seduced by the apparently glamorous lives of the famous, and terrified by the prospect of living pointless banal lives without offering anything which will be remembered by future generations. Much of the impulse to carve a special place in the world springs from a deep, albeit unconscious, awareness that life is short and we must take what opportunities come our way, for they may not come again. Phaëthon's impossible dream is perfectly understandable, given the increasing sense of meaninglessness and boredom which besets so many in the modern world. Yet even with the threat of insignificance facing us all, we need to find the courage and humility to recognize that overweening ambition, without training, skill or a sense of real vocation based on real talents, can be a dangerous path. Whether Phaëthon's ruin is taken as an image of financial disaster generated by grandiose dreams, or as an image of professional humiliation generated by aiming beyond the reach of one's talents, this myth tells us, in no uncertain terms, that the sun-chariot is beyond our reach. In the arena of the world we may aspire, rightly and with hope, to become nothing more or less than our human selves.

Chapter Two

GREED AND AMBITION

Greed, whether for physical pleasure or for wealth, is a fundamental attribute of human nature, and so too is the desire to be first and best. It is naive to believe that these things can be made to go away through ideological principles or moral legislation, but we can contain our greed so that it does not injure others. We can harness ambition with ethics so that we make the best of our gifts while benefiting the world around us. Unfortunately, this is not as easy as it sounds, and myth is full of examples of those driven by blind greed and eaten away by uncontrolled ambition, to the point where they not only injure others but destroy themselves. The myths which follow deal with many different facets of greed and ambition, teaching us about both the constructive and destructive expressions of these primal and powerful human needs.

ARACHNE

Talent needs humility

TALENT IS SOMETHING BOTH ENVIABLE AND, IN ITS WAY, RISKY, AS IT CARRIES WITH IT CERTAIN RESPONSIBILITIES AND CHALLENGES. WE NEED TO HONOR OUR GIFTS BY EXPRESSING THEM IN THE FULLEST POSSIBLE WAY. YET WE ALSO NEED TO REMAIN ORDINARY HUMANS, WHICH INVOLVES A CERTAIN HUMILITY. THE GREEK TALE OF ARACHNE AND HER OVERWEENING PRIDE ILLUSTRATES VIVIDLY THAT TALENT WITHOUT HUMILITY MAY NOT ALWAYS BRING SUCCESS. IN FACT, IT MAY INCUR ENMITY AND EVEN RETALIATION FROM OTHERS.

Arachne was fortunate enough to have been blessed with a rare skill in weaving. So clever was she that not only ordinary country folk flocked to see her work, but nymphs from woodland and river came to watch in amazement at how deftly she wove and what wonderful creations came from her needle. Indeed, so high rose her acclaim that it reached the ears of Athene, the goddess of such arts, to whom, many said, Arachne owed her talent. Athene taught human beings to weave, and all who possess such skill owe their gift to this goddess.

But the merest hint of this hurt Arachne's pride and she tossed her head in contempt. 'Athene, indeed! I owe my skill to no one but myself, and there is no one on earth or in heaven with whom I dare not compete. If Athene wishes, let her try her hand against mine.'

Her friends trembled to hear her talk this way and, out of the crowd who had gathered as usual to watch Arachne, came an old woman. 'Be careful what you say, my dear. Age and experience always bring wisdom. Listen to what I say, and own the power of the goddess, for she has graces to give to mortals who honor her. No human work is so good that it cannot be bettered.'

'Foolish old woman, when I want your advice I'll ask for it!' retorted Arachne angrily. 'If Athene wants a contest, let her come.'

'Here I am!' rang out an imperious voice. And there, where the old crone had been, stood the great Athene herself in all her splendid glory. 'Let the contest begin!'

At first Arachne was flustered, but she quickly regained her composure and boldly accepted the challenge. Two looms were set up, and the rivals began to work.

Athene chose for her design the gods ranged upon the Acropolis at Athens, Zeus in all his majesty, Poseidon with his mighty trident and herself calling forth the olive tree as the best gift to man. About this central scene were pictured foolish mortals brought to confusion, rebellious giants turned into mountains, and as a hint to her presumptuous rival, chattering girls changed into screeching birds. Around this ran a border of olive leaves.

Onlookers held their breath as they watched Athene and the boastful Arachne compete at the loom. Although Arachne's work was outstanding, her mockery of the gods proved to be her undoing.

The Fable of Arachne, Diego Velazquez (1599–1660)

Arachne chose to mock the gods in her handiwork, picking out stories in which the gods had shamed themselves: Zeus wooing mortal women in unworthy ways, Apollo humbly serving as a shepherd on earth, Dionysus playing his drunken pranks, all enclosed in a fine border of ivy and flowers. But these irreverent scenes were so beautifully worked with such cunning art that one could believe the animals and foliage were real enough to touch. Her talent was undeniable and Athene, when she rose to examine her rival's work, could not deny it. She pointed an angry finger at Arachne and said, 'Spin forever, and yet be sure that your work, although delicate and beautiful, will only arouse horror and disgust in mankind

and, no matter how intricate and fascinating your tapestries may be, they will only be swept away!'

Arachne realized to her horror that her human features, her human limbs, her human body, were all shrinking away. In less than a minute, she had turned into the first spider on earth, destined to weave without appreciation forever.

COMMENTARY: *Like so many myths, this story is obvious in its meaning that overstepping the boundaries can bring misfortune, for no one is so clever, intelligent, talented or skilled as to be exempt from disaster. 'Pride comes before a fall' says the proverb, and this story illustrates it richly.*

Arachne, like many talented people, began to believe that her talent would make her so special nothing could touch her. And, indeed, her talent was special, for she did win the contest with Athene. Boasting about it, however, cost her her life, doomed for ever to spin cobwebs as if mocking the skill that had evoked Athene's envy. The gods themselves are envious and to deliberately evoke their envy would prove unwise, as Arachne found to her cost.

We may see scenarios being played out in everyday life, when artists of all sorts, be they painters, musicians, singers or actors, get so big for their boots that they believe no one and nothing could ever be better than them. The scenario of the great performer becoming impossible to work with springs to mind. It is not rare to hear of a talented actor or an exquisite model behaving so badly that directors or photographers will not work with them. They may indeed be skilled or beautiful, but at a certain point their other, less-attractive side may outweigh their talent.

THE RING OF POLYCRATES

Arrogance before the gods

THE GREEKS USED THE WORD HUBRIS TO DESCRIBE THE QUALITIES OF
OVERWEENING PRIDE AND FAILURE TO RECOGNIZE LIMITS. TO THEM, HUBRIS
INEVITABLY INCURRED THE WRATH OF THE GODS – BUT THE PUNISHMENT WAS
ALWAYS ARCHITECTED UNKNOWINGLY BY THE INDIVIDUAL HIM- OR HERSELF. THE
STORY OF POLYCRATES ILLUSTRATES NEATLY HOW HUBRIS, COMBINED WITH
ORDINARY HUMAN GREED, LEADS INEVITABLY TO A FALL.

Polycrates, the Tyrant of Samos, appeared to the world to be the most fortunate of all men. He ruled a rich island which he had taken by force from his two brothers; having killed one brother and banished the other, he soon found himself the sole ruler. Hardly a day went by when he did not receive news of his fleet's victory or of a ship arriving in his harbor laden with riches and slaves. He was so rich and powerful that he wished to become lord of all Ionia.

In the fullness of his triumphs, Polycrates offered himself as an ally to Amasis, the great king of Egypt, who initially welcomed his friendship. But King Amasis began to have second thoughts, and soon sent Polycrates a message.

'A man who is always fortunate has a lot to fear. No one rises to such power as yours without making enemies, and even the gods themselves will be jealous of a man who is too successful; good and ill by turn make the common lot of mortals. I have never heard of any so great as to have no cares and yet who came to a happy end. Take my advice: seek out your richest treasure and offer it as a sacrifice to the gods, so that they will not treat you in any adverse way.'

When Polycrates received this message, he thought about it long and hard, and decided that he would follow King Amasis' advice. He selected an emerald seal ring of very great value, one of the treasures he least wanted to lose, and put out to sea in a richly appointed ship. In front of

his courtiers and guards, he threw the ring into the depths of the sea, trusting it would buy him the favor of the gods.

Even before he reached home, however, Polycrates began to regret the loss of his treasured gem and, for many days, he reproached himself for having thrown it away so rashly. A week later, a poor fisherman brought a very large fish to the palace gates, thinking such a gift would please the lord of Samos. When the servants cut up the fish, they found inside its belly the very same emerald ring which had been flung into the sea, and they handed it joyfully to their master.

Polycrates was delighted and took this as a sign that the gods would grant him good luck forever. He wrote joyfully to King Amasis, explaining that he had followed the king's advice, and the gods had sent back his offering. To his surprise, Amasis sent back the herald renouncing the alliance, because here was one who seemed destined to draw some calamity down on his own head.

Yet the tyrant, in his pride, would take no warning. Instead he pursued his quest for power and wealth and, flushed with success, he thought himself invincible. At length, Polycrates received word from King Oroetes of Persia, who proposed an alliance and offered him a great treasure in exchange for his aid. The greedy Polycrates could not resist the opportunity and sent a servant to visit Oroetes and view the treasures he was offering. The servant was shown eight trunks which were, in fact, filled with stones; but the top layer of each trunk was covered in gold and jewels. The servant brought Polycrates a glowing report of the wondrous treasure, and the tyrant decided to set off immediately.

The oracles and omens, however, were adverse to his making the journey, and Polycrates' daughter dreamed that he was raised in the air, washed by Zeus and anointed by the sun. But Polycrates took the dream to presage some great honor and exaltation, and sailed directly to Persia, ignoring all the warnings. Once King Oroetes had him in his hands, he ordered him to be crucified at once. So the man who thought he had nothing to fear from heaven or earth was washed by the sky and anointed by the sun.

COMMENTARY: The fate of Polycrates is self-architected and may be witnessed innumerable times in modern life. How often do businessmen and political leaders overstep the mark and incur disaster because they have failed to recognize when to stop? This problem may afflict any person who has achieved a goal and is now restless to achieve a greater one; for nothing breeds arrogance like success, unless we recognize that certain laws operate within life which will ultimately always remind us of our mortality and limits.

The greatest flaw in Polycrates' nature is neither his greed nor his ambition, which are human and common enough; it is that he does not honor the gods. Honoring the gods does not necessarily mean that we must be of an orthodox religious bent to curtail the natural human inclination to push beyond our limits. But we need to have respect for life and other human beings, and to face with honesty that drive to have power over others which can creep up unconsciously on even the most well-meaning individual. When Amasis advises Polycrates to offer the gods his greatest treasure, the Egyptian king is expressing a profound truth about the human psyche. If we identify our worth with our worldly achievements, we have given away our sense of inner identity and value; but if we can sacrifice this identification, then we are free in our souls and, if fortunate circumstances change to hardship, we still know who we are. During the great stock market crash of 1929, many people hurled themselves from tall buildings to their deaths, because they could see no meaning and value in life or in themselves if their wealth was gone. This reflects a complete identification with the outer trappings of good fortune, and a total lack of any deep inner sense of self-worth.

Polycrates makes his offering out of fear of the gods' wrath, rather than from respect for their power. His choice is a precious ring. But the ring – a symbol we have met already in the story of Siegfried (see pages 91–96) – must be given freely and with a glad heart; otherwise the offering is meaningless. Polycrates regrets throwing his ring away the moment he has done it. A sacrifice must be given with genuinely open hands if it is to be a real sacrifice. It is thus not

Not long after Polycrates had thrown his precious ring into the sea, a poor fisherman caught an enormous fish. Thinking it would please his lordship, the fisherman brought his catch to be served to the court.

The Ring of Polycrates, Giovanni Fedini (fl.1565–99)

surprising that the gods reject the offering and send it back in the body of a fish. And if we understand the gods psychologically, they reflect the deeper unconscious instincts and patterns underpinning individual development. In refusing to honor this deeper Self within, we may indeed unconsciously architect our own downfall.

The arrogance Polycrates displays is nothing short of a blind belief in his own godlike powers. Such a psychological inflation, even on the small scale of everyday life, can destroy our sensitivity to others' signals and erode our ability to judge situations correctly. If we believe we can do anything and have the right to trample over anybody, we will inevitably fail to notice that others are getting angry and are lining up to ensure that we will not achieve what we want. We will make enemies and invoke opposition in the world around us. If we alienate others sufficiently, they will begin to plot our downfall, or refrain from helping us when we are about to step over the edge. And then, if we have still not learned life's lesson about hubris, we may complain to all and sundry about how badly we have been treated; but it is not likely that we will find any sympathy. Power, as they say, corrupts, and absolute power corrupts absolutely. We may start out humble and wishing to do good; yet, once we are intoxicated by the taste of power, we may stop listening to others, and then we begin to make serious mistakes. The story of Polycrates stands as a clear and unambiguous message to all who seek achievement in the world but have not yet learned the self-honesty and humility necessary to ensure that what has been gained will not be lost.

KING MIDAS

Riches alone cannot give happiness

THE WELL-KNOWN GREEK TALE OF KING MIDAS STANDS AS THE DEFINITIVE
MYTHIC STATEMENT THAT TOO MUCH OF A GOOD THING CAN BE AS BAD AS TOO
LITTLE. THE LEGENDARY GREED OF THE PROTAGONIST IS, HOWEVER, EXPIATED AT
THE END – UNLIKE MANY MODERN EXAMPLES – FOR MIDAS, WITH A LITTLE HELP
FROM THE GODS, MANAGES TO LEARN HIS LESSON WELL.

Midas was a pleasure-loving king of Macedonia. In his infancy, a procession of ants was observed carrying grains of wheat up the side of his cradle and placing them between the child's lips as he slept – a prodigy which the soothsayers read as an omen of the great wealth that would accrue to him.

And so it happened. Midas was richer than most people; yet, like so many who have much, his heart was set on having even more. It happened one day that Midas had the opportunity to do service to a god. He found the old satyr Silenus, tutor to the god Dionysus, drunk and disorderly in his rose garden. Instead of reprimanding the satyr, Midas looked after him kindly for five days and nights, richly entertained by Silenus' drunken tales. Afterwards he returned him safely to Dionysus. The god was delighted with Midas for proving such a considerate and jovial companion to the old drunkard, and instantly offered him any reward he would like.

Midas did not hesitate. 'Pray grant that all I touch be turned into gold!'

'So be it!' replied the god, laughing in a manner Midas did not quite like. The king rushed away, impatient to try out his gift.

On his way back to his palace Midas tore a twig off a tree, and lo it turned to shining yellow gold. Gleefully he picked up pebbles, and they too turned into glittering nuggets. He fairly danced into the palace, touching pillars and posts, all of which turned to gold in a flash. He touched all the furniture and was satisfied to see the gleaming results.

Finally, the excitement and exertions of the day took their toll, and he felt hungry and tired. He called for food, and his servants brought him a basin in which to rinse his hands before eating; but the water froze to golden ice. Midas felt a twinge of worry. He remembered Dionysus' laughter, and shuddered. His delight soon turned to despair as he sat down to eat and each delicious mouthful turned to tasteless glittering metal.

Tormented by hunger and thirst, he rose from the mockery of a banquet and, for once, envied the poorest kitchen boy, who was tucking into a satisfying meal. The king was no longer comforted by the sight of his growing treasure; the very sight of gold began to sicken him. He wept bitterly when his youngest daughter rushed up to take his hand and

promptly turned into a golden statue. Darkness fell, and Midas collapsed on his soft couch that at once grew hard and cold. There he tossed restless and shivering, for every blanket he touched turned into a chilly sheet of gold. He was, at once, the richest and the most wretched man alive.

At the first light of dawn, Midas hastened to find Dionysus and earnestly begged him to take back his gift of splendid misery.

Dionysus was highly entertained. 'So often men's dearest wishes prove unwise!' smiled the god. Yet Dionysus remembered Midas' kindness to Silenus and bade him bathe in the pure waters of the River Pactolus. Driven by the gnawings of hunger and thirst, Midas ran to the river, leaving a trail of gold as he ran. He threw himself into the healing waters. As soon as his head plunged beneath the surface, the fatal gift was washed away and, to his great joy, Midas was able to eat and drink again. But the sands of the Pactolus are bright with gold to this day.

COMMENTARY: *This delightful tale gives us a clear enough message: riches are useless if the most basic needs in life cannot be satisfied. The ordinary, everyday pleasures ultimately make life sweet for rich and poor alike. If these are lacking – or if the capacity to enjoy them has been lost – then no amount of wealth can supply them. On a deeper level, Midas' deadly touch is not merely about greed and the wish to accrue more and yet more wealth. It is also a reflection of something within the man which freezes everything living and warm, and renders simple relating impossible. In this way, many people, driven by the need to accrue wealth, eventually freeze their capacity for simple human enjoyment and interchange; and the food and drink for which they hunger are not physical, but a subtler kind of nourishment without which life is not worth living.*

When Midas touches his daughter, she too turns to gold. People cannot be bought, especially those to whom we turn for the most fundamental ties of affection; and this is an image of 'killing off' a relationship through an

Midas smiled as he sat down at his table and saw all his plates and goblets turned to gold. But as soon as the wine touched his lips, it too turned to gold, and he could not drink a single drop.

King Midas, Nicolas Tournier (1590–1638/9)

overvaluing of money. We may glimpse the glittering traces of King Midas in those individuals who are so preoccupied with making money that they alienate their families and friends, and then wonder why they have become so lonely. This simple tale illustrates graphically how foolish human beings are to think that wealth can buy happiness. Sufficient resources can indeed keep many of life's vicissitudes from us, and those who have suffered from a lack of sufficient funds know too well how the quest for money can dominate life when it is lacking. But 'sufficient' is not a word in Midas' vocabulary. He is not content with being a wealthy king; he wants even more. Thus his greed poisons everything that once gave him pleasure.

Dionysus is an ambiguous god, happy to grant Midas a favor yet, at the same time, amused at the tragic consequences of the king's greed. This deity is lord of chaos and ecstasy, and patron of all those who seek to move beyond their earthly boundaries through drink, drugs, dance and artistic vision. In short, Dionysus is a primal life-force, unconcerned with ordinary morality, but symbolizing the flow of nature itself. He does not advise Midas; he merely lets the king get into a mess and learn from his mistakes. And, in the end, it is Dionysus who releases him through advocating a bath in the pure waters of the Pactolus. When Midas' head is submerged, the curse disguised as a blessing is washed away. In other words, Midas must lose himself in the waters and give up all thoughts of control; only then can he be free to return to his ordinary life. The only antidote to the kind of corrosive greed which afflicts Midas is a letting go of pride and desire on the most profound level. This message, expressed here in mythic form, lies at the core of all the world's great religious teachings.

How many times do we hear people talking of how happy they will be when they win the lottery? They want to believe that wealth will solve all their problems; yet we hear equally often that the winners are more miserable than ever, because they have lost all their friends and can no longer trust others' love and loyalty. Riches do not automatically bring misery. But nor do they automatically bring happiness, unless the individual is capable of retaining a capacity for ordinary contentment in everyday life. Ultimately, the story of King Midas is not about the supposed evils of wealth, but about the power of greed to chill and taint everything that we experience as beautiful and worthwhile.

THE CORRUPTION OF ANDVARI

Power is no substitute for love

THE NORSE MYTH OF THE DWARF ANDVARI'S GOLD FORMS THE BASIS FOR THE
FIRST OPERA IN RICHARD WAGNER'S GREAT CYCLE, 'THE RING OF THE NIEBELUNG',
ALTHOUGH IN HIS VERSION THE DWARF IS CALLED ALBERICH. BUT WHETHER WE
LOOK TO THE ORIGINAL TALE OR LISTEN TO WAGNER'S OPERA, HERE IS A STORY OF
BITTERNESS AND GREED. IT HAS MUCH TO TEACH US ABOUT THE DEEPER ROOTS
OF DESTRUCTIVE AMBITION AND THE CORRUPTION THAT WARPS THE SOUL WHEN
THWARTED LOVE IS TRANSFORMED INTO A DRIVE FOR POWER.

T he dwarf Andvari possessed a great hoard of gold, as well as the power to make yet more; but he did not come by this wealth without bitter cost – nor, in the end, could he keep it. One day, when swimming in the river to catch a fish for his dinner, Andvari spied something shining and glittering on the river bed; it was the gold of the river nymphs, who loved the precious metal for its brightness and joy. Even more enticing to the dwarf were the nymphs themselves, who swam gracefully around him and teased him with flirtatious smiles and compliments. But each time he sought to seize one, she wriggled nimbly out of the way, and Andvari was left breathless and frustrated. Still they teased and tempted him; and all the while, flaunting themselves before him, they also insulted him, mocking his twisted limbs and dark, ugly face. Andvari became angry, and a black hatred filled his mind and heart; and his eyes fixed once again on the glittering gold at the bottom of the river.

Quickly, the dwarf dived down, seized the gold and began to swim to the surface of the water. The nymphs cried out for the return of their toy, but Andvari ignored them. They called and cajoled, and promised him sensuous delights if he would return their treasure to them. But their rejection and scorn had made Andvari bitter. He knew that he was ugly and that no female would ever desire him. If he wished for love, he would have to buy it.

The river nymphs tempted Andvari with their graceful beauty, but teased him by slipping through his eager fingers, leaving him feeling frustrated and foolish.

The Water Nymph, *Guillaume Seignac (fl.c.1900)*

Andvari turned on the nymphs and shouted mightily so all the gods could hear, 'I want none of you and your delights! I abjure love! Before all the gods, I swear that gold alone will I love, and the power which the gold can bring me!' And with these words, which were binding because they were heard in all the realms of heaven and earth, Andvari stole the gold and took it away to his realm. There, with many spells and incantations, he forged it into a magic ring which gave him power over all the other dwarfs and also the power to create endless piles of gold nuggets.

Andvari would have lived thus forever, gnawed by bitterness, turning his fellow dwarfs into slaves and filling the caverns of his dark realm with growing piles of gold. But events were occurring in the realm of the sky-gods which were destined to intrude upon the dwarf's preoccupations. Odin, king of heaven and ruler of all the upper realms, had got himself into trouble and had to buy his way out; and to do so he needed a great deal of gold. He turned to his clever and devious advisor, Loki the fire-god, who promptly advised him that the necessary quantity of gold was available in the realm of the dwarfs. All the gods knew what Andvari had done, although none, up to that point, had seen fit to interfere with what went on in the realms below the earth.

With Odin's permission, Loki hatched a plan; for he knew that Andvari was wily and that the gold would not be easy to obtain. First he travelled beneath the sea to visit the palace of the sea-goddess Ran. 'The gods are in danger!' he told Ran breathlessly. 'Odin himself lies bound, and only your net can save them!'

The sea-goddess opened her cold, pale eyes very wide. She was not well versed in what went on in heaven, so she did not know whether Loki told the truth. But the fire-god was persuasion itself. 'Lend me your drowning net which you use to snare men. I can use it to save gods.'

Thus Ran parted with her net, and Loki left the hall beneath the waves quickly in case she changed her mind. Then he headed for the realm of the dwarfs. He picked his way down a chain of dripping tunnels and through a maze of twilit chambers until he came to a massive cavern beneath the earth. Its roof was supported by columns of rock thicker than tree trunks, and its corners were still and dark. Loki saw a large, silent pool filled with water that seemed to spring from nowhere and flow nowhere. He knew that Andvari was as at home in the element of water as he was in the tunnels beneath the earth, and he also knew that the dwarf would sense his coming and hide. Loki spread Ran's finely meshed net and cast it into the pool. He dragged it and pulled it up, and there, furiously lashing and writhing, was the dwarf. Loki disentangled him, keeping a firm hold all the while on the back of his neck.

'What do you want?' whined Andvari. Although he had a very shrewd idea of why the fire-god had come.

'What I want is your gold,' said Loki. 'Otherwise I will wring you out like a piece of washing. All your gold.'

Andvari shuddered. He led Loki out of the echoing chamber and down a twisting passage into his smithy. It was hot and smoky, but piles and piles of gold nuggets gleamed in the firelight.

'Gather it up,' said Loki, kicking one of the nuggets.

Andvari scrambled about, cursing and moaning. He made a pile of nuggets and small bars of gold, of objects already made and objects half-made. Loki looked at the stack and was well satisfied. 'Is that all?' the fire-god asked.

Andvari said nothing. He stowed the gold into two old sacks and stood them in front of Loki.

'What about that ring?' said Loki, pointing at the dwarf's closed right hand. 'I saw you hide it.'

Andvari shook his head.

'Put it in the sack,' said Loki.

'Let me keep it,' begged Andvari. 'Just this ring. Let me keep it. Then I'll be able to make more gold again.'

But Loki, understanding immediately that the ring was magical, stepped forward and forced open Andvari's fist and seized the little, twisted ring. One never knew when the heaven gods might need more gold. The ring was marvellously wrought, and Loki slipped it onto his own little finger. 'What is not freely given must be taken by force,' he said.

'Nothing was freely given,' said Andvari. But Loki ignored this and, shouldering the sacks, turned towards the door of the smithy.

'You will regret taking my ring!' yelled the dwarf. 'My curse is on that ring and on that gold! It will destroy whoever owns it! No one will win joy with my wealth!'

But Loki merely turned around again and, with Andvari's oaths and curses echoing in his ears, made his way out of the world of the dwarfs and back to the heavens, where Odin sat impatiently waiting.

COMMENTARY: The dwarf Andvari is, sadly, like many humans who, embittered by an early experience of rejection or disappointment in personal life, become dwarfed in soul and give themselves over entirely to power. When he cannot have love, Andvari opts for wealth and lordship over his fellows instead; yet his wealth gives him no joy and, inevitably, it is wrenched from him by others who equally have no ethics about how they obtain their power. This myth is a dark evocation of life in the material jungle and it may be witnessed in the modern worlds of business, finance and politics virtually any day in the week. It may also be witnessed in the small but equally dark manoeuvrings within families, especially when there is an inheritance open to question or a division of property following a divorce. In short, Andvari is a symbol of that within us which responds to personal disappointment with rage and bitterness, and with a consequent loss of real feeling for our fellow human beings.

In the myth of Siegfried (see pages 91–6) we explored the symbolism of the gold of the river nymphs. This 'natural' gold, lying innocent and unformed on the river bed, is an image of those natural resources which lie sleeping within each individual and also within the collective human psyche. The gold is also an image of the natural resources of our planet. Such resources may be left untapped or may be used for good or ill if they are 'brought up' into consciousness and forged into implements of civilization or destruction. Andvari, because he feels ugly and misshapen, abjures love forever and swears he will love only gold. As a mythic image, his ugliness is a quality within, which responds to the scornful teasing of the nymphs with hatred and rage. Even if we possess such primitive dark qualities – which, after all, are really the dark side of being human – we do not need to act on them or to renounce our highest values because we cannot make life give us just what we want when we want it. Andvari's soul is dwarfed because he does not have the generosity, tolerance or inner confidence to ignore the nymphs' teasing. He takes it bitterly because he is already bitter. Andvari teaches us that we cannot justify all human destructiveness by pointing to a hurtful or difficult early environment. There is something deeper, some quality within the individual human character, which chooses to react to such early hurts with either hatred or understanding. We all face such choices, possibly many times in life, and we may shape our future through them.

Because Andvari comes by his gold dishonestly, he draws no sympathy from the gods; and when the time comes for Odin to find a ready source of gold, he has no qualms about robbing Andvari, because the dwarf himself is a thief. Thus, like attracts like, and the dwarf unwittingly determines his own future by his decision to side with the darkness within. We do not need to look to some religious formula of divine rewards and punishments to understand the inner logic of this; our actions in the world generate consequences and, ultimately, we are likely to be treated as we ourselves treat others. Because Andvari has no love left in him, he is not treated with love; and as he enslaves his fellow dwarfs, so too does the fire-god Loki enslave him and wrench his gold from him.

Living in the world may involve learning some hard lessons, and this myth describes one of the most important. An intense craving for wealth and power is often the twisted by-product of emotional pain and bitterness, and it can make us justify behavior that disconnects us from any real relationship with our fellow humans. It is, in the deepest sense, a kind of 'pact with the devil', although the devil, as presented in this tale, is within the individual. Global examples of this are everywhere: companies manufacturing deadly armaments to sell to known dictators, or exploiting poor populations of other countries in order to create wealth at home.

We may also observe ourselves in this story, in the way we treat those who work for us, in our attitudes towards money in everyday transactions, and in the manner in which we momentarily forget our ideals because someone has made us an offer we cannot refuse. Such convenient lapses often arise from a deep but unconscious core of bitterness and anger at other human beings because we do not have the happiness we think we deserve. Yet such behavior may, ultimately, engender its own dark reward, sooner or later. Even if Loki had not come to steal the gold, we might fruitfully contemplate what kind of life Andvari would have gone on living in his dark cavern beneath the earth, friendless and lonely, with only his gold to comfort him. The story of Andvari teaches us that it is not money which is the root of all evil; it is the manner in which we use it to vindicate, justify or compensate for our inability to forgive.

Chapter Three

RESPONSIBILITY

Worldly achievement involves not only risks and rewards, but also responsibility, of an inner as well as an outer kind. When we seek positions of power, we are entering a realm which is deeper and more complex than simply winning a prize or enjoying something we have wanted for a long time. Power invariably concerns how we treat others and, at the most profound level, constellates the ideals we espouse and the commitment we make to life. Power, in short, is a form of service. Mythic tales are full of descriptions of the vicissitudes of power and, usually, include the involvement of a god. This tells us that power is also connected with something higher and that, if we wish to handle power with decency, we need to retain humility, wisdom and a sense of honor towards those whom we both rule and serve.

KING MINOS AND THE BULL

Handling power with integrity

THIS FAMOUS GREEK MYTH ILLUSTRATES VIVIDLY WHAT CAN HAPPEN WHEN PROMISES TO THE GODS ARE NOT HONORED AND POWER IS HANDLED IRRESPONSIBLY. WE ARE TOLD THAT POWER CORRUPTS, BUT WHAT IS THE NATURE OF THAT CORRUPTION? HERE WE SEE ITS DEEPER SIDE, WHEN CORRUPTION AFFLICTS THOSE IN POWER. THE CHOICES MINOS MAKES, AND THE CONSEQUENCES HE INVOKES, REVEAL THE PROFOUND IMPORTANCE OF MAINTAINING LOYALTY TOWARDS THE HIGHER CAUSE ONE SERVES.

Zeus, king of heaven, saw the beautiful Princess Europa and desired her. But the girl was not easily seduced, so Zeus disguised himself as a pure white bull and carried her across the sea to the island of Crete. There he ravished her; but so great was her attraction that he returned again and again to visit her, which was not usual for this fickle god. In time, Europa bore him three sons – Minos, Rhadamanthys and Sarpedon – all of whom were adopted by the Cretan King Asterios, who fell in love with Europa and married her.

When the boys grew up, there was an inevitable dispute over the succession to the throne after their adoptive father Asterios died. Minos, the eldest, settled the issue by praying to Poseidon, god of the sea, for a

divine sign. Poseidon promised that he would send a bull from the sea as a sign to all the world that Minos' claim to the throne was favored by the divine powers. Minos, in turn, agreed to sacrifice this bull directly back to the god, to affirm his loyalty to Poseidon and his recognition that his right to rule derived from the lord of the ocean depths. Thus Minos was to demonstrate to all and sundry that his power was not his alone, and that he must use it responsibly.

Poseidon was greatly angered when Minos cheated him of his promised sacrifice, and in punishment the god inflicted on Minos' wife Pasiphaë an irresistible desire to mate with the white bull.

The Passions of Pasiphaë, *Master of the Campana Cassoni (fl.c.1510)*

face the humiliation of defeat. We may not always read about the consequences of such actions in the daily newspapers. The outcome may be secret and lie at the heart of one's personal life. But there is an old saying that the mills of God grind slowly but grind exceedingly small.

The story of Minos teaches us that handling power with integrity is not simply something we do publicly to impress others. It is an inner commitment to whatever we choose to call God, whether we use religious terminology or the more objective language of humanitarian concerns. If the commitment is sincere, and we keep loyal to the dictates of our hearts, then we renew our inner power and authenticity. If we are hypocrites who promise many things solely to win votes, we may fool some; but we cannot fool our own souls, and we will be left discomfited, unhappy and plagued by our consciences.

The Minotaur, with its bull's head on a human body, is a tragic mythic image of humanity driven blindly by its instincts, having lost the capacity for reflection, ethics and respect for other living things.

DETAIL The Minotaur, G. F. Watts (1895)

KING ARTHUR'S PEACETIME ARMY

After the goal is reached, what then?

THIS LITTLE TALE FROM THE ARTHURIAN LEGENDS – ALTHOUGH IT CONTAINS
MAINLY A DIALOGUE BETWEEN KING ARTHUR AND HIS QUEEN, AND OFFERS US
LITTLE ACTION – PROVIDES A PROFOUND COMMENTARY ON HUMAN NATURE. IN
PARTICULAR, IT REVEALS VERY SUCCINCTLY WHAT SO OFTEN HAPPENS WHEN
WE HAVE FINALLY GOT WHERE WE WANT TO BE, AND DISCOVER THAT IT IS
STRUGGLE, NOT SATIATION, WHICH HONES AND SHARPENS OUR CHARACTERS
AND OUR HEARTS.

After many long and turbulent years, King Arthur had achieved peace. Through nobility, good fortune and force of arms, he had destroyed or made peace with all his enemies – both inside his realm and beyond – and had established, throughout Britain, his right to rule. To achieve this goal, Arthur had gathered around him the best knights and the toughest fighters in the world. All had lived up to their high reputations and fought bravely and brilliantly for their king.

Having successfully made peace through war, King Arthur now faced the dilemma of what to do with his soldiers in times of peace. He could not entirely disband his army in a world where violence may have abated for a time, but still slept uneasily, ready to be awakened. But, on the other hand, he found it difficult, if not impossible, to keep the strength and temper of his men at a peak without fighting; for nothing rusts so quickly as an unused sword or an idle soldier.

Arthur was having to learn, as all leaders must, that peace, not war, is the destroyer of men; security rather than danger is the mother of cowardice; and plenty, rather than need, brings fear and unease. And he learned, with sorrow, that the peace all Britain had long wished for – peace, so painfully fought for – created more bitterness than ever did the bloody struggle of achieving it. King Arthur watched with growing apprehension and unhappiness as his brave young knights, who would

otherwise have filled the fighting ranks to battle with a worthy enemy, now became bored, idle and aggressive, dissipating their strength in a mire of complaints and petty quarrels.

Even Lancelot, his greatest knight, grew despondent, for he could find no opposing sword to keep his own sword sharp. He was like a tiger without prey, and even this noble and courageous fighter grew restless and irritable, and then angry. He suffered pains in his body and exhibited flaws in his disposition which were not there before.

Queen Guinevere, who loved Lancelot and understood men, was saddened to see him destroying himself little by little. She talked to Arthur about it and heard of his concern about the young knights.

'I wish I could understand it,' Arthur said. 'They eat well, sleep in comfort, make love when and to whom they wish. They feed appetites already half satiated and no longer have to suffer all the pain and hunger, weariness and discipline of the past. Yet still they are not content. They complain that the times are against them.'

'And so the times are,' replied the queen.

'What do you mean?' asked Arthur.

'They are idle, my lord. They have achieved a long-cherished dream and now have nothing further to give their hearts to. There is an emptiness that always follows a dream fulfilled. The times make no demand on them now. The fiercest hound, the fastest horse, the best of women, the bravest knight – none can resist the corrosive acid of idleness. Even Sir Lancelot grumbles like a spoiled child in sedentary discontent.'

'What can I do?' cried the king. 'I fear that the noblest fellowship in the world is crumbling. In the dark days, I prayed and worked and fought for peace. Now I have it, and we are not at peace within. Sometimes I find myself wishing for war to solve my difficulties.'

'You are not the first ruler to think thus, nor will you be the last,' said Queen Guinevere. 'We have general peace, it is true; but, as a healthy man has small pains to plague him just a little, so is peace a tapestry of small wars. There are tiny wars occurring all around us. A man batters his neighbour's head in over a lost cow, and a woman poisons her neighbour

because she has a fairer face. Then a family feud begins and continues for generations. These tiny wars are everywhere, always too small for an army, yet always too big for any one person to set right. What the knights need is a quest.'

'But the young knights laugh at old-fashioned questing, and the old knights have seen real war.'

'It is one thing to strive for greatness, but quite another to try to be not small. I think that all people want to be larger than themselves, but they can only be this if they are part of something immeasurably larger than themselves. The best knight in the world, if unchallenged, finds himself shrinking. We must seek a way to declare a great war on little things. We must discover those banners under which small evils enlist to feed a great invisible wrong – the small evils which break out in every community. Against this we could raise a fighting army, although the battles might be small and subtle and scarcely noticeable. We could call it the King's Justice; and every knight would be the personal agent and keeper of this Justice. Each man would be responsible for it. Then every knight would be an instrument of something larger than himself.'

'I wonder how I could declare this war,' mused King Arthur.

'Start with the best knight in the world: Sir Lancelot. And let him take the worst knight as his companion. His nephew Sir Lyonel is a likely candidate, as he is the laziest and the most worthless. Then the worst will have to aspire to the best.'

'The worst and the best,' smiled Arthur. 'It is a powerful combination. Such an alliance would be unbeatable.'

'It is only through such alliances that wars can be fought at all, my lord,' replied the queen.

And so it was done. The knights now had a new goal towards which to aspire and a new vision to inspire them. But this new war was one which

The Knights of the Round Table swore an oath to keep the laws, to use violence only with good purpose, to be merciful, to protect the weak, and never to fight an unjust cause or injure others for personal gain.

The Knights of the Round Table from 'History of the Holy Grail' (15th century)

was never-ending, because there was no single enemy with whom to do battle, only the petty meannesses of the undeveloped human heart.

COMMENTARY: *The aftermath of great achievement is often a profound depression; and we are at greatest risk of inner corruption when we are idle, rather than when we are struggling. This is the deep but unwelcome truth which Arthur discovers and which Guinevere, already cauterized by her forbidden love for Lancelot, has the insight to foresee. When we have longed to reach a goal for many years and finally get there after many battles and hardships, we expect to feel content, fulfilled and at peace. Yet, all too often, the opposite happens, and we cannot understand why, having climbed to the top of the mountain, the vista seems only grey, bleak and without hope. Whether it is a position of worldly responsibility or the acquisition of material objects, so many of us are driven – or so we believe – by the need to have something, to win something, to gain something. Yet this tale reveals a secret about the human heart: it is not the prize, but the struggle, which makes us feel most alive and to which we offer our greatest love and commitment. And, although we are reluctant to admit it, it is struggle which brings out the best in us.*

We may see this pattern in many highly successful people who have battled for many years to gain recognition or wealth and, having achieved it, begin to slide into emotional misery, physical illness and what can best be described as a darkness of the soul. Arthur's fighting knights are, in a sense, symbolic of the motivated side of Arthur himself, full of courage and aspiration, willing to suffer all kinds of hardships to win the great fight. What does one do with this powerful, impetuous, noble spirit when there is nothing to fight for? In worldly terms, an army in peacetime can be a serious problem, for the aggression and martial spirit which make men and women good soldiers turns sour if there is nothing to do battle with. But we do not have to be soldiers to experience this problem. All highly motivated people run the risk of the inner defeat which comes when the prize has been won and there is no longer any meaning to one's life.

Guinevere knows that there is only one possible answer. In order for us to renew our commitment to life and rediscover the sense of a future full of potentials, we must find a new goal; but this new goal must be bigger than our

personal aspirations if it is to prove as effective a motivator as the goal we have just achieved. What is portrayed here is the need for all human beings to first fulfill their individual ambitions and then to recognize that they belong to a larger community and need to make some contribution to that greater whole in order to allow life to flow within once again. Arthur's peace comes when the king has arrived at middle age; and this involvement in the life of the larger world is perhaps a task which is best approached when we too have managed to win at least some of our personal battles and have already discovered our natures, resources and limitations through individual achievement. With power comes responsibility, and with achievement comes the need to turn within and discover what the achievement has really been for, and whom and what it really serves.

THE JUDGEMENT OF SOLOMON

Responsibility requires wisdom

THE BIBLICAL TALE OF THE JUDGEMENT OF KING SOLOMON IS A SHINING EXAMPLE
OF THE IMPORTANCE OF HUMILITY AND WISDOM WHEN WE ARE FORTUNATE
ENOUGH TO RECEIVE THE REINS OF POWER. SOLOMON RULES NOT JUST WITH HIS
MIND, BUT ALSO WITH HIS HEART; AND HIS WISDOM IS A GIFT FROM GOD BECAUSE
HE IS DEVOID OF ARROGANCE AND GREED. IN THIS RESPECT, HE IS A RARE FIGURE
AMONG RULERS, ANCIENT OR MODERN.

hen his father King David died, Solomon became king over all Israel. And the Lord appeared to Solomon in a dream and said, 'Ask what I shall give you.'

And King Solomon said, 'You have showed your servant, my father David, great mercy. Now you have made me king; and I am but a little child; I know not how to go out or come in. Give me, therefore, an understanding heart to judge my people, that I may discern between good and bad.'

And this speech pleased the Lord, who said, 'Because you have asked this thing, and have not asked for yourself long life or riches, or for the lives of your enemies, I have done according to your words. I have given you a wise and understanding heart.'

And Solomon awoke from his dream.

Then there came to him two women who were harlots and stood before him. And the first woman said, 'O Lord, I and this woman dwell in one house; and I was delivered of a child in the house. And it came to pass that on the third day after I was delivered, this woman was delivered also. We were together and there was no stranger with us in the house. And this woman's child died in the night. And she arose at midnight and took my son from beside me, while I slept, and laid her dead child on my bosom. And when I rose in the morning to nurse my child, behold, it was dead; but when I considered it, I knew it was not my son.'

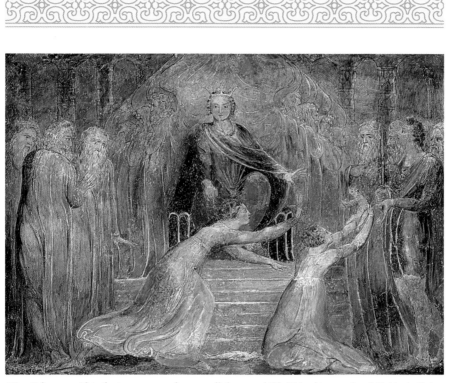

King Solomon said to the two women who quarrelled over a child, 'Take this sword and divide the living child between you.' Thus, in his wisdom, he allowed the identity of the true mother to be revealed.

DETAIL The Judgement of Solomon, William Blake (1757–1827)

And the second woman said, 'No, the living child is my son, and the dead one is your son.'

And the first woman said, 'No, the dead one is your son, and the living one is my son.' And thus they argued before the king.

Then Solomon said, 'One of you says, "This is my son that lives," and the other says, "No, it is my son that lives." Bring me a sword!' And they brought a sword before the king. And Solomon said, 'Divide the living child in two, and give half to one, and half to the other.'

Then spoke the first woman, 'O Lord, give her the living child and in no wise slay it! I would rather it lived and was not mine, than that it was harmed.'

PART V

RITES OF PASSAGE

The great conundrums of life – the mystery of human suffering, the quest
for a sense of deeper or higher reality, the enigma of death – have occupied
philosophical, theological and psychological thought for many centuries.
Myth offers us rich insights into these rites of passage, and can give us
subtle but profound guidance in those spheres of life where we are
confronted with the unanswerable. Human beings may grow and be
enriched through such critical junctures in their lives, but it is not always
easy to find the elusive glimpse of meaning which can allow us to make
something constructive out of frustrating or painful experiences. Instead, we
may become disillusioned and even bitter, because we have failed to
understand the deeper levels and potential inherent in such difficult
crossroads in life. Because life's mysteries are paradoxical, mythic tales
about the encounter with those powers greater than ourselves can give us a
broader and more inclusive vision than the more didactic answers of science
or even conventional religious teaching. There is great strength to be found
in the human soul, but it is often called into being only by the realization
that there is a meaning, if not an answer, embedded in that which we find
most baffling in life.

The image of Charon, the old ferryman who rowed the souls of the dead across the Styx and into the
underworld, portrays our intuitive sense of death as an initiatory rite of passage into another realm.
DETAIL Charon, Joachim Patenier (1487–1524)

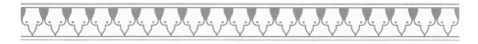

Chapter One

SEPARATION, LOSS AND SUFFERING

Separation and loss are archetypal human experiences, and it is unlikely
that any human being passes through life without some suffering of this
kind. Established religious doctrines have always sought to provide answers
to the mystery of why we suffer, especially when the suffering seems unfair
or unmerited; and such answers, although often unsatisfactory to the
inquiring mind, have provided some comfort over the ages to those who seek
alleviation of their pain. Myth, however, unlike religious dogma, has never
offered answers about why we suffer, or how we may avoid it, or what we
will be given by God in recompense. On the other hand, the transformative
effect of suffering may be glimpsed in many myths, suggesting that some
deeper purpose or function lies embedded in those experiences which cause us
the greatest pain. There is a curiously healing quality about myths which
tell stories of separation and loss, for in them we may discover a mirror of
our own circumstances, and realize that we are not alone. It may be, if we
consider deeply enough the perspective offered by myth, that the only true
healing for human suffering arises from human sharing and human
compassion, rather than specious, easy answers which profess to explain
away one of life's greatest enigmas.

JOB'S TRIALS

The enigma of suffering

THE BIBLICAL STORY OF JOB PRESENTS US WITH A STARK PICTURE OF HOW
UNFAIR LIFE CAN BE, AND HOW OUR CHILDLIKE DREAMS THAT GOODNESS IS
ALWAYS REWARDED AND WICKEDNESS ALWAYS PUNISHED CAN LEAD US INTO
DISILLUSIONMENT AND BITTERNESS. JOB, HOWEVER, NEVER LOSES HIS FAITH
IN GOD, NO MATTER WHAT SUFFERING HE MUST ENDURE. AND, ALTHOUGH THE
MYSTERY REMAINS OF WHY HE MUST UNDERGO THE TRIALS HE DOES, HIS FAITH
IN THE WISDOM OF THE DIVINE – OR, PUT ANOTHER WAY, HIS TRUST IN LIFE –
NEVER FAILS HIM.

There was a man in the land of Uz, whose name was Job; and he was perfect and upright, and feared God, and eschewed evil. He had seven sons and three daughters, and he was a wealthy man with many animals and a very great household; indeed, he was the greatest of all the men of the East.

But Job's prosperity and comfort were doomed to come to an end. One day the angels presented themselves before the throne of God, and Satan was with them. When the Lord asked him whence he had come, Satan said, 'I have been wandering across the face of the earth, observing what takes place there.'

And the Lord said to Satan, 'Have you seen my servant Job during the course of your travels? There is none like him on all the earth – a perfect and an upright man, one who fears God and eschews evil.'

Then Satan said, 'Does Job fear God for nothing? You have protected and blessed him; but put forth your hand now and take away all that he has, and he will curse you to your face.'

The Lord was stung by this reply, and said to Satan, 'Very well, then, test him; all that he has is in your power. But only upon his body do not put forth your hand.' And with great satisfaction, Satan went from the presence of God.

Then misfortune began to strike Job. His oxen and asses and camels were stolen; his servants were slain; and a fire fell from heaven and consumed all his sheep. Then his sons and daughters were all killed when a great wind struck the house in which they were eating and drinking.

Then Job tore his mantle and shaved his head, and threw himself down upon the ground. He said, 'Naked I came from my mother's womb, and naked shall I return thither; the Lord gave, and the Lord has taken away; blessed be the name of the Lord.' And Satan was proven wrong, for during all these disasters, Job never cursed God.

Then Satan came again before the Lord, and the Lord said: 'Am I not proven right about my servant Job? There is none like him on all the earth. He holds fast to his integrity, although you have moved against him and destroyed all he has without cause.'

And Satan answered, 'Yes, indeed, all that a man has will he give for his life. But put forth your hand now and touch his bones and his flesh, and he will curse you to your face.'

The Lord said, 'Very well; his bones and his flesh are in your hands; but save his life.'

And Satan went forth from the presence of the Lord, and cursed Job with sore boils from the soles of his feet to the crown of his head.

Job sat down among the ashes and prayed to the Lord. Then his wife said to him, 'Do you still retain your integrity? Curse God, and die.'

But Job replied, 'You speak foolishly. Shall we receive good at the hand of God, and not suffering as well?' For despite his great pain, Job would not curse God.

Then Job's friends came to mourn with him and comfort him. But they could only offer him false reassurance. They pretended to have the wisdom to understand the workings of God, but they really knew nothing. They suggested that Job had sinned unwittingly and drawn punishment

Although he found himself naked, sick, alone and wretched, bereft of family and worldly goods, Job never once reviled God or lost his faith and trust in the Lord.

Job, Leon Joseph Florentin Bonnat (1833–1922)

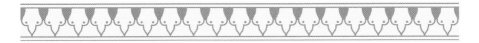

down on his head, or that God was testing him and would eventually reward him. Their words brought Job no comfort, only sorrow.

But the Lord was angry at these men's specious words, and spoke to Job out of the whirlwind, and said, 'Who are these who offer counsel without knowledge? What do they or you know of the power of God? Where were you when I laid the foundations of the earth? Do you know the ordinances of heaven?' And many more questions like these did the Lord ask of Job.

Then Job said, 'What shall I answer? I will lay my hand over my mouth, and I will say no more.'

Then the Lord gave back to Job as much as he had had before Satan had destroyed all he possessed. And in time he had seven more sons and three more daughters, and he lived for a hundred and forty years, and saw his sons and his sons' sons and even unto four generations. So Job died, being old and full of days.

COMMENTARY: *Outside the world of Walt Disney the evil often go unpunished, and the good are unfairly struck down. Young, talented, fine people die of horrible diseases, yet ruthless dictators, responsible for thousands of murders, live to ripe old ages and die comfortably in their beds. This stark dimension of life has provided the fuel for millennia of religious controversy; and although the precise definition of goodness continues to elude even the most self-righteous of religious teachers, we humans persist in hoping that, if we could only discover the formula, we would escape life's vicissitudes.*

The story of Job teaches us that the roots of human suffering and inequality do not lie in something as simple as having sinned and therefore merited punishment. Job has not sinned, yet he suffers. The strange and disturbing dialogue between God and Satan reveals a cosmos devoid of the kind of morality with which we try to gird ourselves in the hope of heavenly reward. There is neither logic, reason nor compassion in God's willingness to hand Job's fate over to Satan, save that Satan has stung him with the suggestion that Job will lose his faith if God is not so kind to him. Yet despite the less than attractive dimension of deity presented in this story, Job does not question the nature or majesty of God.

God is God, and no solution for the enigma of suffering can be found in trying to discover where one's secret sin lies. This is tantamount to saying that there is no reason for suffering; it simply is, because it is a part of life. This is a hard pill to swallow for those brought up on the idea of a Santa Claus-like God; and it requires a humility before life's mysteries which may only be found through pain, loss, deep questioning and an acceptance of reality as it is.

Job's friends mean well, as do most of us; yet they can offer only shallow interpretations which do not deeply touch the suffering individual. At such moments the well-intentioned words of friends and counsellors may give us little, if they are spoken in an attempt by these helpful souls to diffuse their own fear of pain by trying to silence our pain. Mourning has its own laws and timing, and the only real comfort may lie in silence and the capacity to simply be with those who are suffering. We insult others in our efforts to come up with simple solutions or promises of future reward in return for present suffering; and this story tells us that we also insult the divine when we try to provide human answers for cosmic mysteries.

At the end of the story, Job's wealth is restored, and he has a new family. His deceased children do not, however, rise from the dead, and it is clear than even God cannot undo what has been done. We cannot erase the past or magically make our wounds heal or our misery become unremembered. What Job goes through does indeed make him a man, and what we are really seeing in this ancient story is the process of maturing which we must all, sooner or later, undergo. We may not suffer the kind of extreme tragedies that afflict Job. But sooner or later life's unfairness will touch us, and we will feel pain which is unmerited, and suffer losses which we have done nothing to deserve. Whether our trust in life is rooted in a belief in God or simply springs from faith in human potential, Job's tale teaches us that we must somehow find this trust without rational explanations or promises of eventual reward. Only then are we restored to ourselves, and can find the strength to renew our lives after suffering and loss.

ORPHEUS AND EURYDICE

Dealing with grief

THE SAD GREEK TALE OF ORPHEUS AND HIS LOST WIFE EURYDICE TEACHES US
ABOUT THE BITTER-SWEET PAIN OF GRIEF AND LOSS, AND THE INEVITABILITY OF
ENDINGS DESPITE ANY ATTEMPTS WE MAKE TO HOLD ON TO WHAT IS PASSING
FROM OUR LIVES. THIS MYTH OFFERS NO EASY SOLUTIONS ABOUT HOW TO DEAL
WITH LOSS; BUT THERE ARE GENTLE HINTS THAT MAY HELP US UNDERSTAND THE
MYSTERIOUS WAY IN WHICH WHAT WE ARE ABLE TO LET GO OF MAY CONTINUE TO
LIVE, YET WHAT WE CLING TO BEYOND ITS APPOINTED TIME MAY DIE WITHIN US.

O rpheus of Thrace was famed for playing the sweetest music in the
world. He was the son of the muse Calliope and the Thracian
King Oeagrus, although some whispered that he was really the
son of Apollo the sun-god. His skill on the golden lyre which had been
given to him by Apollo was so enchanting that even rushing streams stood
still to listen, and rocks and trees would uproot themselves to follow his
exquisite music.

A singer who could breathe life into a stone had no problem in winning
the love of the fair Eurydice, and at first their marriage was blissful. But
sadly, their joy was brief; for Eurydice was bitten by a snake, and no
remedy could hold her to the world of the living. Grief-stricken, Orpheus
followed her to her grave, playing mournful airs that deeply moved the
hearts of all those who watched the funeral procession. Then, as life
seemed to hold no light for him without Eurydice, Orpheus sought the
very gates of Hades, searching for his lost love where no living human
being may go till the day of his or her own death.

Orpheus played so poignantly that the stern boatman Charon, who

Unable to find meaning in life without his beloved Eurydice, and weary with mourning at her tomb,
Orpheus followed her beyond the grave into Hades' sunless realm.

DETAIL Orpheus at the Tomb of Eurydice, Gustave Moreau (1826–98)

ferried the souls of the dead across the river Styx, forgot to check whether Orpheus had the required coin on his tongue. Enchanted by the magical notes, the old boatman rowed the singer unquestioningly across the black river which divides the sunlit world from the cold realms of Hades. So moving were the notes from Orpheus' golden lyre that the iron bars of the gates of death slid back of their own accord, and Cerberus, the three-headed dog who guards death's gloomy portals, sank down without even baring his teeth, rendered docile by the soothing music. And so it was that Orpheus was able to pass unchecked into the world of the shades. For a few blessed moments, the damned in Tartaros were relieved of their endless torment, and even the hard heart of Hades, lord of the under-world, was momentarily softened. Orpheus knelt humbly at the throne of the king and queen of the dead, praying and pleading with his most mystical of melodies that Eurydice might be allowed to return with him to the land of the living. Persephone, mistress of the underworld, whispered a word in her husband's ear, and the lyre of Orpheus was interrupted by a deep, hollow voice. All the realms of the underworld fell silent to hear Hades' decree.

'So be it, Orpheus! Return to the world above, and Eurydice shall follow you as your shadow! But do not stop, do not speak, and above all, do not look back until you have gained the upper air. For if you do, you shall never see her face again. Go without delay, and believe that on your silent path you will not be alone.'

Orpheus, in awe and gratitude, turned his back on death's throne and made his way through the chill gloom towards the faint glimmer of light that marked the path to the daylight world. He proceeded through the silent halls, his own footsteps echoing dreadfully as he hurried towards the light that shone more and more clearly as he neared his destination. Then, just as he was about to step into the light, he was afflicted with agonizing doubt. What if Hades had tricked him? What if Eurydice was not really behind him? He could not help himself. He turned around and, as he did, he saw Eurydice fading away, arms outstretched beseechingly, dying for a second time. This time the gates of the underworld were

closed to him, and he returned alone and inconsolable to the sunlit world above, in which, for many years, no sun would shine.

In time Orpheus became a priest, teaching the mysteries of life and death and preaching the evil of sacrificial murder to the men of Thrace. He brought joy to many through his music, and he healed and comforted many more; yet he could not heal himself of his despair, because he had lost his one chance of cheating death. His own death was violent, for the god Dionysus resented a mortal receiving the worship and adoration befitting a deity. Dionysus' mad female followers tore Orpheus limb from limb, and the Muses buried his broken body at the foot of Mount Olympus, where the nightingales are said to sing more sweetly than anywhere else in the world.

COMMENTARY: The myth of Orpheus strikes a deep chord in us. It raises our hope that we can perhaps cheat death and circumvent inevitable loss, and then dashes that hope. Orpheus is so talented and special – surely he, if no one else, could make an exception to the rule that every human being must one day die. We often believe that, if we could only make ourselves talented or special enough – perhaps by perfecting some work of art, or by becoming very rich and powerful, or by being very beautiful, or by being sufficiently good and righteous – we could somehow be exempt from grief and loss. Orpheus' music resonates with us because, like him, we feel – secretly if not consciously – that we are exceptions. 'I know everyone has to die,' we say, 'but in this case, surely I, and those I love, could be spared. I can't really believe it will happen to me and my loved ones.' We do not wish to believe that such awful feelings of grief or sorrow cannot be avoided, and that experiences of separation and loss do not discriminate between humans because of merit.

And yet, the story of Orpheus and his lost love Eurydice teaches us that, because we are humans, we are doomed to face loss and death. It is Orpheus' and Eurydice's humanity that makes it inevitable that they must suffer, lose and die. The nature of Eurydice's death underlines the unfairness and unpredictability of life, of which death is an inevitable part. Orpheus' chances look quite encouraging at first, for his music makes even stern Hades relent. And yet, at the last moment,

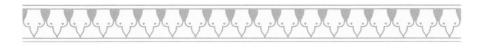

he loses faith and looks back – and all is lost. We think, 'If only he had not looked back ...'. Yet we know deep down that it was inevitable, because Orpheus is human, and no human is capable of such absolute trust in the invisible. Even the Christian story of Jesus' crucifixion tells us that doubt is inevitable, and that the moment will come, born of the extremity of pain, when faith dissolves and darkness descends.

There is a disturbing paradox embedded in this story. We must not look back, for in looking back we suffer our grief and loss all over again; yet if we do not look back, can we truly cheat death? And is any human truly able to refrain from looking back? Perhaps, if we understand the promised resurrection of Eurydice psychologically, we can get a glimpse of the wisdom hidden in this tale. When we look over our shoulders and long for the past to be redone – the perennial 'If only ...' which afflicts us all at one time or another – we condemn ourselves to a replay of our sorrow and a renewed sense of our impotence in the face of the inevitable. If we accept what we have lost and keep our faces turned towards the future, then those whom we have lost are forever with us, for we remember the joy and the love. Such memories cannot be destroyed, and we carry within us all those whom we have loved and whose love has changed us in some way. Perhaps that is the deeper meaning of Eurydice's return to the daylight world – not as a fully resurrected living being, but as a living part of Orpheus' heart and soul. In this sense, brooding over our losses condemns us to live with our suffering, with no help and no release, and we have lost more than if we can carry the loss with faith that life will continue to hold a purpose.

It may be inevitable that, when we suffer loss, we must live in darkness for a time and work through those stages of grief which have their own timing and cycle. Grief is a complex process and may involve rage, despair, idealization, denial, guilt, self-blame, blame of others and a time of depression and numbness before life stirs in us again. It is not a consistent process, for our pain may rise up and flood us at unexpected moments, and we need to be prepared to allow this.

Beset by sudden terrible doubt, Orpheus could no longer bear the suspense of not knowing whether Eurydice followed him on the path from the underworld; so he turned back, and thus lost her forever.

DETAIL Orpheus and Eurydice, Enrico Scuri Bergamo (1805–84)

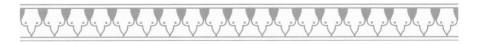

This may also be a way of understanding Hades' command, 'Do not look back!' For if we look back we are really attempting to freeze the moment and short-circuit the process of grief, which carries with it the potential for healing only if it is allowed to follow its own timing. We become uncomfortable when others grieve longer than we think they should. We have ideas about how long we are permitted to mourn and what we should be feeling about those we have lost. Yet every person is different, and the process enacts itself differently in each of us. To stop looking back requires us to relinquish the blind belief that life will make an exception for us; and we may be asked to trust in the natural process of mourning, however long it takes and whatever unacceptable emotions it raises in us. In this way, we do indeed discover an eternal life in the love we have shared with those we have lost. Finally, we come to the other side of grief, to find that serene acceptance, rather than bitter resignation, has allowed life to flow within once again.

CHIRON THE CENTAUR

Facing the unfairness of life

THE UNFAIRNESS OF LIFE IS SOMETHING WITH WHICH WE HAVE MUCH DIFFICULTY RECONCILING OURSELVES. WE PERPETUALLY TRY TO RATIONALIZE LIFE'S UNFAIRNESS THROUGH DOCTRINES AND PHILOSOPHIES WHICH CAN RESTORE OUR FAITH IN THE EQUALITY OF THE UNIVERSE – USUALLY CONVINCING OURSELVES THAT THE GOOD ARE ULTIMATELY REWARDED, IN THE NEXT LIFE IF NOT IN THIS ONE, AND THE BAD ULTIMATELY PUNISHED. THE GREEK MYTH OF CHIRON, LIKE THE BIBLICAL TALE OF JOB, IS A STORY OF UNFAIR PAIN AND SUFFERING. FAR FROM ENCOURAGING OUR NAIVETY, IT TEACHES US THAT THERE MAY BE NO REASON FOR UNFAIR SUFFERING. THERE MAY, HOWEVER, BE A MEANING, DEPENDENT ON WHETHER WE ALLOW OUR SUFFERING TO TRANSFORM US FROM WITHIN.

I n a cave high on the snowy peaks of Mount Pelion lived Chiron, the oldest and wisest of the centaurs – a mysterious race, half-horse and half-human in appearance. These centaurs were the children of Cronus, who raped a nymph by turning himself into a horse; and thus the descendants of this union were half-animal and half-divine.

While most of the other centaurs were wild and savage, Chiron was unusual in his wisdom and gentleness, and he was a friend to humans. He possessed rare skill in playing the harp, and often delivered profound counsels in human speech accompanied by the sweet music of this instrument. He knew all the secrets of herbal lore and could heal many illnesses that human medicine could not alleviate; and he understood the wisdom of the stars, and taught the art of astrology. So great was his fame that many a king's son was entrusted to his care. From Chiron these young pupils learned to fear the gods, to respect old age and to stand by

OVERLEAF *The strange creatures called centaurs, half divine and half beast, were untamed and often savage, indulging in drunken revelry and brutal fighting.*
Battle of the Centaurs, Arnold Böcklin (1827–1901)

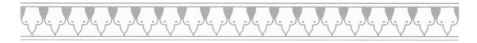

one another in pain and hardship. The wise old centaur taught them to make music, to hold themselves with grace in dance, to wrestle, box and run, to climb the high rocks and to hunt wild beasts in the mountain forests. They learned to read the omens in the heavens and to find those plants which could offer an antidote to infection and pain. The youths Chiron educated learned to laugh in the face of danger, to scorn sloth and greed, and to face all that came to them with courage and good cheer. They grew up skillful and strong, modest as well as brave, and were fit to rule by having learned how to obey.

Among Chiron's greatest friends was the powerful hero Herakles. This giant of a man had been battling with a formidable monster called the Hydra, and, having finally killed the beast, Herakles had dipped some of his arrows in the Hydra's poisonous blood to give them an extra layer of deadliness. Now, on his way to visit his friend Chiron, the hero was waylaid by a tribe of wild, savage centaurs; and a great battle ensued, with Herakles standing alone against the attacking horde. Chiron, when he heard the sounds of battle, emerged from his cave and, raising his hands in a gesture of peace, moved between Herakles and a centaur at whom the hero had aimed an arrow. But the arrow was already speeding on its course, and it struck Chiron full in the thigh.

Chiron would have died instantly had he been wholly animal or wholly human. But he was semi-divine, and the gift of eternal life now proved to be a terrible burden to him. The wound was truly agonizing, and the centaur retreated howling into his cave. This wise healer could find no antidote for the Hydra's poison, and no cure for the excruciating pain. He had no choice but to live with it, for he could not die like other mortal creatures. His pain urged him to try many new remedies, some of which were of great value to others who suffered; but none of them could ease his own suffering.

In desperation, Chiron begged for death from Zeus, king of the gods. Zeus, taking compassion on him, permitted him to enter the halls of the underworld like ordinary mortals, and so Chiron was finally released from suffering through death.

COMMENTARY: This dark myth is not easy to come to terms with. It seems terribly unfair that a good creature like Chiron, wise and civilized, should have to suffer merely because he is in the wrong place at the wrong time. When we encounter such events in the modern world, they fill us with helpless rage and bewilderment. 'Why did this terrible thing happen to someone so young ... so kind ... so good? Why did it not happen to someone bad or unworthy?' We want to believe in the fairness of life, because this belief makes life seem controllable. If we are good and are rewarded, then all we have to do to be rewarded is to be good. That is simple and within our control. The idea of being good, and then being hit with some accident that ruins our lives, is virtually insupportable. Collective catastrophes, whether of human invention (such as war) or precipitated by Nature herself (such as earthquakes, droughts and floods) confront us with life's profound unfairness on a global level. However badly we want to believe in a just cosmos, sooner or later we will meet the enigma of unfair suffering.

When something unfair happens, we have no choice but to suffer it, whether we 'deserve' it or not. At first, we may seek to blame someone or something, and attempt to alleviate our distress by finding a scapegoat on whom we can pin the responsibility. We blame parents, society, the government or a minority group, anything else that comes readily to hand, because we simply cannot countenance a situation where blame is inappropriate. The only possible response, in the end, is understanding and compassion. The word 'compassion' comes from a Latin root which means 'to suffer with'. Unfair suffering is shared by us all and it can open up a deep sense of connection with other living things. Although we may never discover any justification for such unmerited pain, we may glimpse its ultimate transformative power in the way it can cleanse and transform the human heart.

Embedded in this story is the suggestion that there is a price to be paid for attempting to civilize the savage side of human nature. Although this price is unquestionably unfair, there is an inevitability about the sacrifice because that is the nature of life. Struggle is necessary between the conscious ego – symbolized by Herakles – and the destructive instinctual forces within human beings – symbolized by the wild centaurs – if we are to create a better world for ourselves. And sometimes unfair pain and loss are the result of that struggle. Only if we

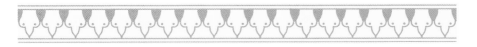

view the story from a broader perspective can we glimpse any deeper purpose in it, although we may find no fairness.

Chiron's voluntary death may be seen as a profound symbol; he exchanges his immortality for the fate of all mortal creatures. We may view this death as a psychological transformation, an inner acceptance of human limits. Only when we think we are so special that we are exempt from life's vicissitudes, do we suffer the true poison of Chiron's wound. This poison may be understood as the bitterness of corrosive ongoing resentment. If we expect to be protected from life, then we will become bitter and filled with poison when we discover we are not so special after all. When unfair suffering enters our lives, the inevitable human response of 'why me?' may have to be replaced by the wiser question, 'why not me?' Chiron's gifts and immortal nature do not protect him from life, nor can our own gifts or 'higher' spirituality. We too may need to accept our mortal limits and undergo the inner death and transformation which allows us to make peace with living ordinary human lives.

Although the centaur is a fantastic creature, the myth of Chiron is really a myth of humanity. We are a mixture of opposites and contradictions, half bestial and half divine, with a capacity for great wisdom and goodness and an equal capacity for savagery and brutality. The wild centaurs with whom Herakles battles are within us as much as Chiron's nobility. These opposites are inextricably linked in human beings and can never be fully untangled. No matter how wise we are, we have the capacity to be savage to one another, and we share in this collective duality even if, as individuals, we choose to align ourselves with the light. Thus we can all suffer unfair pain, physical or emotional, and, once hurt in this way, we can never truly be healed, because our innocence can never be restored. It is up to us to choose the healing path of compassion and acceptance of mortal limits rather than the lingering corruption of inner resentment towards life.

Chiron, the wise centaur, was gentle and compassionate towards human pain. Having suffered so deeply himself, he felt empathy and concern for others who were wounded and needed his help.

DETAIL Mount Helicon with God Pegasus and Centaur Chiron,
Giovanni M. Falconetto (16th century)

Chapter Two

THE SPIRITUAL QUEST

The spiritual quest has provided one of the great themes of literature and art over the millennia, for there is something irrepressible within the human soul that never ceases to aspire to something greater than itself, nor ever relinquishes its belief that something eternal survives beyond the death of the mortal body. Perhaps this is the greatest difference between us and the other animals with whom we share this planet. But such a quest is not simply a desire to serve God. It can also involve a quest for knowledge — not only knowledge of the divine couched in conventional religious terms, but also the kind of knowledge of the laws underpinning reality that the world's greatest scientists and psychologists pursue. And the quest for knowledge may take us on dark paths as well as paths lit by sunlight, and may reveal to us the evil that lies within us as well as the good. The myths which follow all deal with the spiritual quest, and all three involve a self-confrontation which throws into sharp relief the deep paradox of dark and light which lies at the core of the human soul.

THE FORTUNES OF DR FAUSTUS

Good is incomprehensible without evil

THE MYSTERIOUS BATTLE BETWEEN GOOD AND EVIL WITHIN THE HUMAN SOUL IS
PORTRAYED IN MYTH NOWHERE BETTER THAN IN THE STORY OF DR FAUSTUS.
MARLOWE'S GREAT TRAGEDY, DR FAUSTUS, AND GOETHE'S SUBLIME EPIC POEM,
FAUST, WERE BOTH DRAWN FROM THIS MEDIEVAL TALE ABOUT A MAN WHOSE
SPIRITUAL QUEST ULTIMATELY LED HIM TO SELL HIS SOUL TO THE DEVIL. HIS
EVENTUAL RECOGNITION OF THE ARIDITY OF EARTHLY PLEASURES AND HIS FINAL
REDEMPTION THROUGH REMORSE AND COMPASSION REMAIN A POWERFUL IMAGE
OF THE NEED TO COMPREHEND BOTH THE DARK AND THE LIGHT IN ORDER TO
FIND INNER PEACE.

There once was a brilliant philosopher and student of theology called Dr Faustus. But the teachings which the philosophers and theologians offered about the nature of God and the meaning of life could not satisfy his inquiring intellect. Moreover, his pride was as great as his knowledge, and he desired to discover the answers to life's greatest mysteries by his own efforts rather than receiving them from those whom he secretly despised; for thus he could claim all the credit.

So, in time, Dr Faustus abandoned his theology and became a student of hermetic magic; for he hoped to find the secret of life in alchemical experiments and the forbidden knowledge of magic and sorcery passed down from the ancient Egyptians. Yet even these forbidden researches could not teach him all he wished to know, and he sank into a deep melancholy, calling on the infernal spirits in his despair. In response to his summons, a black dog mysteriously appeared in the scholar's study, which then metamorphosed into a strange figure who announced himself as Mephistopheles, the spirit of evil and negation. Mephistopheles was forever on the lookout for human souls whom he could win over to the darkness, thus cheating God; and Faustus wanted Mephistopheles' knowledge of life's secrets and the nature of the divine. Thus a pact was

When Faustus saw the agony he had inflicted on the unhappy Gretchen, he began to experience real remorse for the first time, born out of genuine love for the doomed girl.

Gretchen in Prison, from Goethe's 'Faust', von Josef Fay (1813–75)

made between them, signed in blood, and Mephistopheles agreed to serve Faustus in this world while Faustus agreed to serve Mephistopheles in the next. Mephistopheles knew full well what price Faustus would pay, but the philosopher had not yet understood that it was his immortal soul which he was signing away unto eternity.

For a time, Faustus was excited by the magic and mysteries which Mephistopheles showed him, and believed that at last he was getting close to knowing the secrets of God. But the dark spirit of negation gradually eroded the scholar's will and lured him into deeper and deeper sensuality and pride, and all sense of a spiritual quest was lost. Faustus desired a young girl called Gretchen, whom Mephistopheles contrived to lure into

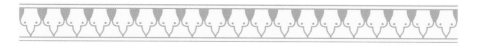

the scholar's hands. She became pregnant by Faustus and, when he abandoned her, she went mad and killed her infant in despair, and was then executed for her crime. Realizing the terrible destruction he had wrought on an innocent human life, Faustus suffered a deep and bitter remorse; for, although he was in the hands of Mephistopheles, he had begun to truly love the girl, and thus something in his soul was kept free of corruption. And this Mephistopheles had not anticipated, since the redemptive power of love was not something the spirit of negation had any knowledge of.

But such was the power Mephistopheles held over Faustus that, for many years, the philosopher indulged every sensual pleasure and penetrated every secret mystery. All that he had wanted to know, he learned; and he understood the glorious heights of heaven and the shrouded bowels of the underworld. However, the remorse he felt about the death of Gretchen grew like a canker inside him, and in spite of his corruption something within him continued to long for the light. As the scholar grew older, Mephistopheles waited with patience and satisfaction, for the time would soon arrive when the scholar would face death, and then his soul would belong to the darkness. But at the final moment, when Faustus at last confronted the true consequences of the pact which he had made, so filled with remorse and love and suffering was he that his soul slipped from Mephistopheles' grasp and was born aloft to the heavenly spheres.

COMMENTARY: *The story of Dr Faustus is a mythic metaphor for every human being's struggle to find the light in the midst of darkness. Faustus is a paradigm of the inner world of all of us, full of conflict between our egocentric desires and our longing to serve something higher and greater than ourselves. Although the original myth has its roots in medieval Christianity and, therefore, presents good and evil in a somewhat simplistic way, nevertheless the message transcends any specific religious doctrine, particularly if it is understood psychologically. Faustus is a symbol of the questing spirit within each human being, courageous and individualistic enough to reject the dogma offered by conventional religious*

authorities, yet dangerously arrogant in assuming that it can defy fundamental human morality in the name of knowledge. We may condemn Faustus for his greed and arrogance, yet we must admire him for his courage and willingness to risk his soul in order to penetrate to the heart of life's mysteries. Here we are presented with the profound paradox of good and evil, for in order to truly understand the former, we must also recognize the latter; and in order to make that recognition, we must meet it first in the secret darkness of our own hearts.

Faustus' disillusionment with conventional philosophical and theological offerings reflects the dilemma of a fine intellect which cannot simply 'believe' because one is told to do so. The spiritual quest, if it is truly heartfelt, arises not from a childlike acceptance of beliefs, but from disillusionment and a profound desire to understand life's paradoxes. Many people never move beyond childlike belief, for it is more comforting to be given simple answers to moral and spiritual dilemmas; and while such people may risk no danger inwardly, they can never really know what life is about, nor find any peace when confronted with the unanswerable questions invoked by unfair suffering. Many of the world's great religions condemn such questioning, as did the medieval Church of Faustus' time. Questioning involves danger, but it also opens up the potential for a real experience of the soul and the inner world.

Power corrupts – a fact no less true on the spiritual plane than on the material one. Faust's new power pushes him over the moral edge, and he is impervious to the destruction he inflicts on Gretchen. Yet he does love her, and cannot entirely ignore what he has done; and this little seed of remorse, born from compassion, is ultimately what allows him to cheat the Devil and find forgiveness and redemption. Thus it is not 'good works' which save him, but the fact that, despite being steeped in pride and sensuality, he can still love and feel remorse. We are taught that we must be 'good' in terms of our actions if we are to be acceptable in the eyes of God. Yet the story of Faustus teaches us that goodness is relative to the definitions of morality espoused by any society at any epoch of history. Love and remorse, however, are not confined to the doctrines of any specific culture or religion. They allow us to taste of both light and darkness and somehow retain the integrity of the soul. It is possible that any honest spiritual quest will lead us into our own potential for darkness and destruction, and that only through

facing these things, and perhaps even feeling, for a time, that we are irredeemable – our own 'pact with the devil' – can we experience what might be called grace. Grace, although the term is Christian, is something not limited to Christianity; it is a mysterious inner release which arises from within and which makes sense not only of our goodness, but of our evil as well.

Thus the myth of Dr Faustus is not the simple morality tale it might first appear. It is an inner journey and, as with all myths when viewed on a psychological level, all the characters are within each of us. Faustus and Mephistopheles are two sides of the same coin, and reflect two dimensions of the human being. The spirit of negation – which we may all experience when we view life as worthless and others as insignificant – may be found in every one of us. We may invoke Mephistopheles within, every time we become disillusioned with life. But Mephistopheles is not merely the Devil. In Goethe's great drama, Mephistopheles says to Faust, 'I am that spirit which wills forever evil yet does forever good.' It is through the agency of our inner darkness that we may eventually find our way to the light.

THE BUDDHA'S ENLIGHTENMENT

The wheel of rebirth

IN PART TWO, WE MET THE YOUNG BUDDHA, THEN CALLED SIDDHARTHA, AS HE LEFT HIS HOME AND FAMILY TO PURSUE HIS DESTINY. NOW WE SEE THE BUDDHA FINALLY ACHIEVE THAT WHICH HE HAS SOUGHT THROUGH STRUGGLE AND SUFFERING: AN UNDERSTANDING OF THE MEANING OF SUFFERING AND THE ULTIMATE PURPOSE OF LIFE. THE BUDDHA'S ENLIGHTENMENT MAY BE TAKEN AS AN ACTUAL EVENT, A RELIGIOUS PARABLE OR A MYTH IN THE MOST PROFOUND PSYCHOLOGICAL SENSE; OR ONE MAY FIND TRUTH IN ALL THREE INTERPRETATIONS. AS MYTH, THE TALE PRESENTS US WITH A PARADIGM OF EVERY HUMAN SOUL'S JOURNEY FROM THE DARKNESS OF IGNORANCE TO A TRANSFORMATIVE COMPREHENSION OF THE CYCLE OF LIFE AND DEATH.

After Prince Siddhartha left his family to seek understanding of the mystery of human suffering, he became a monk and he sought wisdom through following various doctrines and various teachers. But these did not teach him what he was seeking. He continued to wander and then remained for six years on the bank of a river where he practised terrible austerities which reduced his body almost to nothing. For he believed, as many religious people do, that if he denied every desire of the body, he would eventually invigorate the life of the spirit.

But in time he realized that such excessive self-punishment only destroys a person's strength and, instead of freeing the mind, makes it impotent. Siddhartha knew that he must get beyond asceticism, just as he had got beyond worldly life. Exhausted and thin as a skeleton, he accepted a bowl of rice offered to him by a village girl who was moved to compassion by his weakness. Then he bathed in the river. Five disciples who had shared his austerities abandoned him, feeling betrayed by what they deemed to be his self-indulgence. Perhaps, they said to each other, he was not so enlightened after all.

Siddhartha then started for a place called Bodhi-Gaya, where he might find the Tree of Wisdom. As he passed through the forest, such light emanated from his body that the birds were attracted and flew in circles around him, and the animals escorted him. Then he reached the sacred fig tree. He set a bundle of new-mown hay down and sat on it, uttering this vow, 'Here, on this seat, may my body dry up, may my skin and flesh waste away if I raise my body from this seat until I have attained the knowledge I seek!' And the earth quaked six times as he uttered this pronouncement.

A demon called Mara, knowing that Siddhartha's enlightenment would mean his own destruction, decided to interfere. He sent his three beautiful daughters to tempt Siddhartha. The girls sang and danced before him, but

When dawn rose over the sacred tree, Siddhartha, now become the Buddha, had achieved perfect enlightenment. Rays of light shone from his body, reaching the outermost confines of space.

DETAIL The Buddha, Odilon Redon (1840–1916)

Siddhartha remained unmoved in heart and countenance, calm as a lotus on the smooth waters of a lake. The demon's daughters retired defeated. Then the demon sent an army of horrible devils who surrounded the sacred fig tree and threatened Siddhartha. But so profound was Siddhartha's serenity that they found themselves paralysed, with their arms bound to their sides. Finally the demon Mara rode down from the clouds and hurled his terrible weapon – a huge disk which could cut a mountain in two. But this weapon was impotent against Siddhartha. It was changed into a garland of flowers and hung suspended above Siddhartha's head.

The demon was finally beaten. The motionless Siddhartha remained in meditation under the sacred fig tree. Night came, and with it the enlightenment which he sought rose slowly in his heart. First he knew the exact conditions of all living beings, and then the causes of their rebirth into the world of form. Throughout the world and in all ages, he beheld sentient beings live, die and reincarnate. He remembered his own previous existences and grasped the inevitable links of causes and effects. As he meditated on human suffering he was enlightened as to how it came about and the means which might allow it to cease.

When the dawn came, Siddhartha had achieved perfect enlightenment, and had become the Buddha. For seven days he remained in meditation, and then stayed near the sacred tree for another four weeks. He knew that two paths were open to him. He could at once enter nirvana, the state of ultimate bliss; or he could renounce his own deliverance for a time and remain on earth to teach others what he had learned. The demon Mara urged him to leave the world, but the gods united to implore him, and the Buddha at last yielded to his ultimate destiny as a teacher. For the rest of his life he laboured to teach men and women the mystery of suffering and rebirth. Finally, at the age of eighty, he felt he had grown old, and prepared for his end. He lay down beside a river, and the trees about him were immediately covered with flowers. He entered into meditation, then into ecstasy and, finally, passed into nirvana. His body was burned on a funeral pyre which lighted itself and was extinguished at the right

moment by a miraculous rain. Thus one human being trod the thorny path to achieve enlightenment and then turned back, sacrificing for a time his own reward, in order to bring light to the darkness in which other human beings lived.

COMMENTARY: *The story of the Buddha's enlightenment has offered wisdom and serenity to millions of believers, yet one does not have to be a practising Buddhist to discover in this story important psychological truths. Siddhartha first attempts to find the answers to his questions through espousing conventionally accepted doctrines – precisely the way many spiritual quests begin. Yet we too – if we are committed to the truth as Siddhartha is, and not merely seeking comfort for our own suffering – may find that such offerings cannot satisfy us. We then begin to look for answers outside the teachings of established religious structures.*

Next, Siddhartha attempts to achieve spiritual enlightenment through denying his physical needs and desires. This too is often a stage along the path for many people, for in the West we have inherited a centuries-old tradition that perceives the physical body as the root of all evil, and physical pleasure as an interference to the spiritual life. Yet Siddhartha recognizes that he must abjure asceticism as he has abjured conventional religious doctrines, because the life of the body is also divine and it is foolishness at best, and arrogance at worst, to imagine we can find God through denying or even destroying God's creation. Psychologically, wholeness rather than extreme imbalance is the ideal towards which the sensible individual aspires; for the spirit cannot live when the body is wretched and ill. But sometimes we may have to discover this through hard experience, as Siddhartha did. When he finally allows himself to accept the bowl of rice and bathes in the river, his more rigid-minded disciples leave him. In the same way, we may find that we are made to feel outcast from an established religious path if we dare to contradict the dogma and acknowledge needs and desires which have been labelled 'bad' or 'sinful'.

The great symbol of the Tree of Wisdom, under which Siddhartha achieves enlightenment, echoes the images of many other myths. The Tree of Knowledge may be found in the story of Adam and Eve (see pages 74–9); the Tree of Immortality lies at the bottom of the sea, beckoning to Gilgamesh (see pages

102–6); the World-Tree Yggdrasil holds up the cosmos in Norse and Teutonic myth. For millennia the human imagination has envisaged the source of life and wisdom as a tree, perhaps because the tree portrays a fundamental duality which also lies at the core of the human soul. Its roots are in the earth but its branches aspire towards heaven. And it is a living thing, not an intellectual construction, and the spiritual truths which Siddhartha seeks can be found only through such contact with organic life.

The demon Mara, viewed psychologically, is a dimension of Siddhartha himself. Like Mephistopheles in the story of Faustus, he is the personification of inner darkness, and attempts to corrupt Siddhartha in the same way that Mephistopheles corrupts Faustus. But, unlike Faustus, Siddhartha's focus is inward, rendering him immune to the demon's threats. What might this mean for the ordinary individual seeking spiritual answers? Siddhartha's absolute serenity reflects his total commitment to his quest. It is an issue of focusing, of priorities and of giving central importance to the mysteries he is contemplating. We will find no inner serenity if we are constantly distracted by our own internal demons, be they physical temptations or fears and anxieties. Inner focus is not the same as rigid asceticism; it is an attitude, a state of mind, rather than a prescribed set of disciplines. And perhaps this is why the Buddha alone could do what he did; for such total focus on the importance of the inner world comes hard to us, especially when we are young. Intense inner effort of this kind may indeed only be possible in the second half of life, when we are weary with satiation, and the suffering of others begins to mean more to us than our own small worldly pleasures and pains. The stages through which Siddhartha passes are stages of life experience, each of which is necessary for him to move into the next stage. He must try everything before he is ready to relinquish everything for what he is seeking.

We may not be able to achieve the kind of enlightenment described by the story of the Buddha; it may even be arrogant to try. Whether perceived as a mythic image or a great religious avatar, the Buddha is a paradigm rather than an ordinary mortal. But understanding our lives from a larger perspective, with an awareness of the chain of cause and effect which lies behind so much human suffering, may be possible for all of us — if we are prepared to quietly and unobtrusively place our quest for understanding at the center of our lives.

PARSIFAL

The finding of the Grail

IN PART TWO, WE MET THE YOUNG PARSIFAL AS HE RODE OFF TO MANY ADVENTURES. THEN PARSIFAL STUMBLED ONTO THE GRAIL CASTLE AND SAW A VISION OF A WOUNDED KING AND A GRAIL, TO WHICH HE COULD NOT RESPOND WITH THE RIGHT QUESTIONS. OFTEN A VISION OF SPIRITUAL REALITY ARISES SPONTANEOUSLY IN YOUTH, BUT WE LACK THE MATURITY TO UNDERSTAND OR ASK WHAT IT MEANS FOR US. NOW WE MEET PARSIFAL IN LATER LIFE, TEMPERED BY HIS STRUGGLES AND SUFFERING, AND FINALLY ABLE TO ASK WHAT THE GRAIL MIGHT REALLY MEAN.

The young Parsifal rode away from the Grail Castle without comprehending what he saw there. In the woods he met a beautiful girl, who, on hearing he had visited the Grail Castle but had learned nothing, was aghast at his foolishness. 'Unfortunate man!' she exclaimed. 'So much would have been restored if you had only asked. The sick king would have been healed and all would have been well. But now worse troubles will result. You have behaved with incompetence.'

In shame, Parsifal continued on his way. After a time, he met another woman, but this one was hideous to behold, as if she had been spawned in hell. In her hand she carried a whip. She, too, reviled Parsifal for not having asked about the Grail, warning him that many would suffer because of his selfishness and stupidity.

For five years, Parsifal wandered and, during this time, he lost all remembrance of God. He only looked for violent deeds and curious adventures. One day he met three knights with their ladies, all on foot and wearing penitential garments. The company was amazed that Parsifal should be strolling around armed on the holy day of Good Friday. Did he not know that on this day one should carry no arms? They had just come from a holy hermit, to whom they had made their confessions and from whom they had received absolution. On hearing this, Parsifal wept and

desired to visit the hermit. He found the old man and admitted that for five years he had quite forgotten God and done nothing but evil. When the hermit asked him why, Parsifal told him that he had once visited the Fisher King and saw the Grail, but did not ask about them. The omission weighed so heavily on him that he had abandoned his faith in God.

The hermit, knowing of Parsifal's history, granted him absolution, and Parsifal again set out on his way. He was still not yet in a position to ask the decisive question, but he had acquired hope once more.

After this, Parsifal was determined to find the Grail Castle once again so that he could redeem his earlier failure. He met many more adventures, but always the Grail dominated his thoughts. Then, one day, he met a damsel seated beneath an oak tree. Because he was kind to her, she gave him a ring with a magic stone in it that allowed him to ride over a strange bridge of glass and across a dangerous second bridge that turned around on its own axis. The next morning, lost in a mysterious wood, Parsifal prayed to God to lead him to the Grail Castle. He rode on and, towards evening, saw a magical tree in the distance on which many lights were burning. There he met a hunter, who told him that he was at last near the Grail Castle. Finally he arrived at the castle. Servants led him to the Grail King, seated on a purple couch. Parsifal now viewed the sick king with compassion, feeling pain because of the king's pain, and sorrowing because of the king's long sorrows. When pressed, he humbly gave the king an account of his long adventures and spoke openly of his failures. Then he asked, at last, what ailed the king and, most importantly, what the Grail was and whom it served. At these words, the sick king sprang up, healed, and embraced Parsifal. The king then revealed that he was Parsifal's grandfather and that he would remain alive for only three more days, and then Parsifal would wear the crown and rule the kingdom.

And thus Parsifal, who began his journeying young and foolish, at last understood that the Grail was a vision of his own immortal spirit, recognized only through suffering and understanding, and serving the whole of life; and that by finally asking the meaning of this vision he had redeemed his own darkness and earned the right to be a fitting vessel for the light.

COMMENTARY: In this story, the long and thorny path to re-finding the Grail Castle is not followed by achieving heroic deeds. Step by step, it is accomplished through Parsifal's encounters with women. This tells us something profoundly important about the spiritual quest: it is constellated and facilitated not through asceticism or denial of earthly life, but through relationship. Whatever one's sex, it is through emotional involvement with others that one begins to discover one's priorities and, as life moves beyond youth and into middle age, remorse about one's insensitivity and callous acts begins to shift something deep in the soul.

The myth of the Grail has been interpreted on many different levels over the centuries, and all of them have some truth. From a psychological perspective, it is an inner journey, and, although the imagery of the original story is Christian, this inner journey is compatible with any deep religious faith, orthodox or unorthodox. It is really a journey about discovering compassion, which can only occur if we allow ourselves to feel with others and suffer the consequences of our own actions. It is compassion which allows Parsifal to respond in the right way to the sick king, and it is compassion which allows all of us to see beyond our own concerns to the waste land around us and the need of all human beings to find some small ray of light to illuminate their mortal journey. The sick king and the Grail are images within Parsifal himself, as they are within each of us. The king represents the spiritual sickness of meaninglessness, and the Grail is the ever-flowing cup of unity with the rest of life which is the only antidote to meaninglessness. We have many religious terms to describe the basic experience of compassion, but perhaps religious terminology is unnecessary; for all our most transformative experiences arise from that mysterious sense of unity which can occur when we share another's pain and joy. Meaning and compassion are thus inextricably linked in this myth.

The sick king is healed at the end of the story, but he willingly accepts death so that the crown can pass to his grandson. Here, as in the story of Chiron which we met earlier (see pages 243–9), is another presentation of death as a symbol of transformation. That which was injured may now heal and pass away, and that which is renewed and full of hope may now govern the motives by which we live. Thus the suffering which we experience in life, which seems to be so irrevocably wounding, may be relinquished so that life can begin again in a spirit of hope

Because he was kind to her, the lovely damsel gave Parsifal a ring with a magic stone which allowed him to cross the dangerous bridge of glass and at last find the Grail Castle.

The Temptation of Sir Percival, Arthur Hacker (1858–1919)

and generosity. It is right and fitting that the youthful Parsifal behaves like a youth, and his mistakes and foolishness are appropriate for this time of life. It is also right and fitting that gradually, as he grows older and experiences increasing weariness and cynicism, the spiritual quest begins to replace his earlier determination to be a great knight and receive recognition in the outer world. Thus we too may ask, at a certain point when we grow weary of accumulating possessions or striving for worldly success, what purpose our lives truly serve.

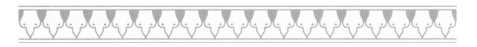

Chapter Three

THE FINAL JOURNEY

Whatever our skills, efforts, aspirations and actions in life, death comes to meet us all. Strong or weak, clever or ignorant, wealthy or poor, good or evil, we must all eventually bow to the great leveller. Death is the only absolute constant in life, and yet remains life's greatest enigma – for no matter how scientifically sophisticated we become, we cannot solve the mystery of what happens to us when the body dies. Human beings have long believed that something survives beyond the physical shell, and myths have always expressed in imaginative forms our human fears, fantasies and expectations of death. Religions have always attempted to offer certainties about an afterlife, teaching us that our adherence to particular dogmas during life will guarantee favorable conditions after death. Myth presents us with an alternative: metaphors and images which guarantee nothing, but somehow communicate a meaning and value to death which renders it part of life and a necessary chapter in a greater cosmic cycle. The three myths which follow all concern the subject of death. While none offers answers, all remind us of the profound paradox of death, which combines the transient nature of mortal life with the eternal and indestructible nature of the greater life of which we are a part.

MAUI AND THE DEATH GODDESS

The inevitability of death

THIS MAORI TALE FROM NEW ZEALAND TELLS US THAT, NO MATTER HOW CLEVER OR COURAGEOUS WE MAY BE, NO HUMAN BEING CAN AVOID THE INEVITABILITY OF DEATH. IN FACT, THE STORY OF MAUI SUGGESTS THAT THE HARDER WE TRY TO ESCAPE OR DENY OUR MORTALITY, THE CLOSER WE COME TO CREATING OUR INEVITABLE END. MAUI, LIKE SO MANY MYTHICAL HEROES, IS FULL OF ARROGANCE AND REFUSES TO ACCEPT HIS MORTAL LIMITS. BUT, AS EVER, NATURE HAS THE LAST LAUGH.

One evening, the great hero Maui was looking uncharacteristically glum and moody. His father, surprised to see him so depressed, asked him what the matter was.

'Why, Father,' replied Maui, 'while we are sitting here chatting, human beings are treading the gloomy path to death.'

'Alas, my son, all men and women are doomed to die,' said his father. 'Sooner or later they drop as ripe fruit from the tree, and are gathered up by the Great Mother of Night, the goddess Hinenuitepo.'

Maui stood up impatiently, and began pacing up and down. 'But must it always be so?' he said. 'If Death were to die, would we humans not then live forever?'

His father's brow clouded. 'Take my warning, son. Such thoughts are dangerous. No man can conquer Death.'

'But you are talking about ordinary men, Father. If that man were I – what then?'

His father sighed deeply and with much sorrow. 'My dear Maui, like any ordinary man you must die too.'

'I am no ordinary man. My mother prophesied that I would live forever. Anyway, no ordinary man could perform the feats I have. Did I not conquer fire, subdue the sun, even fish up land from the sea? What is Death to me but another adversary to outwit?'

His father's tone grew sharp. 'You are not in the upper world now, but in the lower world, where your cunning may not help you. Your mother did prophesy that you would live forever. But when I baptized you, my mind went blank, and I left out a passage of the incantation. By this omission, Maui, I undid the prophecy. And this is how I know you must die like other men at the hand of goddess Hinenuitepo. She is terrible beyond imagination, with flashing eyes, hair of kelp, teeth as sharp as obsidian, and with the evil grin of a barracuda. In all aspects she is monstrous, except her body, which is like that of an old woman.'

A plan was already taking root in Maui's mind, and his father knew he was plotting one of his tricks. He also knew advice was useless, and already he mourned for Maui in his heart. 'Farewell, my last-born and power of my old age,' he said, 'for truly you were born to die.'

Maui paid no attention. Off he went to the woods to share his scheme with his close companions – the many hundreds of fantail birds who lived amongst the trees. He told the birds of his plan and of the part they must play, and, filled with confidence, Maui and the birds set off through the forest. As they drew closer to the sleeping goddess of death, the excited chatter of the birds died away, until hardly a rustle of wings was heard. The air grew chilly and heavy as Maui passed through the bent trees, bearded with lichen, that surrounded the clearing where the goddess lay. Maui shivered as he saw her asleep in the doorway of her house, just as his father had described her. Her terrible eyes were lidded, and her lower jaw, slack with sleep, hung down, exposing her sharp teeth in a horrible grin. As she breathed out heavily, an icy draught swept across the clearing.

Maui held up his hand as a signal for the birds to stop, and whispered, 'My little friends, there she lies asleep – Hinenuitepo, the Great Mother of Night. Remember my words, for my life is in your hands. I will enter her body, but on no account must you laugh until I have passed through her body and out through her mouth. Then you can laugh, if you must. But if you laugh before then, I shall die.'

By this time the little birds were very frightened, and begged him to give up his plan, which now seemed quite mad. But Maui scoffed at their

Maui shared his daring plan to outwit death, the Great Mother of Night, with the hundreds of birds who lived in the depths of the impenetrable forest.

South Island, New Zealand, Eugen von Guerard (1811–1901)

fear, only reminding them that on no account must they laugh too soon. Then Maui approached the goddess. Quickly he stripped off his clothes until he stood naked, his skin shimmering in the light escaping from beneath her eyelids. Then, with a mocking smile, he stooped and quickly made his way, head first, into her body. His shoulders and chest soon disappeared. The birds were amazed at Maui's nimbleness. Some dared not watch, peeking through their feathers. Others choked back the laughter that threatened to overwhelm them. The sound of tittering was beginning to rise, and the goddess stirred. The birds shrank back and held their breath. The goddess settled down again, and they came back to watch Maui's progress, for now he was thrusting his head into the throat

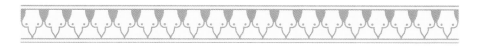

of the goddess. The birds shook with silent laughter, and thinking that victory was in sight for Maui, they desperately controlled themselves. Then Maui gave a heave, and pushed upwards with his shoulders so that his face suddenly appeared in the mouth of the goddess.

It was too much for the fantails. They burst into shrill laughter. At once the goddess awoke and understood what was happening. She closed her thighs on Maui, and broke his body in two. So ended, in laughter and disgrace, Maui's attempt to conquer death, and, because of his failure, men and women continue to tread the dark path to Hinenuitepo.

COMMENTARY: Maui's tragi-comic end reminds us that our attempts to conquer death are futile. Archetypal stories such as this one demonstrate that in all corners of the world people are the same, with a universal fear of death and a universal hope that somehow, be it through bravery, cunning, goodness or majesty, death can be conquered. And no matter how many times we fail, the hope persists that one day we will discover the secret of immortality. We hear news of a wonder-drug which cures all ills and rush hopefully to our doctors; we are cryogenically preserved in the hope that we can be revived in years to come; we try all kinds of diets and vitamins, exercises and regimens; we seek spiritual healers and miracle cures in the hope that our bodies will be freed of the ravages of age. We are, after all, no different from Maui.

But perhaps this story can teach us that it is more productive to live our lives to the full, and experience the richness which is available to everyone every day regardless of material circumstances, rather than spending so much time and energy trying to outwit death. And, in many ways, the fear of death is the same as the fear of life, for if we are unable to fully live in the present and unwilling to accept our mortality, we are not truly living. Then we truly have reason to fear the end of life; for we know we have wasted the gift of life we have been given.

The strange method by which Maui seeks to conquer the Mother of Night is really an image of returning to the womb, for Maui enters her body through the same gateway by which he left his mother's body at birth. This mysterious equation of birth and death in an ancient Maori myth echoes what modern psychological thought has only recently formulated: that the timeless place from

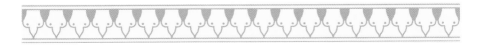

which we emerge at birth and the immortality which we seek after death are, in the human imagination, the same. The longing for immortality is also a longing to return to the womb; and although Maui seeks to be made immortal through his act, he is really secretly seeking death. Immortality is a static place, where nothing changes and nothing grows. It is like the original Paradise garden, where Adam and Eve exist in complete innocence and unconsciousness; and it is like life in the waters of the womb before birth. And there are many people who want life to be this way – static and unchanging, without conflict, eternally the same. This is a kind of death-in-life. Maui's longing for immortality is really a refusal to live life as an independent human being. Thus his death is inevitable, for death is, on some profound level, what he really wants. Although his many feats in myth portray him as a great hero and culture-bringer, his character is strangely close to those very ordinary human beings of any epoch and culture who keep hoping that the womb-like bliss they cannot achieve in the present will somehow be within their grasp if they can only find the magic formula that will allow them to live forever.

Maui's mother prophesied eternal life for him. Yet his father made a human error – he forgot the words which would ensure his son's immortality. Maui's father acknowledged this failure and, in doing so, affirmed his humanity. But Maui did not. His arrogance, or what the Greeks might have called his hubris, urged him to attempt the impossible. And, as always in myth, such arrogance was swiftly corrected by the gods.

The little birds have the last laugh in this tale in more ways than one; for they understand the absurdity of our strivings for immortality, and can hear the cosmic laughter which echoes throughout the vaults of heaven when we attempt to become what we are not.

ER AMONG THE DEAD

Death is the beginning of life

THE MYTH OF ER IS TOLD BY PLATO IN 'THE REPUBLIC'. IT GIVES US A RICH AND
COMPLEX VISION OF DEATH AND THE AFTERLIFE WHICH RAISES IMPORTANT
QUESTIONS ABOUT SOME OF THE MORE SIMPLISTIC WAYS IN WHICH WE VIEW THIS
MOST PROFOUND OF LIFE'S MYSTERIES. WHATEVER WE WERE TAUGHT IN
CHILDHOOD, AND WHATEVER WE BELIEVE AS ADULTS ABOUT WHAT AWAITS US
AFTER DEATH, THE STORY OF ER TELLS US THAT THE COSMOS IS A UNITY AND THAT
WE ARE PART OF A GREATER WHOLE WHICH MOVES ACCORDING TO ORDERLY AND
HARMONIOUS LAWS. DEATH, IN THIS GREAT AND ORDERLY SYSTEM, IS MERELY A
STAGE IN THE CONTINUUM OF THE GREATER UNITY.

Er was a brave warrior who fell in battle. As he was assumed to be dead, he was duly laid on a funeral pyre. There his body lay for twelve days, mysteriously uncorrupted. And on the twelfth day Er amazed his friends by waking up and telling them the story of his journey to the world of the shades.

His soul had passed out of his body to join a crowd of other souls in a strange and wonderful landscape where two chasms opened down through the earth and two passages led up towards the heavens. Here sat the judges who pronounced each person's sentence. The souls of the just were instructed to take one of the upward ways, each soul bearing a scroll outlining its blessedness. But others carried records of their evil deeds and were told to descend underground through one of the downward paths. When it came to Er's turn, however, the judges decided that he should bear back to the living world a report of what he saw and heard among the dead.

He saw how the newly dead went their separate ways, some upwards to the heavens and some downwards to the underworld. Through the other opening to the underworld, shades rose up from the depths, covered in dust and filth, meeting those who descended shining and pure from the

other heavenly path. On the plain they mingled, recognizing those they had known in life, eagerly exchanging news. The just were full of joy, while the evildoers tearfully lamented what they had borne for a thousand years. Er learned that each deed done in life must be recompensed during a tenfold term of shadowy life, with harsh punishments for those who were wicked and rich rewards for those who had benefited their fellow humans.

The souls who were destined to return to earth for another incarnation remained in this place for a time and then set out for a pillar of light that came into view glowing like a rainbow, but more brilliant and more ethereal. This pillar of light, Er learned, is the axis of heaven and earth; and in the middle hangs the adamantine spindle of Necessity, which she turns on her knees to keep eight variously colored circles whirling. These circles are the courses of the sun, the moon, the planets and the fixed stars. With each circle whirls a Siren, chanting on a single note, so that their eight voices mingle in harmony to make the Music of the Spheres. Around the throne of Necessity sit her three daughters, the Fates – Lachesis, Clotho and Atropos. Their voices keep time with the Sirens. Lachesis sings the past, Clotho the present, and Atropos the future, while from time to time all three touch the spindle to keep it turning.

As Er watched, the souls presented themselves before Lachesis, who had on her knees the lots to be drawn by each. A herald then made a proclamation to them all. 'Wandering souls,' cried the herald, 'you are about to enter a new mortal body. Each may choose his own lot in turn; but the choice will be irrevocable. Virtue has no respect for persons; it cleaves to who honors it, and flies from the despiser. On your own heads be your fortune: the gods are not to blame.'

First the souls drew lots for the order in which they should choose, except Er, who was bidden to stand and watch. The herald conjured

While Er languished between the worlds of the dead and the living, he saw the great goddess Necessity, also called Nemesis, presiding over all creation and turning the spindle of the universe.

Nemesis, Albrecht Dürer (1471–1528)

images before them of all the conditions of human life – tyranny, beggary, fame, beauty, riches, poverty, health and sickness. There were animal lives, too, mixed up with men's and women's. The herald, minister of the Fates, now urged the souls not to choose hastily.

But the first soul in line eagerly chose a life that promised great wealth and power. Then, having looked closer into this lot, he found that he was destined to devour his own children, among other enormities; whereupon he cried out bitterly, accusing fortune, the gods and, indeed, everything other than his own folly for such a choice. This soul had come from Elysium and, in his former life, had lived in a well-ordered state, where he owed his virtue to custom and collective expectation rather than to inner wisdom. So, indeed, it was with many of the souls from Elysium who went wrong in their choice, because, although 'good' by popular definition, they lacked experience of the evils of life. On the other hand, those released from the world below had often been schooled, by their own suffering and the suffering of others, to be more genuinely kind and compassionate. And so it was that most of the souls exchanged a good lot for an evil one, or an evil one for a good.

Er was filled with both pity and amusement when he saw how the souls made their choices, apparently guided by some recollection of a former life. He saw Orpheus (*see page 236*) pick out the body of a swan, as if in hatred of the women who had torn him to pieces, not caring to owe his birth to such a one. Agamemnon (*see page 67*) did likewise, selecting the life of an eagle, for his former fate had soured him, too, against humankind. And so it went on, with wily Odysseus coming last of all. He, remembering the past mishaps that had sickened his soul towards adventuring, carefully searched out, in an out-of-the-way corner, a quiet, simple life, which all the other souls had despised. Then he exclaimed that, had he had first choice, he would have asked for no better.

When all the souls had made their choice, they passed in order before Lachesis, who gave to each the guardian genius that should accompany him or her through life and carry out the destiny bound up with that soul's chosen lot. This genius led the soul to Clotho, who, with a turn of the

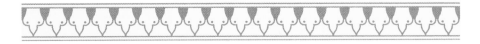

spindle, confirmed their choice. Each soul had to touch the spindle and was then brought to Atropos, who twisted the thread between her fingers to make unbreakable what Clotho had spun. Lastly, each soul with its genius bowed before the throne of Necessity. Then they passed on to the bare plain of Lethe and spent the night by the River of Forgetfulness, whose water cannot be borne away in any vessel. From its stream each had to drink, and almost all rashly drank too deep, and therefore lost all memory of what had gone before. Then they fell asleep. But towards midnight a din of thunder and earthquake roused the souls, who were scattered here and there like shooting stars to the different spots where they should be reborn.

As for Er, he was not instructed to drink the waters of Lethe. Yet he did not know how his soul came back to his body. All at once, opening his eyes, he found himself alive, stretched out on his funeral pyre.

COMMENTARY: Plato's tale of Er is often understood by scholars to be an intellectual construction designed to communicate specific Platonic ideas. Yet the image of a vast and orderly cosmos — where what is above in the heavens is reflected in what is below on earth and where every human action carries antecedents and consequences — is no construction of Plato's. It is an ancient cosmic vision which is truly mythic in nature. Its essence is that each human soul, as part of a larger unity, must take responsibility for its own fate, and we cannot blame either circumstance or God for the situations in which we find ourselves. Although we may, like the souls in the story, have drunk too deeply of the waters of Lethe and have forgotten the history we trail behind us, the roots of our present necessity may indeed lie in the past — whether in a former life or in the ancestral and family psyche from which we have emerged. At least half the world's population believes in reincarnation, although the Judeo-Christian West ordinarily think of this as the prerogative of the 'mystical' East. Yet Plato was Greek, and the myth he presented lies deep in the Western psyche, resurfacing in modern times to bring individual responsibility and choice back to the center of life.

The myth of Er presents us with death as a prelude to life, and life as a prelude to death. Life and death are thus different chapters in a cyclical story, each one a

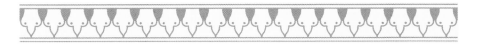

transition governed by an orderly cosmic pattern. Death is thus a rite of passage, and an ending only in the sense that a chapter of the story has come to a close. There is a clearly defined morality in this myth, since the evildoers suffer in the underworld and the good enjoy the bliss of the higher spheres; but neither remains there for eternity, and even the rewards and punishments which await the newly dead are paradoxical in their meaning. We accrue wisdom through the suffering generated by our mistakes, and make mistakes because we do not understand the meaning of suffering. The good can incur evil because they are ignorant of evil, and the evil can be transformed by the consequences of their actions. For those who accept the philosophy of reincarnation, these deep truths may be understood as relevant to how we live our lives here and now, since we are creating the future out of the present and the past. But they may also be understood as relevant to a single life, which is also a cyclical process with chapters which begin and end; and in the course of a single lifetime we may cause suffering and suffer ourselves, learn wisdom and choose rightly, or profess to be good and choose wrongly because the goodness is only skin-deep.

The myth of Er raises many more questions than it answers, and we will never know for sure where this myth came from or what Plato intended by including it in his work. But this grand vision of a cosmos governed by Necessity and reflected in the orderly patterns of the planets, presents us with a very important perception of death. If we live our lives without understanding how we are connected to each other and how every action carries consequences, then we will have every reason to fear death – either because some dire punishment awaits us, or because we must go into the dark knowing that, during our lives, we have done nothing to dispel the darkness of the world around us. As well as presenting us with a very different and complex vision of death, the story of Er is a myth about how to live life.

Deep within the earth, the three Fates, daughters of Necessity, spun, measured and cut the thread which signified the allotted span of each human being's life.

A Golden Thread, J. M. Strudwick (c.1885)

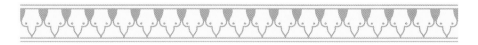

INDRA AND THE PARADE OF ANTS

The play of unending life

THE HINDU STORY OF INDRA AND THE PARADE OF ANTS IS ONE OF THE MOST
DELICATE BUT PROFOUND MYTHIC PRESENTATIONS OF THE CONTINUITY OF LIFE. IT
OFFERS US A GRAND COSMIC PICTURE OF THE EBB AND FLOW OF ALL THINGS – BUT
NOT AS AN ATTEMPT TO DIMINISH THE SUFFERINGS OF LIFE, OR PROMISE US
REWARDS AFTER DEATH. THIS IS A VISION OF THE TRUE NATURE OF ETERNITY AND
TIME. IN THIS STORY, A LONG ONE BUT WELL WORTH REFLECTION, EVEN THE KING
OF THE GODS IS HUMBLED AND BROUGHT TO A KNOWLEDGE OF HIS PROPER ROLE
IN THE GREAT PLAY OF UNENDING LIFE.

Indra, king of the gods, slew the giant dragon that had held all the waters of heaven captive in its belly. The god flung his thunderbolt into the midst of the ungainly coils, and the monster shattered like a stack of withered rushes. The waters burst free and streamed across the land, to circulate once more through the body of the world. This flood is the flood of life and belongs to all. It is the sap of field and forest, the blood coursing in the veins. The monster had appropriated the common benefit, but now was slain, and the juices again were pouring. The gods returned to the summit of the central mountain of the earth and reigned from on high.

The first act of Indra was to rebuild the mansions of the city of the gods, which had cracked and crumbled during the supremacy of the dragon. All the divinities of heaven acclaimed Indra their saviour. Greatly elated in his triumph and the knowledge of his strength, he summoned Vishvakarman, the god of arts and crafts, to erect a palace which should befit his unequalled splendor.

Vishvakarman constructed a shining residence, marvellous with palaces, gardens, lakes and towers. But as the work progressed, Indra's demands grew more exacting, and his vision vaster. He required more pavilions, ponds, groves and pleasure grounds. The divine craftsman,

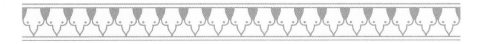

finally brought to despair, sought succour from above. He turned to Brahma, the great creator-god, who abides far above Indra's sphere of ambition, strife and glory.

After listening to the craftsman-god's complaint, Brahma said to him, 'Go home in peace. You will soon be relieved of your burden.' Brahma, in turn, went to seek Vishnu, the Supreme Being, of whom Brahma himself was but an agent. Vishnu in turn let it be known that Vishvakarman's request would be fulfilled.

Early next morning, a boy carrying the staff of a pilgrim made his appearance at the gate of Indra. The boy was only ten years old, but radiant with the lustre of wisdom. The king of the gods bowed to the holy child, who cheerfully gave his blessing. Then the king of the gods said, 'O venerable boy, tell me of the purpose of your coming.'

The beautiful child replied, 'O king of gods, I have heard of the mighty palace you are building, and have come to ask some questions. How many years will it take to complete? What further feats of engineering will the craftsman-god Vishvakarman be required to perform? O Highest of the Gods, no Indra before you has ever succeeded in completing such a palace as yours is to be.'

Indra was amused by the boy's pretension to a knowledge of Indras earlier than himself. 'Tell me, child!' he said. 'Are they then so very many, the Indras you have seen or heard of?'

The boy nodded. 'Yes, indeed, many have I seen.' The words sent a slow chill through Indra's veins. 'I knew your father,' continued the boy, 'Old Tortoise Man, progenitor of all the creatures of the earth. I knew your grandfather, Beam of Celestial Light, the son of Brahma. And I know Brahma, brought forth from Vishnu, and I know Vishnu himself, the Supreme Being. O king of gods, I have known the dreadful dissolution of the universe. I have seen all perish, again and again, at the end of every cycle. At that terrible time every single atom dissolves into the pure waters of eternity, whence everything originally arose. Who can count the universes that have passed away or the creations that have risen afresh from the formless abyss of the waters? Who will number the passing ages

of the world? And who will search through the wide infinities of space to count the universes side by side, each with its Brahma and its Vishnu? Who will count the Indras in them all, ascending to godly kingship one by one, and one by one passing away?'

While the boy spoke thus, a parade of ants had made its appearance in the hall. In military array, they moved across the floor. The boy noted them and laughed. Then he subsided into a profoundly thoughtful silence.

'Why do you laugh?' stammered Indra, for the proud king's throat had gone dry. 'Who are you?'

The boy said: 'I laughed because of the ants. But I cannot tell you the reason, for it is a secret which lies buried in the wisdom of the ages, and is not revealed even to the saints.'

'O child,' Indra pleaded, with a new and visible humility. 'I do not know who you are. Reveal to me this secret of the ages, this light that dispels the dark.'

'I saw the ants,' replied the boy, 'filing in long parade. Each was once an Indra. Like you, each once ascended to the rank of a king of the gods. But now, through many rebirths, each has again become an ant. Piety and high deeds elevate living beings to the glorious realm of the celestial mansions. But wicked acts sink them into the worlds beneath, into pits of pain and sorrow. It is by deeds that one merits happiness or anguish, and becomes a master or a serf. This is the whole substance of the secret. Life in the cycle of countless rebirths is like a vision in a dream. The gods, the trees, the stones are alike apparitions in this fantasy. But Death administers the law of time and is the master of all. Perishable as bubbles are the good and evil of the beings of the dream. Hence the wise are attached to neither evil nor good. The wise are not attached to anything at all.'

The boy concluded this appalling lesson and quietly regarded his host. The king of the gods, for all his splendor, had been reduced in his own

Indra did not realize that, although a god, he too belonged to the unending cosmic cycle of countless rebirths, and would therefore one day bow to Death, the master of all.

Krishna on the bird Garuda overcomes Indra on his elephant, from the 'Hariansa' (c.1590)

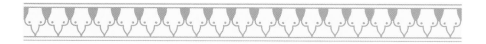

regard to insignificance. And then another apparition entered Indra's hall. The newcomer was a hermit, with matted hair and ragged clothes. A strange circle of hair grew on the old man's chest. He squatted on the floor between Indra and the boy, remaining motionless as a rock. Then the boy asked the hermit his name and purpose, and what was the meaning of the strange circle of hair on his chest.

The old man smiled. 'I am a brahmin. My name is Hairy, and I have come here to behold Indra. Since I know that I am short-lived, I possess no home, build no house, do not marry, and seek no livelihood. I exist by begging alms. This circle of hair on my chest teaches wisdom. With the fall of an Indra, one hair drops. That is why, at the center, all the hairs have gone. When the present Brahma has expired, I myself shall die. What use, therefore, is a wife or a son or a house? Each flicker of the eyelids of the great Supreme Being Vishnu registers the passing of a Brahma. Everything else is an insubstantial cloud, taking shape and again dissolving. Every joy, even the heavenly, is as fragile as a dream. I do not crave to experience the various blissful forms of redemption. I crave nothing at all and devote myself exclusively to meditating on the incomparable feet of highest Vishnu.'

Abruptly the holy man vanished and, simultaneously, the boy vanished as well. The king of the gods was alone, baffled and amazed. He pondered, and wondered whether it had been a dream. But he no longer felt any wish to magnify his heavenly splendor. He summoned Vishvakarman and heaped gifts on him, then sent the craftsman-god home.

Indra now desired redemption. He had acquired wisdom and, in his bitterness, wished only to be free. He resolved to leave the burden of his office to his son and to retire to the hermit life of the wilderness. But his beautiful queen was overcome with grief. She implored the king's spiritual advisor, Brihaspati, the lord of Magic Wisdom, to divert her husband's mind from its stern resolve. The resourceful Brihaspati spoke to Indra of the virtues of the spiritual life; but he also spoke of the virtues of the secular life, and gave to each its due. Indra relented, and his queen

was restored to joy. And thus Indra fulfilled that which he had been created to do in the transient universe of which he was a part, and no longer felt fearful or enraged about the parade of ants, or the Indras who had been before and would be again and again unto eternity.

COMMENTARY: The myth of Indra and the parade of ants needs little elaboration; it speaks for itself, reminding us that all our little human efforts to understand what the cosmos might mean, and all our struggles to claim a place of importance in the world, pale into insignificance before the great mystery that is life itself. One does not need to believe in the Hindu gods to grasp what this tale teaches: that wisdom and fulfillment lie in living a balanced life, mindful of both body and spirit, and content to be what we are. Great or small, human or ant, god or human, each spark of life is part of a vast living unity whose intentions and workings are orderly yet ultimately beyond our grasp. Because we are human, we must strive and, perhaps, like Indra, build palaces or, like Faustus, seek knowledge or, like the noble souls in Plato's tale, serve humanity. But while we are fulfilling that individual destiny which is unique to each one of us, it is a good idea to keep things in perspective. Remember the parade of ants.

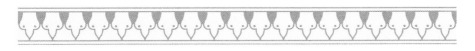

BIBLIOGRAPHY AND FURTHER READING

The Acts of King Arthur and his Noble Knights, John Steinbeck. New York: Noonday Press, 1993. London: Heinemann Ltd, 1979.

Celtic Myth and Legend, Charles Squire. Van Nuys, CA: Newcastle Publishing Co., 1987.

Classical Mythology, A. R. Hope Moncrieff. London: Studio Editions Ltd, 1994.

Gods and Heroes, Gustav Schwab. New York: Pantheon Books, 1977. London: Random House, 1977.

The Greek Myths, Robert Graves. New York: Penguin, 1993. London: Penguin, 1977.

The Illustrated Encyclopedia of Myths and Legends, Arthur Cotterell. New York: Macmillan, 1996. London: Macmillan, 1996.

King Arthur and the Grail, Richard Cavendish. London: Weidenfeld and Nicolson, 1978.

Larousse World Mythology, Pierre Grimal (ed.). London: Hamlyn, 1989.

Maori Legends, Alistair Campbell. Paraparaumu, New Zealand: Viking Sevenseas Ltd, 1969.

Myths and Symbols in Indian Art and Civilization, Heinrich Zimmer. Princeton, NJ: Princeton University Press, 1992.

Myths of Babylonia and Assyria, Donald A. McKenzie. London: Gresham Publishing Co., 1933.

The Niebelungenlied. New York: The Heritage Press, 1961. London: Penguin, 1965.

The Norse Myths, Kevin Crossley-Holland. New York: Random House, 1981. London: Penguin, 1980.

The Prophet, Kahlil Gibran. New York: Random House, 1996. London: Heinemann Ltd, 1973.

Sources of the Grail, John Matthews (ed.). Hudson, NY: Lindisfarne Books, 1977. Edinburgh: Floris Books, 1996.

INDEX

ACKNOWLEDGEMENTS

With thanks to the authors of all the books of myths which appear in the Bibliography, to whom we are heavily indebted. Thanks also to Ian Jackson and Sophie Bevan for their help and support in this project, and to Barbara Levy for her encouragement.

EDDISON·SADD EDITIONS

Editorial Director Ian Jackson
Editor Sophie Bevan
Art Director Elaine Partington
Designer Brazzle Atkins
Picture Researcher Liz Eddison
Production Karyn Claridge and Charles James

PICTURE CREDITS